SHARING THE COMMON POOL

River Books, sponsored by

THE MEADOWS CENTER
FOR WATER AND THE ENVIRONMENT
TEXAS STATE UNIVERSITY

Andrew Sansom, General Editor

A list of titles in this series may be found

at the end of the book.

Publication of this book was generously supported by
The Cynthia and George Mitchell Foundation.

Water Rights in the Everyday Lives of Texans

CHARLES R. PORTER JR.

FOREWORD BY ANDREW SANSOM

Texas A&M University Press College Station

Sharing the Common Pool

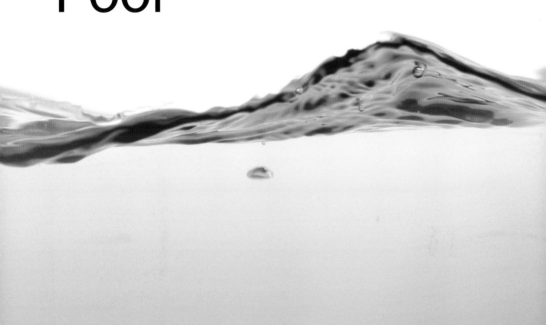

This paper meets the requirements of
ANSI/NISO Z39.48-1992 (Permanence of Paper).
Binding materials have been chosen for durability.
Manufactured in China by Everbest Printing Co.
through Four Colour Print Group

Library of Congress Cataloging-in-Publication Data
Porter, Charles R., Jr., 1952– author.
Sharing the common pool : water rights in the everyday lives
of Texans / Charles R. Porter ; Foreword by Andrew Sansom.
pages cm. — (River books)
Includes bibliographical references and index.
ISBN 978-1-62349-137-6 (flex : alk. paper) —
ISBN 978-1-62349-170-3 (e-book)
1. Water rights—Texas. I. Title.
KFT1323.W2P67 2014
346.76404'691—dc23
2013040751

CONTENTS

FOREWORD

I cross the Blanco River twice each day, driving from my home in Austin to work at Texas State University in San Marcos. Sometimes there is water in the river and sometimes there is not.

The Blanco originates out in Kendall County, just below the Gillespie County line, south of Fredericksburg. It flows in a southeasterly direction toward Hays County, where I work, and before it gets to the county line, most of the river flow goes back underground through the river bed. The now-underground river continues to flow in the same direction and emerges again to the surface from the iconic spring at Jacob's Well in the little village of Woodcreek. From there, the water flows down Cypress Creek through the city of Wimberley, where it again becomes the Blanco.

Under current Texas law, if you tried to get a water rights permit for water in the Blanco from the Texas Commission on Environmental Quality, you would probably be unsuccessful, because the surface water in the river, considered the property of the state, is largely committed. On the other hand, if you wanted to drill a well up above Jacob's Well, you could pump just about as much water as you are man or woman enough to pump with barely any regulatory constraints at all, because the state courts have ruled that underground water is the property of the landowner.

And it's the same water.

Although this bizarre situation is illustrative of the most daunting conflict in Texas water law, it is only one of many peculiarities standing in the way of developing a water strategy for Texas that ensures both continued economic growth and environmental protection. To some extent, as Charles Porter points out in this easy-to-understand description of Texas water rights, this situation arises from a system that dates all the way back to when we were a colony of Spain, yet it affects a modern society that bears absolutely no resemblance to the lives and times of those who created it so long ago.

As I write, Texas is facing a continuing drought that has stretched our water supplies to the limit and has no end in sight. We can only hope that, due to changing climate, it is not the "new normal" and that, some-day soon, it will end. Thankfully, state leaders have become increasingly focused on the issue and have begun to take steps to address our water needs by enabling the financing of new water infrastructure projects in the years ahead. Unfortunately, we simply cannot build enough stuff to work our way out of the most critical natural resource issue facing the coming generation. It will require the attention of every one of us as we try to move forward through a dense thicket of confusing, conflicting, and evolving water policies.

That is why *Sharing the Common Pool: Water Rights in the Lives of Everyday Texans* is so timely. On these pages, Porter makes often-arcane laws and regulations understandable for the layperson and thus pro-vides a most valuable service to those average Texans who seek to be better informed about this vital issue.

Eventually, the Blanco joins the San Marcos River, which flows on down to its confluence with the Guadalupe, one of Texas' most beloved watercourses. The Guadalupe provides water to cities like Seguin and Victoria on its way to the Gulf, where it ultimately nourishes the estu-aries of San Antonio Bay and the habitat of a rich assemblage of coastal organisms, including the Whooping Crane. Thus, the river, which inter-mittently flows both underground and on the surface and whose waters are claimed in the one case by the state and in the other by private citi-zens, must be managed in the years ahead to continue to meet all the demands that are placed on it in the context of laws that are ambiguous at best. The more we can help our citizens understand our quirky system of managing our water resources, the better off we'll be, and that is what this volume in our River Books series is designed to do.

—*Andrew Sansom*
General Editor, River Books

ACKNOWLEDGMENTS

My thanks go to many people for their contributions to this book and my research. My wife, Constance Porter, was my strong beacon of strength over the years of travel and work on the manuscript. Kirk Holland was my stalwart mentor, teaching me the intricate and nuanced world of groundwater conservation district rules and management. Russ Johnson clued me in to the past pivotal court cases and ongoing cases that created the legal doctrine of water rights in Texas, which continues to emerge. Stacey Steinbach was another strong supporter of my efforts and gave me invaluable insight into groundwater issues. Lynne Fahlquist of the United States Geological Survey opened door after door for my research efforts, arranging countless speaking engagements. Mark Strama and Paul Workman of the Texas House of Representatives offered me the opportunity to teach and lecture about water rights and participated in forums to explore water policy. With the help and introduction of Charles Ponzio, former El Paso mayor Bill Tilney kindly gave me eyewitness perspectives on water issues in far West Texas and water relations with Mexico. Augustus Campbell shared his scholarly expertise on the role of watermasters in Texas surface water management. Susan Conseco and Dylan Drummond offered their scholarly opinions on groundwater ownership. Bill Nelson and Terry Newton of Del Rio offered their point of view on Val Verde County water issues. Todd Votteler and Jim Murphy of the Guadalupe Blanco River Authority encouraged me and provided insight into the critical issues they face daily. Tom Hatfield's fine work on the history of the 1950s drought seasoned my efforts. Water law scholars and practicing attorneys such as Tim Brown, Ed McCarthy, Jason Hill, and Russ Johnson graciously spent hours with me, discussing the nuances of the statutes and court cases. Many others encouraged me, provided information, and generously offered their time and thoughts. Above all, the unrelenting support and guidance of Shannon Davies of Texas A&M University Press, along with my many friends there, took this book from an imaginary project to fruition. To all my friends and supporters I give my heartfelt appreciation.

SHARING THE COMMON POOL

INTRODUCTION

Today close to 90 percent of Texans live in an "urban" area.[1] Water rights are generally overlooked by urbanites because their water is immediately available from the "taps" in their homes. The size of the monthly water bill and any emergency rules concerning irrigation of plants and grass are usually the only limitations people living in cities experience in regard to their right to use water. If city dwellers pay their water bill on time and follow the landscape watering rules, then their water right is generally secure and hardly ever comes to mind.

People living in the "country" have a different and sometimes more respectful attitude toward water. The domestic, livestock, and irrigation water used by people living in rural areas flows from their own underground wells or, less often, from nearby surface water. These people tend to be more aware of their water rights because access to the water, the quality of the water they draw and use, and the daily maintenance of the pumps and storage tanks are their sole responsibility.

Whether someone's water source is from a seemingly unlimited municipal supply or from a private rural well, the right to the water *does affect everyone* living in drought-prone Texas. Why? Because all water comes from one hydrologic cycle as it circulates from the land to the sky and back again, and water at all times exists in nature conjunctively, or interconnected.[2] Water is the ultimate zero-sum game: the volume of water used by one right holder sourced from our common pool of water ultimately diminishes, to some degree or other, the volume of water available to other water rights holders.[3]

Almost all Texans, when asked, profess confusion about water rights. Water rights in Texas vary: between water flowing on the surface and water underground, from regulatory agency to regulatory agency, from place to place, and from time to time. A good example of the conventional wisdom that water rights in Texas are convoluted and at times in the recent past incomprehensible is found in a 1955 ruling made by federal judge James V. Allred, a former attorney general and governor of Texas. Allred wrote, "For years it has been a matter of common knowledge that the Texas water laws and decisions are in hopeless confusion;

that even if they are clear as some attorneys profess to believe them, their application and administration would be difficult."[4] When a well-known jurist such as Judge Allred expresses confusion and frustration with our water laws and decisions, *in a published decision,* it is understandable why the general public may share his feelings. However, few Texans today understand the wider view of the legal, social, and economic consequences of our water rights system.

I grew up in Texas during the drought of the 1950s and have witnessed countless droughts and dry spells my entire life. I tolerated the recurring times of little or no moisture and suffered both financially and spiritually through them. I, like most Texans, accept drought as a way of life, a demon that cannot be exorcised from "our parts." Water rights are the most fundamental stick in the "bundle of sticks" that determines all the "property rights" and represents much of the market value of any real property in Texas.[5] I learned from personal experience supported by historical research that the market value of land is diminished by limited accessibility to water. The consequences of lower real estate values are far reaching for all of us since much of the funding for the public services we hold dear (e.g., public school education) are based upon ad valorem taxation of real property.[6]

Remember to seek advice from your attorney on water issues. It is very helpful to have a basic knowledge of water rights so you can ask pertinent questions and be conversant in the subject. I write and teach about water use and water rights at St. Edward's University, such as the course "Water Rights for Texas Agents," and am a certified instructor for the Texas Real Estate Commission, teaching courses for continuing education credit for real estate licensees. I taught a seminar on the fundamentals of water rights before the 82nd Session of the Texas legislature in 2011 and have given dozens of lectures around Texas to public agencies, trade associations, and private groups about the importance of water rights to our lives, about right-of-way issues in water infrastructure projects, and on the history of the development of water rights. All across the state, Texans have demonstrated to me their strong desire to understand more about the mystery of water rights.

Why else is it important to know about water rights in Texas? Texans buy, lease, and sell real estate thousands of times daily. In addition to the significant impact water rights have on the value of property, statutory obligations have created a need to understand water rights because all known defects in real property must be disclosed to any potential purchaser during the time the purchasers are making their decision to buy. This duty to disclose any known defect, *including a defect in water rights,* is shared by sellers, lessors, and their real estate agents. Buyers and lessees must know about the water rights to a property they are considering, so they must know what questions to ask. Chapter 9 discusses disclosure in everyday real estate transactions in detail. As water becomes scarcer throughout the state due to population growth and inevitably recurring droughts, the need for sellers, buyers, and real estate agents to fully understand the water situation associated with any property for sale has become critical.

Texans must keep one other very important consideration in mind—several US government agencies can have supralegal (superior; from Latin *supra,* meaning "above") authority over some areas of Texas water policy either directly or indirectly. Agencies such as the Environmental Protection Agency (EPA) and the US Fish and Wildlife Service (USFWS) promulgate rules that can significantly affect water rights; Congress passes laws that affect water rights; and the federal courts issue rulings, which historically have drastically modified water policy in Texas.

The book is organized in five parts:

- Part 1 provides foundational information about the hydrologic cycle and the unique properties of water and introduces the basis for understanding water rights and water law in general.
- Part 2 explores who owns water in Texas: which water is considered state owned and which is privately owned.
- Part 3 tackles how supply and demand affect us today and will in the future, how we use water, and who regulates our use of water.
- Part 4 gives further detail about the duties of buyers, sellers, and real estate agents and discusses how water rights impact everyday real estate transactions.
- Part 5 recalls past debates in water policy and discusses what debates loom in the future.

Certain legal terms, regulatory phrases, and other industry vocabulary were impossible to avoid in writing this book. For someone to be conversant in the discourse about water rights, this unique vocabulary cannot be ignored, and a cursory understanding of this language helps provide a better understanding of water rights in Texas. A glossary is included in the back of the book.

In summary, this book was written to help readers think about the critical position water rights play in their daily lives; to know what they need to keep in mind when buying, selling, and leasing real property in Texas; and to prepare to participate in the debate over the issues we face in order to secure a sustainable and bright future in our arid, drought-prone state. The book should be looked upon as a primer to gain a broad understanding of how water rights are determined and the obligations and consequences that stem from exercising those rights. To meet the challenge of our future, Texans will be faced with tough budgetary decisions involving new water sources and delivery.

The urgency for the preparedness this book provides is best summed up by Edward G. Vaughan, chairman of the Texas Water Development Board, on September 23, 2011, in his preamble letter to the "Water for Texas 2012 State Water Plan": "The primary message of the 2012 State Water Plan is a simple one: In serious drought conditions, Texas does not and will not have enough water to meet the needs of its people, its businesses, and its agricultural enterprises." This dire forecast of water scarcity to come emphasizes how critical it is for Texans to gain knowledge about their water rights *now*.

We absolutely must act now because water infrastructure improvements and development of new water resources take decades to complete. We also absolutely must act now so that we can all begin to change our behavior in order to conserve our most fundamental and precious life-giving resource. We are under the silent siege of drought; we have to prepare now to adapt to its inexorable hold on our land and economic future.

Part One

NATURAL WATER, HUMAN RULES

1

THE UNIQUE CHARACTERISTICS OF WATER AND WATER RIGHTS IN TEXAS

Determining a water right in Texas depends on which of three geological containers holds the water.[1] The first container is *surface water,* or water that flows on the surface of the ground in a watercourse.[2] The State of Texas owns the water in a watercourse. The assessment of what makes up a watercourse can be complicated, so the safest way to look at ownership of surface water is to consider all water flowing in any stream or area with bed and banks to be surface water. Surface water is not yours to own but, except in unique situations, is owned by the State of Texas. Knowing this may save you many dollars in fines and hours of angst. If you have a question about surface water ownership on real property you own or are considering purchasing, ask the Texas Commission on Environmental Quality (TCEQ) for a determination.

The second geological container is known as *diffused surface water,* or rainwater that runs off your roof or over the surface of your land without flowing in a stream or channel. The water in this container is owned by the landowner.

The third container is *groundwater,* or water held underground in aquifers and pools. Ownership of groundwater in Texas was debated for many decades, but in the fall of 2011 the debate ended for all practical purposes when the Texas legislature passed a bill (generally known as Senate Bill 332 by Fraser), which states, "The legislature recognizes that a landowner owns the groundwater below the surface of the landowner's land as real property."[3] The bill was signed into law by Governor Rick Perry, effective September 1, 2011.

WATER EXISTS IN A CONJUNCTIVE STATE AT ALL TIMES

Water is the ultimate example of an element of nature that exists in a conjunctive state.[4] Surface water, diffused surface water, and groundwater are, have been, or will be ultimately in union with one another; water exists in a conjunctive relationship in all three geological containers all the time. Diffused surface water feeds both surface water and groundwater. Groundwater feeds surface water both in the underflow and via natural springs. As water flows downhill above or below ground, the containers feed and deplete each other visibly and invisibly. This conjunctive relationship is a key concept that must be grasped in order to understand water rights in Texas. This law of nature, when applied to water ownership in Texas, complicates the debate since even with modern technology we cannot yet "see" underground.

Another fundamental concept about water that prudent policymakers should keep in mind is that it *ignores political boundaries.* Setting workable public water policy based upon surface political boundaries and not upon the boundaries of the common pool of water in a given river basin, watershed, or underground aquifer is problematic. The water one user draws from a common pool affects the other users of that common pool, much like sharing a milkshake with your sibling while using separate straws simultaneously.

THE HYDROLOGIC CYCLE

Every human being, creature, and plant on earth shares a common pool, draws from it all the time, and is utterly dependent upon it for existence. Water is the "common denominator" of all life on earth. Water exists in one constantly churning hydrologic system. Kirk Holland, general manager of the Barton Springs/Edwards Aquifer Conservation District, describes this cycle and the challenge it creates for humans: "God made one hydrologic system in Texas—where precipitation, ground-

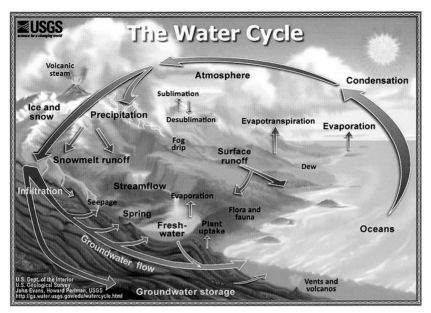

The hydrologic cycle. Courtesy United States Geological Survey.

water, surface water, and the bays and estuaries are all interconnected such that changes in one affect the others, on varying time scales. So we humans should also create a water resource management system that integrates all those components, even though each has its own differing characteristics. That task requires a level of perfection that humans so far have been incapable of achieving."[5] The water in this common pool is in constant motion and relentlessly seeks a downhill path to the ocean on the surface and below the ground. Water in its hydrologic cycle changes from gas to liquid to solid effortlessly and with absolute reliability, like the earth's other constant we can rely upon—gravity.

Human use of water affects the hydrologic cycle, usually quite drastically. Water is in constant motion flowing through this cycle. As water moves through the cycle in Texas, its ownership continuously changes.

OWNERSHIP OF A WATER MOLECULE IN TEXAS

Imagine tracking one water molecule in various stages in the hydrologic cycle in Texas. As the water flows through the cycle, rights to this water molecule change between private and public ownership. The fugitive nature of the molecule is a root cause of some of the confusion over water rights in Texas. For example, when the water molecule comes to a landowner's property via a rain shower and does not enter into a watercourse, then this water molecule is owned by the private landowner and is considered diffused surface water. If that same water molecule percolates into the soil before it evaporates to join the gaseous stage of the hydrologic cycle, it becomes groundwater, which is also owned by the private landowner.[6] However, if and when the same water molecule runs off the landowner's property and into a watercourse or stream, thereby becoming part of the flow, the molecule enters the geological container known as surface water and is owned by the State of Texas. Even when landowners have an adjudicated right to surface water in Texas, they hold only a "usufruct" right, or a right to "use" surface water, not to own the surface water itself.[7]

Natural springs are the most cherished and by far the most visible intersection of a water molecule's change in ownership as it flows through the cycle. While the molecule is in the ground before it emerges from a spring, it is groundwater owned by the landowner. When the water molecule emerges from the spring into a pool without running into a watercourse or stream in Texas, the water molecule remains the landowner's property. Once the water molecule emerges from the spring and flows into a watercourse or stream, the State then owns it. The significance of the one water molecule example is that water exists in a conjunctive relationship, resulting in an ever-changing chain of title in Texas. As former Texas attorney general and Supreme Court justice Will Wilson, an expert on water rights in Texas whose expertise and keen thinking on water has never been given the credit it deserves, said, "Both legislative and judicial attempts to engraft workable property concepts upon the hydrological cycle have encountered what initially appear to be insuperable difficulties. The first of these is caused by the physical fact that water in its natural state is in constant motion and is not subject to branding or other identification. Claims of property ownership are usually noted by fences, gates, locked doors, and other tags. Water's ownership is difficult to successfully identify as it travels through the hydrological cycle in Texas."[8]

Water also responds instantly to the pressure of a water well pump. In the illustration, the water well appears to be outside the underflow of the stream; however, the impact of the water pump on the groundwater table causes the water molecules in the groundwater and the stream to flow toward the pump. In fact, stronger pumps create a cone of depression at their lowest point, causing even greater flow into the well casing

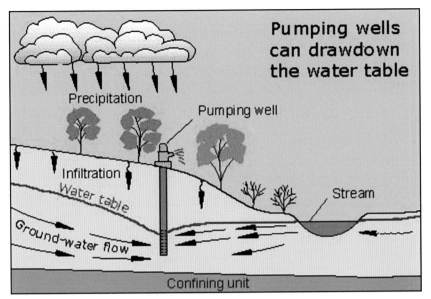

A water well pump's impact on the water table and surface stream.
Courtesy United States Geological Survey.

and potentially depleting the other sources. In the illustration, did the privately owned water well take some of the state-owned stream water? Without doubt, it did. The illustration indicates the difficulty in determining ownership of water due to the conjunctive relationship between geological containers. In other states where all geological containers of water are owned by the state, this confusion is eliminated; these states still face conflicts over water allocation and other issues, but the basic ownership issue is rarely in question.[9]

Water wells can drastically affect surface and spring water many miles away from the actual water wells, as we learned from the drying up of Comanche Springs in Fort Stockton.[10] Comanche Springs draws, or did draw, its water from the Trinity Sands. The farmers and ranchers south and west of the springs tried to save their livestock and crops by drilling wells into the same Trinity Sands during the terrible drought of the 1950s. Comanche Springs fed Comanche Creek, from which farmers held appropriative rights for irrigation of their crops.[11] When the farmers and ranchers drilled their wells, Comanche Springs dried up, which caused Comanche Creek to dry up as well. The courts determined that the irrigators on Comanche Creek were due no compensation from the farmers and ranchers. Until the water molecule emerged from the ground into

Comanche Springs and then ran into Comanche Creek, it was for the taking without liability to water well drillers.

~~~~~ **TEXAS WEATHER AND DROUGHT**

Texas is a border state not only on the ground but also in the atmosphere; our weather constantly changes as the southeast prevailing winds off the Gulf of Mexico meet other winds from the north. We seem to have either floods or droughts—there is nothing normal about Texas weather.

Water is a scarce resource in most areas of Texas west of Interstate Highway 35. Future predictions of population growth coupled with inevitable recurring droughts surely will make per capita availability of water scarcer still. One of the worst droughts on record is commonly referred to as the "50s drought," which devastated many areas of Texas from 1950 to 1957, as shown graphically in the Palmer Drought Severity Index (PDSI) chart.[12] As Elmer Kelton put it, "It crept up out of Mexico, touching first along the brackish Pecos and spreading then in all directions, a cancerous blight burning a scar upon the land. Just another dry spell men said at first. . . . Why worry? they said. It would rain this fall. It always had. But it didn't. And many a boy would become a man before the land was green again."[13] Rural landowners know that rainfall is fickle—so fickle that it can rain on the upper pasture, and the lower pasture just a few hundred yards away can be dry as a bone. It is interesting to study public policy decisions made based upon need and public reactions to the pain of drought at any one time period shown on the index; rainfall or the lack thereof resulted in many famous court decisions and at times was and still is the cause of drastic public reaction.

The chart demonstrates drought conditions in the same location in the San Antonio area from 1900 to 1979. Notice the severity of the 1950s drought. A century earlier in the 1850s, Texas also suffered severe drought. Throughout Texas at that time, farmers lost crops and were forced to default on mortgages.

A True Tale of Drought in the 1850s

A victim of the terrible drought in the 1850s was a man in Seguin who would by the end of the nineteenth century become one of the wealthiest men in Texas, George W. Brackenridge. A young man in his twenties at the time, Brackenridge lost a league of land (4,428.4 acres) to foreclosure because the drought destroyed farm crops on the land. Bracken-

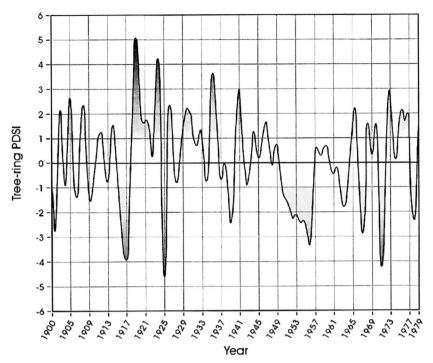

PDSI values in San Antonio, 1900–1979.
Negative PDSI values indicate dry conditions, and positive values
indicate wet conditions. PDSI values generally fall between −6 and +6.
Graph by author.

ridge purchased the land on terms, subdivided it, and then sold the tracts to farmers on terms. When the farmers' crops failed, they could not make their payments to Brackenridge, causing Brackenridge to default on payments to the holder of his note. Brackenridge lost the entire property in foreclosure. He left Seguin a financially broken young man. In fact, he was so broke that he had to walk back home to his parents' house in Texana, near today's La Porte, behind his mule-riding cousin, J. J. Thornton. The lessons Brackenridge learned about water's overwhelming impact on land value etched themselves indelibly into his mind and became the key consideration in most of his business decisions involving land purchases and land lending for the remainder of his life.[14] Brackenridge's purchases of tracts in San Antonio and Austin were located on the San Antonio River and the Colorado River, respectively, due to his experiences in Seguin.

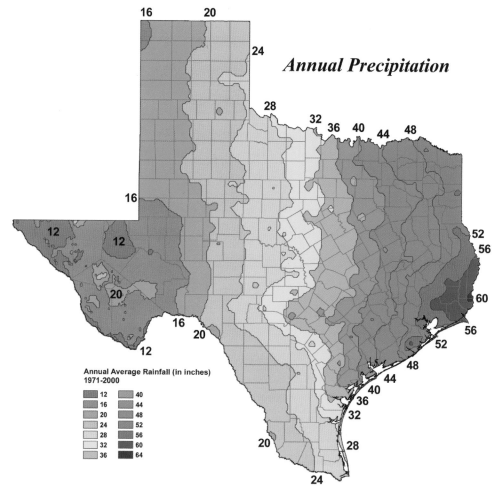

Annual Precipitation

Annual Average Rainfall (in inches)
1971-2000

12	40
16	44
20	48
24	52
28	56
32	60
36	64

Average annual rainfall in Texas. Courtesy Texas Water Development Board.

The Drought of 2010–2011

Severe drought raised its ugly head yet again in the spring and summer of 2011 across Central and South Texas; it just simply stopped raining. In Wilson County, the location of my family farm, we had no rain at all for six months. The even more difficult problem in Wilson County was the lack of almost any kind of moisture; the hot prevailing wind from the southeast dried out and shrank even the 80-year-old siding on our 1926-era farm house. Outdoor burn bans lasted for months. We were all frightened daily that a spark carried by the wind would start a wildfire that would char the entire county.

The drought resulted in one of the most devastating fires in Texas history, the Bastrop fire of September and October 2011. The fire was caused by wind moving power lines at condenser banks that sent sparks and embers onto dry tree debris on the ground. The debris, shrubs, and trees were so dry they were very near their kindling point and quickly ignited.[15] The fire ultimately burned some 34,000 acres. I viewed the monstrous size of this fire from 30 miles away on Red Bud Trail in Austin. The Frost Bank Tower in downtown Austin was dwarfed by the huge smoke cloud generated by the fire — and let me stress again — my view was from 30 miles west of the fire. Including the smaller saplings that burned, as many as a billion trees were destroyed in this fire alone. Earlier that summer fires raged all over Texas; at one time in June, there were 185 simultaneous ongoing wildfires in East Texas alone. By the time of the Bastrop fire, these fires stretched firefighting capabilities to a limit Texans had rarely experienced.

The 2011 drought in Texas was more severe than that in any one year in the 1950s drought. Newspapers, the Internet, blogs, along with television and radio stations, filed daily reports with stories of terrible calamities the drought caused throughout the state. The fires awakened an entire generation of Texas homeowners to the risks and consequences of severe drought that before were generally considered to be only a yearly risk to and tragedy of the homeowners in the California hills. At the time of the Bastrop fire in September, there were still more than 100 other active wildfires across Texas, including some of the June fires in the eastern portion of the state that were still burning.

The illustration shows annual rainfall across Texas. This wide variance in rainfall levels creates a special problem for water policymakers in Texas. In the words of Tom Hatfield, "The worst drought in Beaumont's history could very well set a record for annual rainfall in El Paso."[16]

2

WATER RIGHTS AND
WATER LAW IN GENERAL

Water needs to be viewed as more than an economic resource. This is an appropriate change in thinking for a number of reasons. First, water's life-sustaining function sets it apart from a mere economic commodity. Second, although water is often treated as a property right, water does not fit well into a property construct. —Amy Hardberger, St. Mary's School of Law

What is a "water right"? According to the Texas Water Code, state-owned water is "a right acquired under the laws of this state to impound, divert, or use state water." A more thorough definition is a "right or group of rights designed to protect the use, enjoyment, and in some cases, ownership of water that travels in streams, rivers, lakes, and ponds; gathers on the surface of the earth; or collects underground."[1]

It is very important to keep in mind that water is "fugitive" by nature;[2] that is, it is in constant motion everywhere, even underground. Due to its fugitive nature, water presents a unique ownership problem as described by Sir William Blackstone in 1807: "For water is a moveable wandering thing, and must of necessity continue common by the law of nature; so that I can only have a temporary, transient, usufructuary [*sic*], property therein: wherefore, if a body of water runs out of my pond into another man's, I have no right to reclaim it."[3] Property ownership includes a bundle of rights, one of which can be a right to water.

The basic concept of water rights under English common law differs from the civil law of Spain and the Republic of Mexico. Water rights under English common law were generally riparian in nature.[4] Water rights under Spanish and Mexican civil law were generally appropriative, or based on a grant or license from a sovereign. Since the early 1800s, some western state legislatures and courts have struggled with the conflict between the two legal systems over the rights to water of riparian lands. Texas struggled with this dual system until the Water Rights Adjudication Act of 1967.[5]

The western states adopted English common law, so those who owned land adjacent to water had the right to take the water from flowing streams for irrigation based solely upon their adjacency to it. Under Spanish and Mexican law, however, water could not be taken from a river or stream for irrigation without an *explicit* grant from the sovereign. Many courts in the West have relied upon the customary practices and application of Spanish laws to support their rulings and set legal precedents from time to time on water issues.

As a result, logic-defying and seemingly unfair judicial rulings on water issues in the West have been rendered in the past and continue today. The same holds true for guidance from the legislatures; the lack of legislation on various important water issues stands out most noticeably in Texas and Kansas.[6] Two of the most controversial water issues are rights to irrigate from a flowing stream of surface water and the use of large volumes of groundwater in such quantity that neighboring water wells, springs, and creeks go dry. A primer in water uses helps to lay the groundwork to understand the issues.

There are five basic water uses in Texas: for households, commonly referred to as domestic and livestock use; for irrigation; for municipalities; for industry; and for the environment. Spanish, Republic of Mexico, Texas, and state laws across the western United States have generally concurred on protection of domestic and livestock use of any type of water.

The most heated and challenging disputes have always been over irrigation use, whether from surface water or groundwater. Why? Irrigation of land requires huge amounts of water; its use is considered *artificial.* Domestic use for households and watering livestock is considered *natural.* Until the late nineteenth century, most irrigation water came from rivers and streams. By the end of the first decade of the twentieth century, claims to surface water exceeded the amount of water that flowed in most of the rivers of the western United States. With late nineteenth-century technology, in which deep drilling and large pumping equipment became available across the West, irrigation using groundwater became increasingly popular. For example, irrigation today accounts for almost two-thirds of all groundwater use in Texas; other states similarly use high quantities of groundwater for irrigation purposes. Groundwater irrigation puts pressure on aquifers and can dry up springs and the streams flowing from them across the West during times of drought.

HOW WATER RIGHTS BECAME CONFUSING IN TEXAS

The story of water in the West, and Texas in particular, is one fraught with confusing and conflicting laws and court rulings, a general lack of direction toward a common goal for everyone's benefit, short-sighted legal experimentation that resulted in dual systems of law in many states and territories, and a disjointed approach to water conservation. The myriad of laws, regulations, and court rulings varying from state to state makes the understanding of the history of irrigation in the West since the Mexican War a challenge for even the most learned jurist or legislator.

The basic cause of the confusion in the West, especially in Texas, was the application and misunderstanding of riparian rights under the blended Spanish and English legal concepts. "In its wisdom," wrote water rights expert Garland F. Smith, "the Legislature [in Texas] adopted the Common Law of England, and the courts (with the aid of the Bar) for over a century tried to adapt the non-consumptive riparian doctrine to the consumptive use of irrigation."[7] "Riparian rights under English Common Law consist of a bundle of rights, which include the right to flow [for industries such as mills], to fish, to navigate, and to use the water for irrigation and for domestic purposes."[8]

Then, by passing the Irrigation Act of 1889, Texas officially adopted the Spanish-influenced principle of "prior appropriation,"[9] which provided that all streams "within the arid areas of the state" not already claimed by a landowner were declared the property of the state and therefore subject to state regulation.

> **Prior Appropriation**
>
> "Appropriation" and "appropriated rights" are terms used in water regulation that refer to the granted right to use the water. The system in Texas is like others in the West: first in time (the date of acquisition of the appropriation from the state or granted right to use the water) is first in right. Older or "senior" right holders (those with an appropriated right to use the water) are allocated the water first during restricted flow no matter their location on the stream. For example, if your right to use the Concho River was granted in 1982 and mine was granted in 1992, even if I was upstream of you, I must let the water flow past me until you take your prior appropriated amount. If you need all the flow in the river to fill your senior right, I am out of luck.

Since some of the states in the West officially recognized their mixed Spanish/Anglo heritage, the confusion and frustration over irrigation water and riparian rights to use it were prominent issues in water rights disputes. In England and the eastern coast of the United States, home to naturally well-watered lands with ample rainfall, riparian rights were rarely controversial; there was generally plenty of water for everyone. This was not true in the arid West; riparian rights of irrigation created serious water shortages during the recurring and, at times, lengthy periods of drought. When water was ample, few disputes arose, but when it became scarce due to drought or excessive use by one party over another, conflict exploded.

In Texas, in fact, not until the clarifying historical work of Justice Jack Pope in the 1962 case *State v. Valmont Plantations* (see appendix 1), when the Spanish water rights system was declared to be an appropriative system based only upon specific grants to the use of surface water, did riparian claim alone to irrigation basically end in Texas.

As law professor Hans W. Baade wrote in 1986, "Therefore, while Spanish and Mexican water *law* is entirely unrelated to the substantive contents of the Texas Water Code, water *rights* based on the law of the pre-Independence sovereigns of Texas [Spain and the Republic of Mexico] not only continued to be valid, but indeed had to be ascertained, whenever and wherever there were Spanish or Mexican land grants within a stream or stream segment to be adjudicated." Baade continued: "Water rights claimed to have arisen under Spanish and Mexican era grants had to be ascertained, even at this late date [1967], in terms of the water law of Spain and Mexico at the time and place of the grant of the surface estate pertinent to them."[10] Since title to almost one-sixth of all the land in Texas traces to valid pre-Independence grants, the validity of the water rights associated with these claims was not just one of historical interest but was and still is critical to the livelihood of the landowners.

As a result of Justice Pope's exhaustive research and ruling, the Texas Water Rights Adjudication Act of 1967 was passed in order to finally settle the issue of surface water rights in Texas. After 120 years of disputes in the courts, legislature, and government agencies statewide, the act required that all claims to surface water for irrigation purposes had to be presented to the Texas Water Rights Commission for adjudication between July 1967 and July 1969. The goal was to verify the true claims with a certificate of adjudication to settle the years of costly conflicts between parties claiming surface water rights. Another goal was to fairly and responsibly allocate the finite amount of Texas surface water. Some 10,000 claims were presented during this time, and most were adjudicated as confirmed or denied, but even today a few remain in dispute.[11] Texas is one of the few western states having fully adjudicated surface water rights, which was more easily accomplished in Texas because the federal government owned virtually no land in the state.

In 1913 and again in 1917, after and during other terrible droughts across the state, the Texas legislature extended the state's jurisdiction to regulate surface water use in amendments to the 1889 irrigation act. In 1917, the Texas Constitution (Article 16, Section 59) was amended to create a new duty of the legislature: it was to protect the natural resources of the state by having jurisdiction over all natural resources of the state, including surface water. This constitutional *duty*—not a choice for the legislature, but a duty—forms the modern foundation for all water regulation in the state.

Part Two

WHO OWNS WATER?

WATER: STATE OWNED

*Generally, ownership of water is directly related to its source
and type. It can be generally said that under Texas law,
underground water belongs to the owner of the surface estate,
while surface water belongs to the State of Texas and may
be only used by the landowner with the State's permission.*
—*Russell S. Johnson, attorney at law, April 2010*

First and foremost in understanding water ownership in
Texas is determining the "geological container" in which
the water resides at any point in time. The water molecule changes ownership many times in the hydrologic
cycle depending upon the geological containers it passes
through on its flow to sea level.

With the passage of Senate Bill 332 in 2011, a decades-
long debate on ownership of groundwater came to a
close, and it appears that for now at least, ownership of
water in Texas is clear: Surface water is owned by the
state; groundwater and "diffused" surface water (runoff)
are owned by the surface landowner.

Upper Rio Grande. Photo by author.

~~~~~ **SURFACE WATER IN RIVERS, STREAMS, AND LAKES**

Surface water in Texas lies in a geological container in which water flows in a natural bed such as a river, creek, or even the smallest stream. *Surface water is owned by the State of Texas and held in trust for the people.* This concept of ownership again is not without the earliest of precedents. The colonial Spanish brought this idea with them to Texas, where the king of Spain owned the surface water in trust for all "his" people. The safe assumption a landowner should make is that any water that runs in a "channelized" flow is owned by the State of Texas, including the underflow of any stream or other body of water.

State-owned water is defined in the following way by the Texas Water Code, Section 11.021:

(a) The water of the *ordinary flow,* underflow, and tides of every flowing river, natural stream, and lake, and of every bay or arm of the Gulf of Mexico, and the storm water, floodwater, and rainwater of every river, natural stream, canyon, ravine, depression, and watershed in the state is the property of the state.

(b) Water imported from any source outside the boundaries of the state for use in the state and which is transported through the beds and banks of any navigable stream within the state or by utilizing any facilities owned or operated by the state is the property of the state.

Of course, determining which water is state owned can be more complex than it seems, and contradictory opinions abound. One of the important considerations in determining if the surface water is state owned is whether or not the water is "ordinary" flow, that is, following its normal "watercourse." According to attorney Judon Fambrough of the Texas Real Estate Center at Texas A&M University,

> The key element determining whether surface water belongs to the state is the presence or absence of a watercourse. Texas owns all surface water in a natural body of water or watercourse. According to Texas case law, a watercourse contains three features: a defined bed, visible banks and a permanent supply of water.
>
> The supply of water need not be continuous to satisfy the definition, but a recurring flow is essential. Streams and creeks are publicly owned because they have a permanent supply of water. Draws, gullies, ravines and swales have defined beds and visible banks but they do not have a permanent supply of water. Water in these is considered diffused surface water and is privately owned.[1]

The Texas case that clearly defined "watercourse" was *Domel v. City of Georgetown* (1999), which also quoted an earlier case, *Hoefs v. Short* (1925). To expand on Fambrough's quote, the opinion in *Hoefs v. Short* was that the bed and banks may be "slight, imperceptible, or absent" and that the water current "need not be continuous"; the flow can be "intermittent . . . or even dry for long periods of time" and still be classified as a watercourse; therefore, the water found there is owned by the state. According to the Texas Supreme Court in *Hoefs*, "A permanent source of [water] supply . . . merely means that the stream must be such that similar conditions will produce a flow of water, and that those conditions recur with some regularity, so that they establish and maintain a running stream for considerable periods of time."[2]

The safest position for a landowner or real estate agent to take is that all surface water in *any* defined bed with visible banks could be state-owned water. Why? The repeated and persistent droughts in Texas make it very difficult to determine which flow is recurring. Before making any representations, it is wise to ask for a ruling from the TCEQ if you run across a situation where you are not absolutely sure about whether the water present is "recurring flow."

Floodwaters are also owned by the state when they are from a water-course with a permanent supply of water.[3] Floodwater that pools, however, and is permanently severed from the watercourse becomes the property of the landowner. The ruling in the Lower Guadalupe River adjudication in 1987 provided, "When surface waters or flood waters permanently come to rest in a natural depression, they lose their characteristics as surface or flood waters and become the waters of a lake or pond."[4]

Notice that floodwaters are considered the property of the state. However, under certain circumstances and in specific areas of the state, ownership can be modified according to the Texas Water Code, Section 11.023:

> (c) Unappropriated storm water and floodwater may be appropriated to recharge underground freshwater bearing sands and aquifers in the portion of the Edwards underground reservoir located within Kinney, Uvalde, Medina, Bexar, Comal, and Hays counties if it can be established by expert testimony that an unreasonable loss of state water will not occur and that the water can be withdrawn at a later time for application to a beneficial use. The normal or ordinary flow of a stream or watercourse may never be appropriated, diverted, or used by a permittee for this recharge purpose.

The next line in Section 11.023 is of special interest:

> (d) When it is put or allowed to sink into the ground, water appropriated under Subsection (c) of this section loses its character and classification as storm water or floodwater and is considered percolating groundwater.

The definition of water owned by the State of Texas is further explained in this statement published by the TCEQ: "Additionally, state water injected into the ground for an aquifer storage and recovery project remains state water. State water does not include percolating groundwater; nor does it include diffuse surface rainfall runoff, groundwater seepage, or springwater before it reaches the watercourse."[5] Obviously, any question about the ownership of water on a piece of land, especially land adjacent to a well-known creek, stream, or river, should be directed to the TCEQ. While surface water is owned by the State of Texas, a permit may be obtained for *use* of the water. This permit does not transfer ownership; the right granted to use the water is a usufruct right only.

As mentioned previously, the Water Rights Adjudication Act of 1967 set out the process of proving historical claims to the use of state-owned surface water. The TCEQ's publication G1-228, *Rights to Surface Water in Texas,* details the way in which the water rights commission set up the foundation for the current system of distributing water rights to state-owned surface water under the Adjudication Act. The TCEQ offers this account of the process: "State district courts . . . reviewed all . . . claims and the commission's [Texas Water Commission] recommendations. *Certificates of adjudication* were issued for approved claims. Each of these certificates was assigned a priority date based on when that water use first occurred. Some of the priority dates go back to the time of the first Spanish settlements. Since 1967, the courts have adjudicated about 10,000 claims. The process is complete except in the Upper Rio Grande Basin, where the remaining claims are now being adjudicated."

Texas claimants had to prove two points in the adjudication hearings: (1) that they had used a certain amount of water at a specified rate and for certain purposes from a specific stretch of a river, stream, or reservoir; and (2) the first date they had used that volume of water. The scope of the hearings in 1967 must have been overwhelming to the staff of the water rights commission. But due to the diligent and patient work of hundreds of people, claims to surface water rights in Texas, which had been so hotly disputed in the courts for more than 120 years, have for the most part been settled, and a stable and fair system of allocation and appropriation of adjudicated rights is in place.

Currently, surface water rights in Texas are determined, granted, and administered by the TCEQ. Before using state surface water or in advance of "construction on any project designed for the storage, taking, or diversion of" state surface water, a permit must be obtained from the TCEQ.[6] Surface water rights may be severed from the land and transferred, much like mineral rights, but the water cannot be moved without a permit from the TCEQ. (The first water right severed from the land in Texas occurred in 1742 in Villa San Fernando [San Antonio] and became a standard practice in the state.)

According to the TCEQ, two types of surface water rights are available: perpetual rights, including certificates of adjudication and permits; and limited-term rights, including term permits and temporary permits. These rights to use surface water are appropriated rights. As mentioned

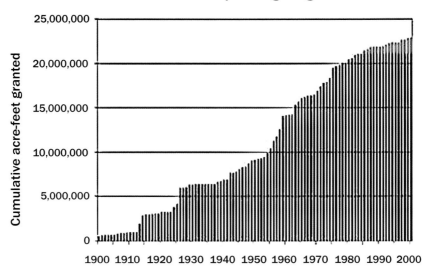

Texas Water Rights Timeline —
All consumptive rights granted

Surface water is fully allocated in Texas. Graphic provided by National Wildlife Federation, Austin, based on data from Texas Commission on Environmental Quality.

earlier, Texas follows the legal concept of prior appropriation: first in time, first in right. Today our surface water rights are fully allocated and at times even overallocated. Of the surface water allocation, irrigation makes up the largest use.

UNDERFLOW

Ordinary flow is water following its normal course in the streambed and is obvious to the observer. Less obvious to the observer is the underflow of the stream, the flow of water underneath the streambed. It is generally not visible and may or may not follow directly below the visible streambed. According to Kirk Holland of the Barton Springs/ Edwards Aquifer Conservation District, underflow is hard to determine. Due to the conjunctive nature of aquifers, streams, and the underflow of streams, at times it is very difficult, even with today's advanced science of hydrogeology, to distinguish when an underflow of a stream is recharging an aquifer or when an aquifer is flowing into the underflow of a stream.[7]

A landowner can divert or capture water from a watercourse in an amount up to 200 acre-feet in a stock pond.[8] One acre-foot of water equals 325,851 gallons of water, or about the amount of water it takes to flood a football field, not counting the end zones, 1 foot deep. The following are the complete TCEQ regulations about this situation:

(a) In accordance with Texas Water Code (TWC), §11.303(1), a person may directly divert and use water from a stream or watercourse for domestic and livestock purposes on land owned by the person and that is adjacent to the stream without obtaining a permit. Manner of diversion may be by pumping or by gravity flow. Such riparian domestic and livestock use is a vested right that predates the prior appropriation system in Texas and is superior to appropriative rights. A vested riparian right is only to the normal flow in the stream, not to the storm water, floodwater, or authorized releases from storage for downstream use.

(b) In accordance with TWC, §11.142, a person may construct on the person's own property a dam or reservoir with a normal storage of not more than 200 acre-feet of state water for domestic and livestock purposes without obtaining a permit. The reservoir may be on-channel, adjacent to the stream, or on a contiguous piece of property through which flows the stream from which the water is diverted. For purposes of this subsection, normal storage means the conservation storage of the reservoir, i.e., the amount of water the reservoir may hold before water is released uncontrolled through a spillway or into a standpipe. A person who temporarily stores more than 200 acre-feet of water in a dam or reservoir having a normal storage of greater than 200 acre-feet is not required to obtain a permit for the dam or reservoir if the person can demonstrate through reservoir capacity data and monthly reservoir water level records maintained by the owner that the person has not stored in the dam or reservoir more than 200 acre-feet of state water on average in any 12-month cycle. Selection of the 12-month cycle shall be at the owner's discretion, but must be consistent from year to year. This exemption does not apply to a commercial operation. Use of land for livestock purposes is not a commercial operation. This domestic and livestock exemption is not available to owners of property sold by a municipality having a population of 250,000 or less and owning land within 5,000 feet of where the shoreline of a lake would be if the lake were filled to its storage capacity, if the property was sold without notice or the solicitation of bids to the person leasing the land, in accordance with Local Government Code, §272.001(h).

(c) A dam constructed in accordance with subsection (b) of this section may not be located on a navigable stream.

(d) The use of a reservoir by free-ranging wild game and fur-bearing animals that may be harvested by hunters and trappers who pay a fee or other compensation to hunt or trap on the property does not constitute a use for which a permit must be obtained for an otherwise exempt domestic and livestock reservoir. Additionally, the use of water that is used in making products from a family garden or orchard that are traded with a neighbor or used in a local bake sale or potluck dinner does not constitute a use for which a permit must be obtained for an otherwise exempt domestic and livestock reservoir.

(e) In accordance with TWC, §11.142(b), a person may construct on the person's property a dam or reservoir with normal storage of not more than 200 acre-feet of water for wildlife management as defined in Texas Tax Code (TTC), §23.51(7), and for fish management purposes, excluding aquaculture or fish farming purposes, if the property on which the dam or reservoir will be constructed is qualified open-space land, as defined by TTC, §23.51. For purposes of this subsection, normal storage means the conservation storage of the reservoir, i.e., the amount of water the reservoir may hold before water is released uncontrolled through a spillway or into a standpipe. This exemption does not apply to a commercial operation. For the purposes of this subsection, commercial operation means the use of land for industrial facilities, industrial parks, aquaculture facilities, fish farming facilities, or housing developments. The incidental use of the reservoir in a manner that does not remove the land from the definition of qualified open-space land as defined by TTC, §23.51, including using a photograph in advertising, does not constitute a use for which a permit must be obtained for an otherwise exempt reservoir.[9]

Any questions a prudent landowner or real estate agent has about diverting surface water into a stock tank should be directed to an attorney or to the TCEQ for a ruling, *prior to* either beginning construction or representing to a potential buyer that the existing condition is legal. Be extraordinarily careful when diverting surface water.[10]

Even though landowners have a right recognized by the state to divert 200 acre-feet of water from a state stream without a permit, it is always a better idea to be sure of compliance to avoid the startlingly high penalties that could be assessed for illegal actions. Before diversion of a stream, it may prove wise to check with the Texas Parks and Wildlife Department and the US Fish and Wildlife Service to be sure the planned diversion does not harm any environmental flow regulations for the particular stream or area in which the land is located. While this seems cumbersome and in many ways unfair to the landowner, the complexities of water rights, regulations, and laws make it essential to thoroughly understand the legality of any plan of action involving water.

≈≈≈≈ **OTHER EXEMPTIONS FROM PERMIT**

The TCEQ lists other published exemptions from permitting use of surface water in Texas:

1. *Domestic and Livestock Use.* Also called D&L use, this refers to water used to water range livestock, meet household needs, or irrigate a yard or home garden.
2. *Wildlife Management.* In 2001, the Legislature added wildlife management as an exempt use. Under this use, you may build on your own property a dam or reservoir that normally holds no more than 200 acre-feet of water. This reservoir must also be on *qualified open-space land,* as defined by Section 23.51 of the Texas Tax Code. If you have questions about whether you qualify for this exemption, contact our Water Rights Permitting & Availability Program.
3. *Emergency Use.* County fire departments, rural fire departments, and other similar public services may draw water from local reservoirs when needed to deal with an emergency.
4. *Other Specified Uses.* The Water Code's less-common exempt uses may under certain conditions include the use of water in fish or shrimp farming, in drilling for and extracting oil, or for sediment controls in surface coal mines. Retaining water with spreader dams or terraced contours is also considered an exempt use. Under these exempt uses, you may take water from a stream. However, if your operation adds sediment or other contaminants to the water before you discharge it, you should determine whether you may need to obtain a water quality permit.[11]

"Navigable" streams in Texas have been a source of much argument, consternation, and rumor about who owns the water they contain. One of the tests to determine who owns the streambed is whether or not the stream is navigable.

Judon Fambrough pointed out in an article in *Tierra Grande,* a publication of the Texas Real Estate Center at Texas A&M University, that navigability is the factor in whether or not a watercourse can be *dammed;* some navigable watercourses may be dammed legally (for livestock or domestic use), but it is illegal to dam a watercourse navigable by certain types of boats such as keelboats, steamboats, and flatboats. He defined "navigable in law" and "navigable in fact." According to Fambrough, "A stream is navigable in law if the average width from its mouth upstream is 30 feet or more. The volume of water carried is irrelevant. . . . A stream is navigable in fact . . . if the volume of water will support shipping, commerce and travel. . . . If a stream is navigable by either definition the state owns the streambed." He went on to mention another potential downside for landowners who legally dam a stream. "Once a navigable stream is dammed, the public has the right of access to the reservoir. However, if the dam is built across a non-navigable stream, the public could be denied access as long as the reservoir does not border on public property." Be doubly sure the "impounded" reservoir is used for livestock or domestic purposes or has a permit from the TCEQ. To repeat: The fines are $5,000 per day per occurrence.[12]

It may appear to be a great idea to dam a stream for personal use. However, remember that if the stream is navigable, then the public has access to it. If privacy is important to a landowner, the landowner should consider the public access seriously before damming up the stream. A prudent landowner or real estate agent should ask the TCEQ for a ruling on the navigability of any stream before construction begins. The Texas General Land Office surveying department is another resource to consider.

〰〰〰 **CITIES AND PRIORITY TO USE SURFACE WATER**

What about a city's rights to surface water? Do cities have a priority to the surface water of the state? The TCEQ's *Rights to Surface Water in Texas* poses this question followed by its answer: "*Don't cities come* before *factories and fields?* Many people mistakenly believe that *how* water is to be used determines when a user can be shut off in a shortage. For example, it is often heard that municipal use carries a higher priority than irrigation or industrial use. In most of Texas, that is not the case. Only in the Middle and Lower Rio Grande basin does purpose of use determine priority—and then for *only* the water stored in Falcon and Amistad reservoirs. In these reservoirs, municipal and industrial rights have priority over irrigation when water shortages require that supplies be allocated." A city's priority to water depends upon the area of the state and its unique geographically written statutes, rules, and regulations. More about municipal use and the water rights of cities can be found in chapter 7.

In summary, the safest assumption any landowner or potential land purchaser should make is that any and all water in streams that have a permanent source of water, for example, from a spring or seep, or running in even the smallest streambed, is owned by the state until a ruling by the TCEQ provides a different determination. Writing to ask for a ruling by the TCEQ will save money in both fines and legal fees. Additional legal fees, fines, and potential damages from a lawsuit brought by a downstream landowner or a new purchaser can be avoided with a ruling in advance of any action to divert or dam a stream.

WATER: PRIVATELY OWNED

In the hydrologic cycle, surface water, before it becomes water in a watercourse, likely gets to the watercourse by running off the ground. Diffused surface water is rainwater or the water in our rare snowmelts—runoff—that stays on a landowner's property before it enters a bed or channelized flow.[1] This diffused surface water is owned by the landowner and is subject to capture without obtaining a permit from the state. If the landowner is able to capture the runoff water, defined as "casual or vagrant" water, before it joins a natural gully, stream, or watercourse, the landowner owns this water.[2] This captured diffused water can be sold or used as the landowner sees fit. However, the moment this captured water enters a watercourse, its ownership transfers to the state. Water left standing in upland areas after a flood recedes may also qualify as diffused surface water, even though actual floodwaters cannot be captured because they are owned by the state.

DIFFUSED SURFACE WATER: "RUNOFF"

Although diffused surface water may be diverted or captured without a permit, the act of diversion cannot cause damage to other landowners. According to the Texas Water Code, Section 11.086,

(a) No person may divert or impound the natural flow of surface waters in this state, or permit a diversion or impounding by him to continue, in a manner that damages the property of another by the overflow of the water diverted or impounded.

(b) A person whose property is injured by an overflow of water caused by an unlawful diversion or impounding has remedies at law and in equity and may recover damages occasioned by the overflow.

(c) The prohibition of Subsection (a) of this section does not in any way affect the construction and maintenance of levees and other improvements to control floods, overflows, and freshets in rivers, creeks, and streams or the construction of canals for conveying water for irrigation or other purposes authorized by this code. However, this subsection does not authorize any person to construct a canal, lateral canal, or ditch that obstructs a river, creek, bayou, gully, slough, ditch, or other well-defined natural drainage.

(d) Where gullies or sloughs have cut away or intersected the banks of a river or creek to allow floodwaters from the river or creek to overflow the land nearby, the owner of the flooded land may fill the mouth of the gullies or sloughs up to the height of the adjoining banks of the river or creek without liability to other property owners.

Dietrich v. Goodman (2003) established that the term "surface water" in the section of the water code just quoted refers to diffused surface water.

Stock tanks are artificially created to capture rainwater or diffused surface water; therefore, the water in the tank is owned by the landowner.[3] Stock tanks are gems in a landowner's pocket, so to speak, and as a hedge against our continuing droughts, it is my opinion one can never build too many stock tanks. They must be maintained, however. A variety of state agencies, such as the Texas Department of Agriculture and the Texas A&M AgriLife Extension Service, can provide guidelines for the design and maintenance of tanks. County extension agents know the local soils and can be very helpful in making decisions about the right depth and lining of a stock tank and in providing all kinds of local, experience-based information. The great news is that the county agents' advice is free.

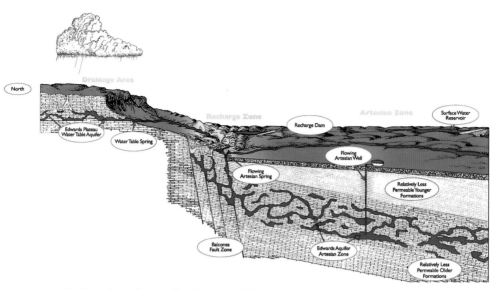

Section of a typical aquifer. Courtesy United States Geological Survey.

〰〰〰 GROUNDWATER

> *Ground water is assuming an interestingly significant role*
> *in our economy; questions involving its ownership and control*
> *have become extremely important.* —Joe R. Greenhill and
> Thomas Gibbs Gee, *"Ownership of Ground Water in Texas"*

Today, groundwater has fully assumed the role these famous jurists mentioned at the height of the nightmarish drought of the 1950s. Allocation and management of groundwater has since been and will remain in the future the focal point of Texas water policies.

Groundwater is the water beneath the land surface that fills the pore spaces of rock and soil material and that supplies wells and springs. Groundwater can be found in pools and aquifers below the surface. Not all groundwater is potable or drinkable by humans; some is brackish or contains mineral salts (not necessarily sodium chloride, or table salt, but all kinds of complex salts), giving the water a bad taste and causing it to be toxic to plants. According to numerous private studies and studies done by state agencies, one of the great hopes we have to remedy future water shortages in Texas is to find more and more economical ways to desalinate the estimated 2.64 billion acre-feet of brackish groundwater in the state.

Much of the state's groundwater is held in aquifers. Of the main Texas aquifers, 9 are classified as major and 23 are classified as minor. These

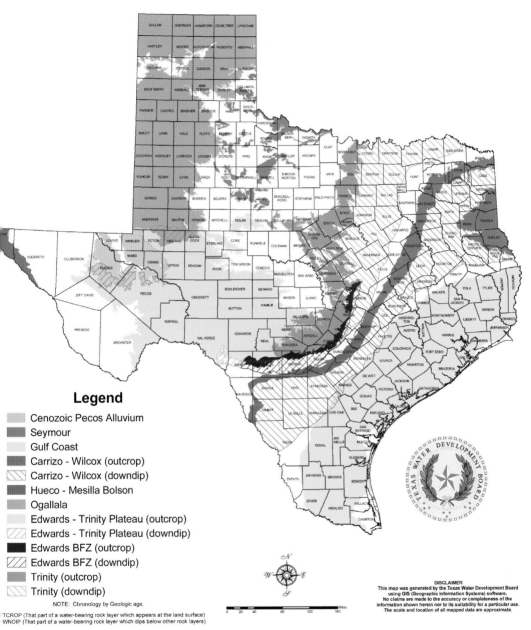

Legend

- Cenozoic Pecos Alluvium
- Seymour
- Gulf Coast
- Carrizo - Wilcox (outcrop)
- Carrizo - Wilcox (downdip)
- Hueco - Mesilla Bolson
- Ogallala
- Edwards - Trinity Plateau (outcrop)
- Edwards - Trinity Plateau (downdip)
- Edwards BFZ (outcrop)
- Edwards BFZ (downdip)
- Trinity (outcrop)
- Trinity (downdip)

NOTE: Chronology by Geologic age.

TCROP (That part of a water-bearing rock layer which appears at the land surface)
WNDIP (That part of a water-bearing rock layer which dips below other rock layers)

Major aquifers of Texas showing groundwater management areas.

Courtesy Texas Water Development Board.

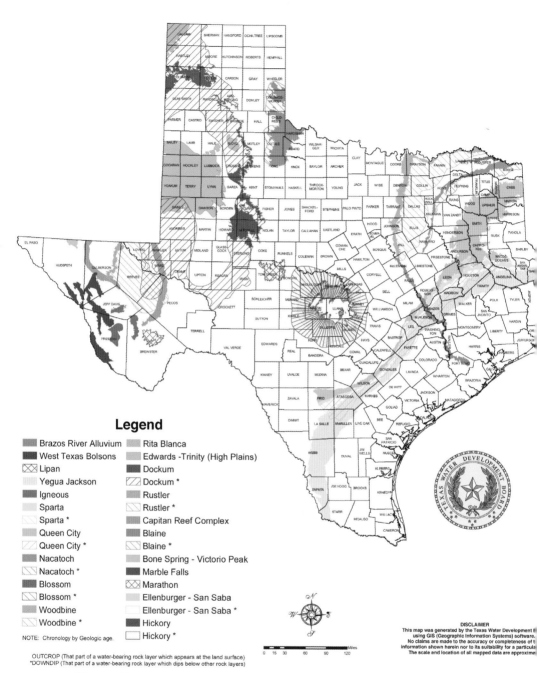

Legend

Brazos River Alluvium	Rita Blanca
West Texas Bolsons	Edwards -Trinity (High Plains)
Lipan	Dockum
Yegua Jackson	Dockum *
Igneous	Rustler
Sparta	Rustler *
Sparta *	Capitan Reef Complex
Queen City	Blaine
Queen City *	Blaine *
Nacatoch	Bone Spring - Victorio Peak
Nacatoch *	Marble Falls
Blossom	Marathon
Blossom *	Ellenburger - San Saba
Woodbine	Ellenburger - San Saba *
Woodbine *	Hickory
	Hickory *

NOTE: Chronology by Geologic age.

OUTCROP (That part of a water-bearing rock layer which appears at the land surface)
*DOWNDIP (That part of a water-bearing rock layer which dips below other rock layers)

Miles
0 15 30   60   90   120

Minor aquifers of Texas showing groundwater management areas.

Courtesy Texas Water Development Board.

aquifers supply 59 percent of all the water used in Texas, and 97 percent of this water is stored in the major aquifers. Irrigators use 79 percent of the water from aquifers; 82 percent of this subtotal is drawn from the Ogallala Aquifer. Municipal demands account for 36 percent of water used from groundwater stored in aquifers.

Texas aquifers vary as to the ability and the rate at which they can replenish or "recharge." The Edwards Aquifer replenishes rather quickly, but the Ogallala has a much slower recharge rate. Some of our aquifers are being "mined"; that is, more water is being taken out than is being replaced by recharge. Some aquifers discharge naturally via springs and seeps, and some make up the base flow for rivers and streams. Therefore, aquifers conjunctively function with all our water sources.

Aquifer Recharge Zones

Recharge zones are the designated and protected areas across the many aquifers in our state through which surface water enters the ground to replenish the groundwater, and the recharge zones of most of our major aquifers are environmentally protected. For example, the Edwards Aquifer recharge zone encompasses a significant area of Central Texas. One method cities and counties use to protect recharge is to place a limit on "impervious" cover—concrete, asphalt, and even in some areas, gravel—allowing greater percolation into the aquifer through natural surfaces. Impervious cover limitations in these zones are critical to this protection strategy. However, these limitations generally decrease commercial property values because of the limit placed upon the size of improvements, and there can be an impact to the tax base as a result, money from which is used for public operations such as schools and hospitals.

An example of the impact of impervious cover limitations is found in the Buda area. As a result of new mapping, the recharge zone has been expanded to the east, closing in on the intersection of SH 967 and SH 1626. A 4.2-acre tract is for sale at this intersection, which fronts on SH 1626. Generally, this tract has an allowable impervious cover of 65 percent of the surface, the minimum amount needed to economically develop a commercial building and parking lot. Land in the area has sold for between $4 and $10 per square foot. The westernmost 5 feet of this tract has recently been included in the aquifer recharge zone, and now this area's allowable impervious cover has dropped to 15 percent. A further movement of the recharge zone a few hundred yards to the east will drop more of the tract from 65 percent allowable impervious cover to 15 percent. Should this event occur, the property's market value will fall by 50 percent or more since the tract will no longer be developable into a viable commercial property such as a retail center or office building. The consequences to the landowner's long-term property value can be devastating; the consequences to the tax base of the Buda Independent School District may be affected as well.

Here lies another example of the choices we have to make as citizens. What do voters value more, the protection and enhancement of the aquifer recharge or support of the ad valorem tax base for schools and other public operations? If the recharge zone is modified and consequently the impervious cover allowed decreases on a given tract of land, should the landowner be compensated for the resulting drop in the value of the land?

Ownership of Groundwater

Groundwater is private property in Texas, owned by the surface owners or their assigns. The ownership of groundwater by the surface landowner in Texas was clarified by the passage of SB 332 in 2011 and further confirmed by the Texas Supreme Court in 2012 in *The Edwards Aquifer Authority and the State of Texas v. Burrell Day and Joel McDaniel.* But the concept of groundwater ownership in Texas has long been a source of conflict and under judicial review several times.

Rule of Capture

After the landmark 1904 decision in *Houston & Texas Central Railroad Company v. East,** Texas has followed the concept of the rule of capture for groundwater, or "he who has the biggest pump gets the water," without liability to his neighbor. The rule of capture is subject to three limitations today:

1. A landowner's pumping of groundwater cannot maliciously be done to harm a neighbor.
2. A landowner's pumping of groundwater cannot be done in a wasteful manner.

Suffice it to say, most landowners in Texas for many years considered groundwater underneath their land to be their property; SB 332 passed easily by a large margin in both houses of the 82nd Texas Legislature. Most Texans have also felt that any taking of that groundwater by eminent domain or other regulatory action should be compensated. In the first sentence of the ruling in the *Day* case, Justice Nathan Hecht wrote, "We decide in this case whether land ownership includes an interest in groundwater in place that cannot be taken for public use without adequate compensation guaranteed by article 1, section 17 (a) of the Texas Constitution. We hold that it does."[4]

The dispute in the case arose in 1996 when landowners Day and McDaniel requested a permit to draw 700 acre-feet of groundwater per year from the Edwards Aquifer, regulated by the then recently formed Edwards Aquifer Authority (EAA), and were granted only 14 acre-feet by the EAA.[5] The issue eventually considered by the Texas Supreme Court was not about the EAA's authority; the court decided EAA's authority was clear, and the EAA had acted properly. The landmark issue that the Texas Supreme Court considered was whether Day had a constitutionally protected interest in the groundwater beneath his property; the court concluded that Day's interest *was* constitutionally protected. The pending issue then became whether the EAA's regulatory scheme had resulted in a taking of Day's constitutionally protected interest, which would have meant that EAA owed Day an amount of monetary com-

3. A landowner's pumping of groundwater cannot be done in a negligent manner that is the proximate cause of a neighboring property's subsidence.**

Groundwater conservation districts (GCDs) may provide additional limitations under the their duly promulgated authorities to determine the amount of water that can be pumped under the rule of capture.

*The *East* case is discussed in detail in chapter 10.

**See appendix 1 for discussion of *Smith-Southwest Industries v. Friendswood Development.*

pensation. Unfortunately, the case settled out of court on June 25, 2013, without addressing this issue.[6]

The *Day* case made it clear that groundwater is owned by the surface landowner and that the ownership interest is constitutionally protected by the State of Texas. The next big question that cases similar to *Day* will determine is this: How much groundwater regulation is too much? Although not all local governments in Texas have chosen to be covered by a GCD, a locally managed GCD is the preferred method of management of groundwater in Texas, as confirmed several times over the last decade by the Texas legislature. Since the EAA is a unique form of groundwater conservation district, every GCD watched the *Day* case closely because it would have determined their limitations in allocating their constituents' privately owned groundwater, especially in light of a significant entrepreneurial effort of those whose business goal is to "harvest, transport, and sell" groundwater to many of Texas' thirsty cities. Because the *Day* case was settled, the GCDs are still left without guidance from the courts on these issues.

5

WATER: SHARED OWNERSHIP

States neighboring Texas claim ownership of their surface water and groundwater. The states share surface water, from major boundary rivers to hundreds of streams and creeks. The Red River and the Sabine River form part of our boundaries with Oklahoma, Arkansas, and Louisiana. Texas shares transboundary aquifers with New Mexico, and the Rio Grande springs from Colorado and New Mexico headwaters. In any dispute between states over surface water, the only court with jurisdiction is the United States Supreme Court.

 OKLAHOMA, ARKANSAS, LOUISIANA, AND NEW MEXICO
To date there have been few disputes with our neighboring states other than some boundary disputes with Oklahoma as the Red River meanders—disputes concerning oil and gas reserve locations. The Sabine River between Texas and Louisiana is located in the wet area of the state in relation to rainfall, so the potential for disputes over water issues is lessened. However, the Sabine springs from headwaters in Texas, and any diversion of Sabine flow would certainly concern Louisiana, as any diversion of the Sabine on the Louisiana side would Texas. The

View from the middle of Amistad Dam looking south. Photo by author.

Canadian River flows through the Texas Panhandle from New Mexico through a large part of Oklahoma. Any diversions by New Mexico and/or Texas concern Oklahoma. In the early twentieth century the Elephant Butte Reservoir on the Rio Grande caused quite a debate, but Texas and New Mexico came to agreement and the reservoir was built.

There are too many creeks and streams that flow in and out of the states to mention, but any question about any stream shared by the states should first be directed to the TCEQ.

≈≈≈ MEXICO

> *The US Border Patrol and the Mexican Army knows borders,*
> *but water does not recognize national boundaries. —Bill Tilney,*
> *former mayor of El Paso and consul general in Ciudad Juárez*

Texas and Mexico share a 1,254-mile boundary along the Rio Grande (Río Bravo in Mexico). The "border" is an area south of a line (IH-10) from El Paso to San Antonio and south and west of a line (IH-37) from San Antonio to Corpus Christi. The population growth along the border has been staggering in the past decade. Areas such as the Rio Grande Valley between McAllen and Brownsville boom even today. McAllen amazingly has the lowest per capita household income (less than $20,000 per year) yet has the highest per capita household retail sales (more than $80,000 per year). This statistic alone indicates the special situation along the Lower Rio Grande; retail purchases by citizens from northern Mexico drive the McAllen economy. El Paso is in a long-term growth period and has recently seen an even greater increase in growth, which is logical as thousands are fleeing drug wars in Juárez to live in El Paso. The US Army base at Fort Bliss continues to grow and bring economic stability to the area, as does the University of Texas at El Paso. The people of the border are a unique blend of Americans and Mexicans who consider the Rio Grande as just another watercourse to cross. Most border people are concerned with their families on either side with much less attention paid to nationalities—their families and friends are simply people, not Mexicans or Americans.

"The essential, defining geographic characteristic of the borderland is its aridity—the scarcity of water."[1] The surface water in the border area is prone to depletion from time to time by drought coupled with irrigation. For years, the only focus has been on surface water; the treaties and agreements with Mexico ignored groundwater and associated aquifers. However, the United States and Mexico share 18 groundwater sources, all of which conjunctively relate in some manner with the shared river, Rio Grande/Río Bravo.

Groundwater conservation districts in Texas regulate groundwater in some areas along the Rio Grande. However, not all the borderlands in Texas along the Rio Grande are subject to GCDs; there is no district in the Del Rio area, for example.

In Mexico, groundwater can be owned privately as it was during Spanish rule, but groundwater underlying public lands is government owned. Mexican law allows the government to regulate groundwater use on a priority basis and may place public use of groundwater above private use as deemed necessary. The 1917 Mexican Constitution states that "underground waters may be brought to the surface by artificial works and utilized by the surface owner, but if the public interest so requires or use by others is affected, the Federal Executive may regulate its extraction and utilization, and even establish prohibited areas."[2] Since 1917, the Mexican government has in essence federalized groundwater via the 1934 National Water Law and the 1956 Law of Conservation and Groundwater. There is now a National Water Commission in Mexico that exercises even greater control of all water resources in the country.

The significance of the issue of water as a common pool resource shared between nations is illustrated best in El Paso. El Paso and Ciudad Juárez draw water from the same aquifer, the Hueco-Bolson. Ciudad Juárez's population exploded in the 1980s due to the growth of global manufacturing and migration of Mexicans from the interior of Mexico to the border area to seek employment. The aquifer was drawn down significantly, but due to a slowing in the population growth and an actual decline of population in Juárez, much based upon the chaos that is a consequence of the drug cartels and Mexico's war on drugs, the drawdown is "tapering off."[3] The City of El Paso's desalination plant, which makes brackish water drinkable, is also giving the aquifer some needed relief.

For the past 25 years, there has been cross-border water planning between El Paso and Ciudad Juárez, and in 2009 El Paso was host to a binational conference that focused on water and water conservation. One of the major topics was sewage treatment along the border. In our interview, Bill Tilney said, "I am pleased to note that over the past 15 years we have seen sanitary sewage treatment plants and other facilities built along the border to improve health conditions. NAD Bank and commissions along the border have been helpful in that regard, and I was pleased to have worked with Camp, Dresser and McKee, Inc. engineering firm to assist in the construction of some of these facilities. While there are good intentions by Chihuahuan and Texan officials, the bottom line is that given the poverty level in Juárez and the outlying area, providing water to an impoverished population will dictate how water is used there." According to writer S. C. Gwynne, "Sixty percent of the water in that plant [a Ciudad Juárez sewage treatment plant] ends up back in your local rivers. It may dismay you to learn that in many rivers all across the United States and in many parts of the world, *particularly downstream of a major city, much of the water you see is treated effluent.*"[4]

As one who has visited Texas/Mexico border cities for decades, I can attest to sickeningly bad smells from time to time on both sides of the border around the creeks that enter the Rio Grande. Further investigation on my part made me aware of the inadequacy of the sanitary sewage treatment plants on those occasions, again found on both sides of the border.

The only approach to finding a fair long-term solution to water issues between Texas and Mexico is to consider both where the water comes from and in what condition it will be when it returns to the system. Treatment plants cost millions of dollars and take years to build. Both human waste treatment and the effect of runoff from industrial and agricultural activities should be considered. To properly address planning how best to enhance the water shared by Mexico and Texas requires a partnership full of understanding, respect, and concern for the interconnectedness we have with one another.

As discussed in my keynote speeches at Water Workshops in 2009 and 2011, US water relations with Mexico date back to the days of the Mexican War in 1848. Article VII of the Treaty of Guadalupe Hidalgo declared that both nations have the right to navigate the Rio Grande and that neither nation could unilaterally "construct any work that may impede or interrupt, in whole or in part, the exercise of this right." The Gadsden Purchase of 1853 confirmed the same. In 1880, a conflict between Mexican and Texan farmers arose over irrigation from the river. The conflicts continued until 1889, when both nations created the International Boundary Commission (IBC), which eventually became the International Boundary and Water Commission (IBWC).

However, the IBC was not able to settle the disputes between irrigators on either side of the border. At the suggestion of the IBC, the first water distribution treaty was negotiated, the 1906 Rio Grande Convention, a nonbinding agreement with little effect on the water disputes. The limited nature of the 1906 Convention led to the Water Treaty of February 3, 1944, which addressed water across the entire Texas border with Mexico. The treaty allocated water along the Rio Grande between the nations, and Mexico was required to deliver 350,000 acre-feet of Rio Grande water to the United States.

Not addressed in the 1944 treaty were groundwater or transboundary aquifers, of which there are at least seven between the United States and Mexico from Brownsville to San Diego. Finally in 2006, the US Congress passed the United States–Mexico Transboundary Aquifer Assessment Act. This legislation recognized the need to at least "study" the situation; to date no final report has been made.

One of the key recharge sources of the Rio Grande in Mexico is the Río Conchos, a giant river system with headwaters throughout the Sierra Madre range. When the snowmelt is too low to feed the Río Conchos headwaters, the Mexicans fall behind on the amount of water they must release to the Rio Grande. For many years, reports of billions of gallons of water debt generated American complaints. However, as nature has a habit of doing, in just one or two years of good moisture in the Río Conchos basin, Mexico was able to make up the "debt."

Like all other negotiations between people or nations, one of the most critical challenges for any mediator is balance of power between the parties in dispute. In 1944, at the peak of World War II, the United States was the more powerful country in the negotiation of this treaty. Was this power used to the disadvantage of Mexico? Perhaps the more important question is whether or not the 1944 treaty should be modified to better address current situations on the border.

~~~~ **NEIGHBORING WATER MANAGEMENT AGENCIES**

Here is a list of the major agencies that have some jurisdiction over the surface water and transboundary aquifers Texas shares with its neighbors for all three geological containers. Diffused surface water is not managed jointly at this time with any of Texas' neighbors.

Surface Water Management
1. *Internationally:* International Boundary and Water Commission
2. *Nationally:* Comisión Nacional de Aqua (Mexico) and the Bureau of Reclamation (United States)
3. *Between the states in the respective countries:* Rio Grande Compact Commission in the United States and the federal government in Mexico
4. *Internally in the states in the respective countries:* Texas Commission on Environmental Quality, the New Mexico Office of the State Engineer, Junta Central de Aqua y Saneamiento in Chihuahua (Mexico), and in Texas and New Mexico by state watermasters
5. *Locally:* Individual municipalities and irrigation districts in both countries

Groundwater Management
1. *New Mexico:* New Mexico Office of the State Engineer (groundwater is owned by the state in New Mexico and is heavily managed and appropriated)
2. *Texas:* Groundwater conservation districts and the Texas

Commission on Environmental Quality (groundwater is owned in Texas by private individuals, corporations, and cities)

3. *Mexico:* Comisión Nacional de Aqua and irrigation districts to some degree, but both are susceptible to political influence by powerful individuals and other interests

Part Three

HOW IS WATER USED
AND REGULATED?

6

SUPPLY AND DEMAND,
TODAY AND TOMORROW

Why is an understanding of water rights in Texas more important today than ever before in our history? Because Texas currently has a strong economy, and experts project Texas will experience long-term growth.

 GROWTH PROJECTIONS AND WATER SUPPLY

Most experts expect the population of Texas to almost double by 2060. That growth would put tremendous pressure on our water resources, and predictions show a trend downward in the supply of water versus demand over the same time period, even without the recurring droughts. But in drought times, sure to revisit regularly, the predictions are dire indeed. In the state water plan for 2012, water development board chair Edward G. Vaughan wrote in his cover letter this significant statement: "The primary message of the 2012 State Water Plan is a simple one: In serious drought conditions, Texas does not and will not have enough water to meet the needs of its people, its businesses, and its agricultural enterprises. . . . This plan also presents the sobering news of the economic losses likely to occur if these water supply needs cannot be met."[1]

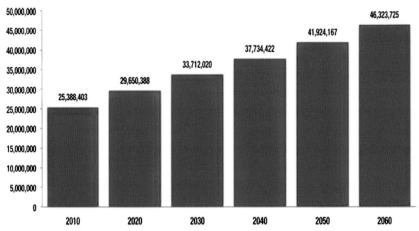

Projected population growth in Texas, 2010–2060.
Courtesy Texas Water Development Board.

Projections indicate that irrigation will hold steady as a major user of water resources over the next 50 years along with a corresponding large growth in municipal use. These statistics clearly demonstrate why water resources in Texas are under pressure now and will be in the future and why water must be protected, enhanced, and conserved.

~~~~~ WATER PLANNING EFFORTS

In June 1997, Governor George W. Bush signed into law Senate Bill 1 (SB 1), comprehensive water legislation enacted by the 75th Texas Legislature. This legislation was an outgrowth of increased awareness of the vulnerability of Texas to drought and to the limits of existing water supplies to meet increasing demands as population grows.

Regional Water Planning Groups

With passage of SB 1, the legislature put in place a "bottom-up" water planning process designed to help ensure that the water needs of all Texans were met as Texas entered the twenty-first century. Governor Bush set up planning groups to work on long-term water strategies for surface water and groundwater. The legislature followed up by creating specific groundwater management areas and regional water planning groups to plan for the long-term future of water in Texas.

The Texas Water Development Board (TWDB) divided the state into 16 regional water planning groups (RWPGs). Senate Bill 1 mandated that individuals representing 11 interest groups serve as members of the

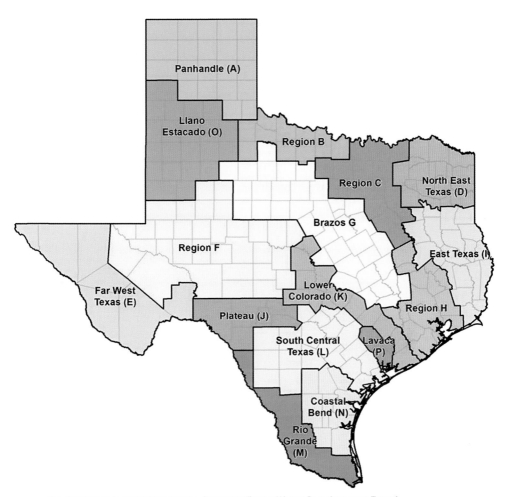

Regional water planning groups. Courtesy Texas Water Development Board.

RWPGs, which would be responsible for deciding how future water needs in their respective regions may be met and would prepare regional water plans for their respective areas. The plans they developed would map out how to conserve water supplies, meet future water supply needs, and respond to future droughts in the planning areas.

The planning process begins with the collection and analysis of various kinds of information related to water demands and supplies. Two basic types of information are needed to determine surface water supplies for regional water planning. First, the total available supply within the region, which comprises the firm yield of individual reservoirs (the maximum water volume a reservoir can provide each year under a repeat of the drought of record), the increased yield due to current system operations, and the "run-of-the-river" supplies (the changing, dynamic surface flow), must be determined. Second, the supply of water currently available to water-user groups as identified by user source and limited by permits, contracts, availability, and infrastructure must be determined.

Each regional water plan includes information about water supplies and demand, water quality problems affecting water supply, and social and economic characteristics of the region. The plan also identifies water supply threats to agriculture and other natural resources. Information concerning current preparations for drought and the status of other water plans in the region are also reviewed.

The following tasks are common to each regional water plan:

- determine water demands;
- determine water supplies available for use during drought of record;
- determine where and when there is a surplus of supply or a need for additional supplies;
- determine social and economic impact of not meeting needs;
- develop specific strategies to meet future near-term needs (less than 30 years);
- develop options to meet long-term future needs (30–50 years);
- determine identified needs with no feasible solutions;
- identify ecologically unique streams and rivers;
- identify unique sites for reservoir construction;
- coordinate with neighboring regions concerning mutual interests and shared resources; and
- propose regulatory, administrative, or legislative recommendations to improve water resource management in the state.

In 2006, the RWPGs in Texas anticipated that the "current" demand of 17 million acre-feet per year in 2010 will increase to 21.6 million acre-feet by the year 2060. According to the more recent chart shown here, the "current" demand in 2010 has already exceeded 18 million acre-feet per year.

State Water Plan

Under SB 1, the TWDB is required to develop a state water plan every five years: "Section 16.051 of the Texas Water Code directs the Texas Water Development Board to prepare, develop, formulate, and adopt a comprehensive State Water Plan that incorporates the regional water plans ap-

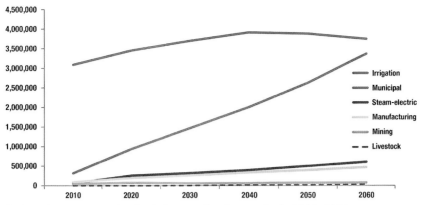

Projected water demand and existing supplies (in acre-feet), 2010–2060.
Courtesy Texas Water Development Board.

proved under Section 16.053. The State Water Plan shall provide for the orderly development, management, and conservation of water resources and preparation for and response to drought conditions, in order that sufficient water will be available at a reasonable cost to ensure public health, safety, and welfare, further economic development, and protect agricultural and natural resources of the entire State." Through the RWPGs, the TWDB developed the most recent plan, for 2012, published in the fall of 2011. Here are a few "quick facts" mentioned in the 2012 plan:

- The population in Texas is expected to increase 82 percent between the years of 2010 and 2060, growing from 25.4 million people to 46.3 million people.
- Water demand is expected to increase by 22 percent,[2] from about 18 million acre-feet per year in 2010 to about 22 million acre-feet per year in 2060.
- Existing water supplies—the amount of water that can be produced with current permits, current contracts, and existing infrastructure during drought—are projected to decrease about 10 percent, from about 17.0 million acre-feet in 2010 to about 15.3 million acre-feet in 2060, due primarily to Ogallala Aquifer depletion and reduced reliance on the Gulf Coast Aquifer.
- If Texas does not implement new water supply projects or management strategies, then homes, businesses, and agricultural enterprises throughout the state are projected to need 8.3 million acre-feet of additional water supply by 2060.

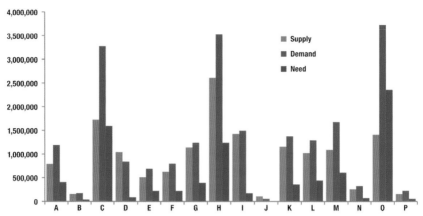

Water needs and supplies in 2060 (in acre-feet per region).
Courtesy Texas Water Development Board.

- The capital cost to design, construct or implement the recommended water management strategies and projects is *$53 billion*. Municipal water providers are expected to need nearly *$27 billion in state financial assistance* to implement these strategies [emphasis added].

Even more troubling for Texas agribusiness is this comment: "Irrigation represents the vast majority (98–99 percent) of unmet needs in all decades [of this plan]. Since irrigation uses 60 percent of the state's total current water demand today (decreasing to 38 percent by 2060),[3] and agriculture is key to our economy, the statement bodes ill for our future.

Some regions in Texas are predicted to have adequate water supplies. However, some, such as Region O, are projected to fall woefully short. One of its most critical water resources is the Ogallala Aquifer, which is shared by several states from Texas to South Dakota.[4]

Funding for Water Shortages

In the fall 2011 election, Texas voters were asked to consider Proposition 2, which would enable the State of Texas to issue $6 billion in general revenue bonds to fund emergency and other water projects for those governmental entities in Texas too small to be able to either obtain credit or pay a reasonable interest rate. It passed. Prop 2 gives TWDB the chance to use the high credit rating of the State of Texas to reduce the cost of borrowing for the smaller political subdivisions around the

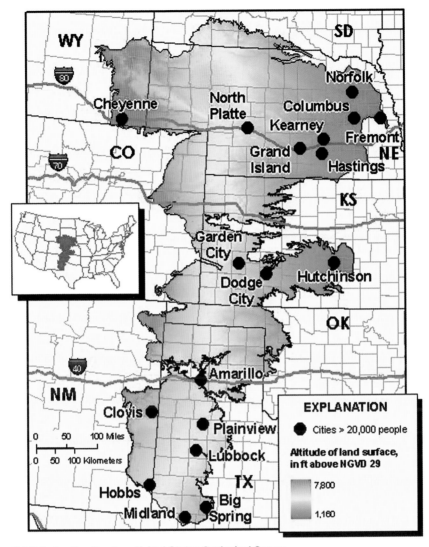

Ogallala Aquifer. Courtesy United States Geological Survey.

Lubbock, a key city in Region O, has experienced water problems since the 1960s. During a dinner meeting in 1979 with a Lubbock businessman, Russell Wolf, I first became aware that Lubbock was already then undergoing critical water shortages. Russell, at that time 75, a well-known and highly respected businessman in both Texas and Louisiana, told me that by the time I was his age (I was 28 at the time) oil shortages would be unimportant to us. Water would be the single most vital resource in short supply, not oil and gas. Russell has been proven correct, albeit, a little earlier than he thought.

state. Other than the cost of the election, the projects supported by these bonds are projected to pay for themselves.

Why do we need the state to help finance these kinds of water-related projects? Consider the situation the small West Texas town of Robert Lee faces. This ranching community of 1,110 residents in Coke County is running out of drinking water. Its sole source of water is the E. V. Spence Reservoir, which in 2011 was almost dry, and the remaining water in it is of poor quality—very salty and thick with debris. When and if it runs out of water, the community runs out of luck as well, with limited or no future growth prospects. No growth in real estate values due to a lack of water results in a loss of tax revenues to support schools and other public services. Without water Robert Lee will inevitably become a ghost town. Robert Lee needs a pipeline to bring at least 150,000 to 200,000 gallons daily to its residents. Bonds issued by a small community like Robert Lee would be very difficult to market, and the interest rate the market would demand will be much higher than the rate the state would have to pay.

Just 12 miles east of Robert Lee lies the "water-rich" town of Bronte, which has 10 groundwater wells to draw from as well as the Oak Creek Reservoir. A pipeline from Bronte to Robert Lee is the type of water-related emergency project ideally suited for the Prop 2 bond funds. Without a doubt, more similar needs will arise in the near future.[5]

HOW WE USE WATER

Most of us are unaware of the number of ways we use water in our society, how vital these uses are to our way of life, and how these uses impact each other because they all draw water from the common pool in the hydrologic cycle. Some uses are highly consumptive (water is removed with no direct return); others are less so. But each and every time we use water, we change it and return it to the hydrological cycle along with the debris and by-products of our daily lives, some of which are toxic. In only the past 34 years, since the passage of environmental protection laws, have we begun to establish the obligations users have to the quality of water when it is returned after use. This return flow of water is still the most overlooked aspect of water management yet may be the most critical for our future.

The major uses of water are for domestic purposes and livestock, which in Texas include wildlife use; for agricultural irrigation; for municipalities; and for industry. The use of water for the environment, referred to as "environmental flows," is now also recognized as one of the most important and legally protected water uses in Texas. In fact, the supralegal authority of the US Fish and Wildlife

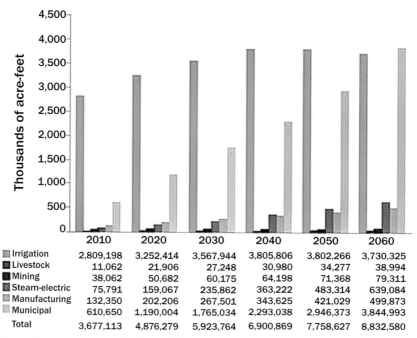

	2010	2020	2030	2040	2050	2060
Irrigation	2,809,198	3,252,414	3,567,944	3,805,806	3,802,266	3,730,325
Livestock	11,062	21,906	27,248	30,980	34,277	38,994
Mining	38,062	50,682	60,175	64,198	71,368	79,311
Steam-electric	75,791	159,067	235,862	363,222	483,314	639,084
Manufacturing	132,350	202,206	267,501	343,625	421,029	499,873
Municipal	610,650	1,190,004	1,765,034	2,293,038	2,946,373	3,844,993
Total	3,677,113	4,876,279	5,923,764	6,900,869	7,758,627	8,832,580

Uses of water (in acre-feet), 2010–2060. Courtesy Texas Water Development Board.

Service has a massive impact on water planning in all Texas water policy, especially in the Edwards Aquifer region and on the coast.

Water rights in Texas vary depending upon how the water is used. The right to domestic and livestock use is generally protected across the state, and this use is allowed in high daily volumes. The most highly consumptive use of water is for agricultural irrigation. While most modern irrigation systems in Texas obtain their water from groundwater sources, irrigation from surface water sources is also allowed based upon the prior appropriation system. Use by cities and municipalities is increasing by leaps and bounds due to the state's growing population. Industrial use is generally not consumptive but can be controversial.

All water in Texas must be used *beneficially,* which is a highly subjective word. When asked how I define "beneficial use," I always say, "Most people define it in one phrase—*my use* (which is of course beneficial . . . yours, maybe not)." Texas laws and regulations define "beneficial use," but, as is usually found in the rules and regulations of our state, any one agency or statute may define the term in a unique way.

The Texas Water Code, Section 11.02, defines it this way: "'Beneficial use' means use of the amount of water which is economically necessary for a purpose authorized by this chapter, when reasonable intelligence and reasonable diligence are used in applying the water to that purpose and shall include conserved water." The definitions of "reasonable intelligence" and "reasonable diligence" are also subjective, and "economically necessary" can again be defined by the two-letter word *my* because we all feel the use *we* put to water is economically necessary. Two universally recognized beneficial uses of water are for agricultural irrigation and for municipal use.

At the same time that most agricultural irrigation systems are obtaining their water from groundwater sources, municipalities are also looking to rural groundwater resources as the most important supply for their future needs. Cities in Texas have a duty to protect and enhance the lives of their citizens and are correct to seek all possible water resources available. Many cities, like Lubbock, El Paso, and San Antonio, consider the search for freshwater sources their top priority. To that end, cities do not hesitate to press their interests in the courts, write new regulations in their municipal codes to expand their jurisdictional boundaries, and lobby continually to seek changes in the state statutes to help remedy their water needs today and in the future.

An example of these efforts occurred in sessions of the legislature when the Texas Water Code was quietly amended to give cities more rights to condemn groundwater found under private property inside their city limits, within their extraterritorial jurisdiction, or even outside those boundaries. These changes to the Water Code received almost no notice by the general public, but they can be highly significant to the water rights of owners with property close to city limits.

<hr>

DOMESTIC AND LIVESTOCK USE

"Domestic and livestock use" is defined in various ways by the Texas Water Code, by the individual local groundwater conservation districts, and by the rules of the Texas Commission on Environmental Quality, each in its own language, and by specially formed agencies such as the Edwards Aquifer Authority. There is no uniform definition of "domestic and livestock use" in Texas because our state varies so greatly geographically. Some sample definitions help illustrate why people take such widely different positions on water issues from time to time.

According to the Texas Water Code, Section 11.023, "State water may be appropriated, stored, or diverted for: . . . domestic and municipal uses, including water for sustaining human life and the life of domestic animals." The key words used here refer to *sustaining life of humans and domestic animals*. The official policy of Texas as outlined in this passage is obviously to protect the most basic need for survival, consumption of potable water. In fact, domestic and livestock use has been protected and guaranteed by all the governments of Texas from the time of Spanish rule, which began actively in the early eighteenth century.

GCDs across the state define "domestic and livestock use" similarly but not uniformly; landowners or lessees must carefully check with the local district to be sure their intended use complies with the local rules. A typical definition of "domestic use" is found in the rules on the Middle Pecos Groundwater Conservation District website. In this district, "'Domestic Use'" means water used by and connected to a household for personal needs or for household purposes such as drinking, bathing, heating, cooking, sanitation or cleaning, and landscape irrigation. Ancillary use may include watering of domestic animals."

The definitions in the districts are generally written to fit the unique local culture and environment. For example, the definition found on the Hill Country Underground Water Conservation District website states that "Domestic Use" is

> use of groundwater by an individual or a household to support essential domestic activity. Such essential domestic activity includes water for uses inside the home; for irrigation of lawns, flower beds, shrubs, trees shading the home, or a family garden and/or orchard with manual sprinklers and garden hoses for watering of domestic animals; for protection of foundations; and for recreation specifically only for swimming pools. Essential domestic activity does not include:
> (A) water used to support activities for which consideration is given or for which the product of the activity is sold;
> (B) the irrigation of lawns or other landscaped areas by sprinkler or other system, whether above ground or below ground, permanent or temporary (other than hand-held hose or single sprinkler attached to a garden hose);
> (C) pond, lake, tank, reservoir, or other confinement which has a capacity greater than 50,000 gallons; and
> (D) non-closed geothermal heating/cooling systems.

Notice that this district's rules do not allow watering lawns with sprinkler systems, while the Middle Pecos district may allow it. Also notice that in the Hill Country example, the district seems to have defined "domestic use" thoroughly, clearly, and concisely, yet this same district does not define "livestock use," even though confusingly the phrase "domestic and livestock use" is mentioned once without further definition of what constitutes "livestock" in a paragraph about well spacing in the latter portions of the rules.

In contrast, and as another example of the variety of local GCD definitions, the Colorado County Groundwater Conservation District rules separately define "livestock use" as follows: "'Livestock Use' means domesticated horses, cattle, goats, sheep, swine, poultry, ostriches, emus, rheas, deer and antelope, and other similar animals involved in farming or ranching operations on land, recorded and taxed in the County as an agricultural land use. Dogs, cats, birds, fish, reptiles, small mammals, potbellied pigs, and other animals typically kept as pets are not considered livestock. Livestock-type animals kept as pets or in a pet-like environment are not considered livestock."[1]

This definition can be confusing and maybe even contrary to locally accepted practices when considering show animals kept by students in Future Farmers of America (FFA). Show animals may not be considered livestock because they are kept in a "pet-like environment" under the rules of the GCD. This definition could be interpreted to include show cattle, pigs, and other FFA members' prize animals. Surely this district would allow these animals to be watered from a water well that is a domestic and livestock use well. It is doubtful many groundwater conservation districts would attempt to stop FFA students from watering their prize livestock.

Ignoring a groundwater conservation district's rules, however, can result in frighteningly high fines, which can mount up quickly. In the Hill Country Underground Water Conservation District the schedule of fines is as follows:

Minor Violation
First occurrence: Up to $50 per day
Second occurrence: Up to $100 per day
Third occurrence: Major violation

Major Violation
First occurrence: Up to $250 per day
Second occurrence: Up to $500 per day
Third occurrence: Civil suit for injunction with penalties up to $10,000 per day

A prudent landowner or lessee must be careful to keep in mind that the rules and regulations change continuously from jurisdiction to jurisdiction, and while GCDs always require and seek public comment, sometimes no public comment is offered. In the world of Texas water now and in the future, keeping up with local rules will be more important than ever before in our history. *Most groundwater conservation districts have websites, and all but a few of the districts publish their rules, amendments, and proposed amendments online.*[2]

The TCEQ, which oversees surface water withdrawals and permits, also has a role in domestic and livestock water regulations. The TCEQ does not define "domestic and livestock" in a glossary per se but refers to it in this way in its Frequently Asked Questions section on its website:

> Do I need a permit to build a pond on my creek?
>
> Possibly. In most cases an impoundment or other appropriation of state water does require a permit. However, §11.142 of the Water Code provides an exemption from permitting for a domestic and livestock reservoir with a capacity of 200 acre-feet or less. The exempt reservoir must be built on the owner's property and not back water up onto any other landowner. The owner may not divert water from the reservoir for any purpose other than domestic and livestock use. *Domestic use does include the watering of a personal lawn or garden and use of water by a household to support domestic activity drinking, washing, and culinary purposes. Livestock use is the use of water for open-range watering of livestock. Irrigation of pasture land for livestock is NOT included in this definition. Any irrigation use (other than that described as domestic use) does require a permit* [emphasis added].[3]

Note the answer to the question includes watering a "personal" lawn or garden and includes "culinary" purposes, a term used in several Texas statutes. Additionally, note the definition of "livestock use" as "open-range watering" of livestock. The definition of "livestock" here is silent concerning pets.

The TCEQ website makes further mention of domestic and livestock use in its rules:

> Sec. 11.142. [Texas Water Code] PERMIT EXEMPTIONS. (a) Without obtaining a permit, a person may construct on the person's own property a dam or reservoir with normal storage of not more than 200 acre-feet of water for domestic and livestock purposes. A person who

temporarily stores more than 200 acre-feet of water in a dam or reservoir described by this subsection is not required to obtain a permit for the dam or reservoir if the person can demonstrate that the person has not stored in the dam or reservoir more than 200 acre-feet of water on average in any 12-month period. This exemption does not apply to a commercial operation.

Still another definition for "domestic and livestock use" is found in Chapter 30 of the Texas Administrative Code, Section 297.1:

> Domestic use is defined as: The use of water by an individual or a household to support domestic activity. Such use may include water for drinking, washing or culinary purposes; for irrigation of lawns, or of a family garden and/or orchard; for watering of domestic animals; and for water recreation including aquatic and wildlife enjoyment. If the water is diverted it must be diverted solely through the efforts of the user. Domestic use does not include water used to support activities for which consideration is given or received or for which the product of the activity is sold.
>
> Livestock use is defined as: The use of water for open-range watering of livestock, exotic livestock, game animals or fur-bearing animals. For purposes of this definition, the terms livestock and exotic livestock are to be used as defined in §142.001 of the Agricultural Code, and the terms game animals and fur-bearing animals are to be used as defined in §63.001 and 71.001, respectively, of the Parks and Wildlife Code.

It is imperative that any landowner or prospective landowner understand the precise definition that any appropriate regulatory agency with jurisdiction over his or her property has for domestic and livestock use. The two ways to determine whether one's desired domestic and livestock water use is within the rules of the regulatory body in whose jurisdiction the land sits is to (1) *seek the advice of an attorney* and/or (2) ask for an official ruling from the governmental entity or entities claiming administrative jurisdiction over the water resources associated with the land. Taking the time to investigate and confirm that one's intended use complies with the statutes, regulations, and rules not only saves a great deal of angst for the landowner or lessee but also can help avoid shockingly high daily fines per occurrence if the intended use is found to be in violation of the rules.

Exemptions

Exemptions to the permitting requirements as they relate to domestic use can be confusing, yet another good reason to hire an attorney to assist in water issues. From the Texas Water Code:

> Sec. 36.117. EXEMPTIONS; EXCEPTION; LIMITATIONS.
>
> (a) A district by rule may provide an exemption from the district's requirement to obtain a drilling permit, an operating permit, or any other permit required by this chapter or the district's rules.
>
> (b) Except as provided by this section, a district shall provide an exemption from the district requirement to obtain a permit for:
>
> (1) drilling or operating a well used solely for domestic use or for providing water for livestock or poultry if the well is:
>
> (A) located or to be located on a tract of land larger than 10 acres; and
>
> (B) drilled, completed, or equipped so that it is incapable of producing more than 25,000 gallons of groundwater a day.[4]

This exemption seems to support a statewide exemption of 25,000 gallons of groundwater a day, but notice the key phrase "may exempt"—it does not mandate this level.

A GCD must exempt from permitting any domestic and livestock water well capable of producing less than 25,000 gallons per day on a 10-acre tract; several limit the exemption for domestic and livestock to 10,000 gallons per day. Some GCDs have declared all wells in their jurisdiction exempt.

Twenty-five thousand gallons per day is an enormous amount of water. To place it in perspective, consider the amount of water five of us, three of which were very active children, used at my home in Houston. In a typical month, with some watering of outdoor plants and a lot of washing machine loads, we used in our heaviest month no more than 15,000 gallons. Using 25,000 gallons per day equates to *750,000* gallons per month, or almost 2 acre-feet per month, which totals 24 acre-feet per year.

Taking it a step further, consider that 1 inch of rainfall over 1 acre of ground brings 27,154 gallons of water. Assume that a person on every day of the year takes the full 25,000 gallons per day of exempt water for domestic or livestock use. Mathematically then, in this situation the property owner is annually taking out of the ground the equivalent of 336 inches of rain a year, or the amount of rain that would classify the property as being in a tropical rainforest![5]

Definitions of "exempt use" may also be responsive to special authorizations made in priority groundwater management areas (PGMAs).[6]

Riparian Right

Surface water rights for domestic and livestock use are exclusive to the property adjacent to the stream from which water is being taken, hence can be referred to as riparian. The use of water for domestic and livestock purposes is the last remaining riparian right in our state, meaning that the right to divert water from a stream for domestic and livestock use cannot be severed from the land or sold; it stays with the property. Water for domestic and livestock use may even be taken from surface waters without a permit since the TCEQ considers this use exempt. Landowners are allowed to divert and/or pump water from streams and rivers for domestic and livestock use and store it in quantities not to exceed 200 acre-feet per year.[7]

As indicated previously, the definition of "domestic and livestock use" varies across the state. The fines for noncompliance with domestic and livestock use under the various district rules at times are issued per day and per occurrence, so the prudent landowner will be very careful to fully understand the local jurisdiction's rules and definitions. In the world of e-mail, it is much easier to gain a written confirmation of your rights pertaining to domestic and livestock use in your groundwater conservation district or special district.

AGRICULTURAL IRRIGATION

In most parts of Texas, irrigation is absolutely critical to agribusiness. Much of Texas is semi-arid land subject to periodic drought; Texas' unreliable moisture makes farming a very risky proposition without irrigation. The Spaniards understood the importance of irrigation when they came to Texas in the seventeenth century; they sought irrigable land first before settling any area.[8]

As a clear example of the difference irrigation makes to crops, the two photographs from the area around Hondo, Texas, in August 2009 show cornfields that share a common property line. The corn in the irrigated field was over 9 feet tall. The corn in the nonirrigated field was barely 2 feet tall. The irrigated cornfield will produce a marketable crop;

Adjacent cornfields in Hondo, with and without irrigation, August 2009.
Photos by author.

the nonirrigated field probably will not. In these photographs, the irrigated field's water source is groundwater distributed by a center-pivot sprinkler system.

Annual irrigation for agribusiness typically uses 60 percent of all the available water resources in Texas. Because irrigation for agriculture uses the most water in our state, it requires special permits from all appropriate jurisdictions. Use of surface water for irrigation is based upon prior appropriation and requires a permit from the TCEQ. Approximately 70 percent of water used for irrigation comes from groundwater sources (simple math calculates that irrigation uses 43 percent of all the groundwater in the state). Water well drilling permits must be obtained from the appropriate local GCDs for water wells used for irrigation. In many districts, including special districts like the Edwards Aquifer Authority, meters are also required to monitor the amount of water withdrawn and ensure that the withdrawals do not exceed the permitted amount. The water well drilling contractor is required to file a well report with the Texas Department of License and Regulation and must give a copy to the owner of the well.[9]

The amount allowed to be withdrawn for irrigation varies among GCDs. For example, in the Uvalde area, irrigation permits are granted by the Uvalde County Underground Water Conservation District. The district rules are similar to those for other GCDs. Section 12.2 (a) Production Limitations, Agricultural Use states: "A well or well system used for irrigation may be permitted to withdraw groundwater in an amount not to exceed a cumulative maximum production level of ten (10) gallons per minute per irrigated acre contiguously owned or operated by the same person, not to exceed two and one half (2½) acre feet per irrigated acre per year, unless an exception has been granted by the District."

In this district, a permit for an irrigation water well may be granted for 2.5 acre-feet per irrigated acre per year. Consider using my previous example that 1 inch of rain equals 27,154 gallons of water on each acre of ground. Since 2.5 acre-feet of water per irrigated acre per year equals a total of 814,627.5 gallons, then the amount of permitted water that can be drawn from groundwater in Uvalde County is the equivalent to 30 inches of rainfall. The average rainfall in the county is posted on the Uvalde County website to be 23.22 inches. From September 2005 to December 2006, Uvalde recorded only 7.85 inches of rain; 2006 was the driest year on record. From September 2007 to December 2008, Uvalde recorded only 14.16 inches of rain, and the year total for 2008 was 11.14 inches, the third driest year on record. Without irrigation over the past years, only the most financially sound farmer could have survived. Being able to draw the equivalent of more than the average annual rainfall in Uvalde gives farming a chance to become an ongoing concern. Uvalde's statistics are typical of the area west of San Antonio to Brackettville.

Due to the expense of operating and maintaining an irrigation system, technology is being developed that is gradually driving all agribusiness operations to better conserve water resources. A good example of the new technology is found in Texas' first GCD, the High Plains Groundwater Conservation District, which was founded in 1951. The High Plains GCD, whose jurisdiction comprises 10,728 square miles of the Panhandle and includes all of six counties and portions of nine other counties, has in place, as of November 2009, some 13,013 center-pivot irrigation systems, 800 of which have been added since 2005. These systems draw water almost exclusively from the Ogallala Aquifer.

High Plains has been a leader in utilizing irrigation conservation methods, which has resulted in between 65 percent and 70 percent of all their permitted center-pivot systems being equipped with high-

Irrigation in San Elizario. Agriculture in the area depends totally on irrigation, which has been stable for the past 20 years. Photo by author.

efficiency (water) application packs.[10] High Plains also conserves water during irrigation sessions by recommending that the center-pivot water nozzles be dropped almost to ground level in "diked" furrows. Diked furrows allow the water to stay in contact with the roots of the crops and keep it from flowing wastefully to the end of the row.

MUNICIPAL USE

Municipal use pertains to water used by cities and municipalities. It is considered a beneficial use and includes residential use; commercial use (such as retail stores and office buildings); and institutional use (such as hospitals, schools, and prisons). Municipal use is for sustaining human life and the life of domestic animals. The Texas Water Code, Section 11.023, lists it as the number-one use for which state water can be appropriated, sharing that position with domestic and livestock use.

Can cities (municipal use) come *before* factories and fields (industrial use and irrigation use) during times of shortage? There is a misconception that at all times municipal use carries a higher priority than irrigation or industrial use. But priority to surface water is subject to prior appropriation—first in time, first in right—even for cities. In shortage periods, however, the 82nd Legislature gave the TCEQ the authority to suspend the right of any person who holds a water right to use the water by adding Section 11.053 to the Water Code on September 1, 2011. In an effort to meet the requirements of implementing this new authority, the TCEQ in April 2012 issued final regulations that added this contentious provision: the executive director may issue an order suspending or adjusting water rights and "may determine not to suspend a junior water right based upon *public health, safety, and welfare concerns.*"[11]

Since some municipalities have rights to surface water that are junior to those of irrigators, stakeholder comments on the initial version of the regulations reflected a belief by agricultural users that the intent of the provision was to establish as policy an implicit preference to urban users over agricultural users. These fears temporarily came to pass on November 14, 2012, when the TCEQ notified certain junior water rights holders in the Brazos River basin below Possum Kingdom Lake with a priority date of 1942 or later that their right to divert or impound water was immediately suspended. At the same time, junior rights for some municipal and power-generating uses were not suspended, in the interest of public health and safety. The Texas Farm Bureau and others filed suit against the TCEQ in December 2012 to nullify the order. On January 29, 2013, the TCEQ rescinded the controversial order, but as of this date, the lawsuit challenging the TCEQ's authority is still pending.

In Texas, farmers frequently hold surface rights to irrigation that are senior to those of municipal users. According to Jeremy Brown of UT Law Grid, "Obviously, this sort of setup is not the best match for a state that is a *highly urbanized* industrial powerhouse faced with a future of increasingly unreliable and inadequate water supplies. The TCEQ drought curtailment rule marks a bold effort to modernize the doctrine. But that doctrine is well established, serving as the basis for an entire system of property rights. It cannot be altered without affecting those property rights, as the Farm Bureau lawsuit argues, or without sending ripples throughout state water policy."[12]

How this controversy is settled in the courts could change a set of property rights that are more than a century old. The Farm Bureau pleadings state: "In spite of such clear legislative direction [the Farm Bureau's interpretation of Section 11.027, which states that the executive director of the TCEQ, *in accordance with the priority of water rights established by Section 11.027*], and in spite of multiple comments from water rights holders and public officials during its rulemaking process, TCEQ gave itself authority to exempt preferred uses from a suspension or curtailment order in adopting its Curtailment Rules. TCEQ claimed that its general police power to protect the public health, safety and welfare allowed it to exempt preferred uses from a priority call."[13] A careful balance of fairness between urban and rural water needs will be debated for many years to come in the legislature and in the courts of Texas. The main battle will be fought mostly over groundwater, but the early skirmishes are being fought over surface water.

INDUSTRIAL USE

The availability of water is critical to industry in Texas. Since surface water is generally fully allocated in Texas today, the only source for water for new industries and the expansion of existing industry in Texas is more than likely to be groundwater, pitting industry against both municipal and rural users.[14]

"Industrial use" refers to water used for activities such as electrical generation and cooling equipment, especially in nuclear power plants. Old-time industrial uses were for mills driven by water wheels to grind corn or wheat into cornmeal and flour. Some of Texas' early textile plants also used water to power their mills. Water uses such as these are not considered consumptive because the water is usually returned to the hydrologic cycle in some fashion, but different industrial processes use water in a variety of ways.

A consumptive use is brewing beer. A study reported that a bottle of beer requires 37 gallons of water, from the water required to grow the ingredients to that used to brew the final product. Early San Antonio was the site of numerous breweries up and down the spring-fed San Antonio River, including the Lone Star and Pearl beer breweries.

Other examples of industrial uses, which represent by no means all of the possible industrial uses, are product manufacturing, including metal and chemical products, petroleum refining, various kinds of food making, and computer chip manufacturing. Industrial use is a beneficial use for which the state may appropriate state waters via a permit. Industries located in most GCDs must acquire permits as well.

Some industrial use does not cause a long-term drain for Texas water resources since many industrial uses are not consumptive. There is always the potential for pollution and environmental damage, but recently the record has been good for Texas industries.

The oil and gas industry is very significant to the health of the economy of Texas and has traditionally been so. Oil and gas drilling operations have special exemptions to consume groundwater for drilling purposes. Recently, due to statewide exploration for oil and gas in the newly discovered shale formations and the huge amount of water this new drilling technology requires, water use for oil and gas has had significant consequences for water planning efforts.

Debates over oil and gas exemptions are coupled with concerns about the Texas rule of capture. In the words of Russ Johnson concerning the Barnett Shale area, "Barnett shale gas well production has generated a ton of concern and controversy. It is not an easy area. First, there is the dominant estate issue, which gives the mineral owner all surface rights (presumably including the right to use groundwater) necessary to extract the minerals, subject to some obvious limitations. Second, to the extent there is a GCD, water use for 'exploration and drilling' is exempt from regulation (with a couple of exceptions in the Barnett Shale area). Water used for production is not exempt from regulation."[15]

Drilling operations in the shale formations of Texas require huge amounts of water to fracture the soft rock and force the natural gas or oil to flow to the surface in a technique called hydrologic fracturing or "fracking." According to an expert petroleum landman, a shale well uses 70,000 gallons of water almost instantly in the earliest stages of fracking.[16] Although some oil companies pay groundwater owners up to $.75 per 42-gallon barrel (a 100,000-gallon draw @$.75 per barrel equals $1,785), the overall depletion of groundwater, especially during a drought, could have long-lasting negative effects that could offset the positive economic benefits of the shale boom. Another consequence for the water-selling landowner could be a lack of water for cattle, resulting in fewer cattle than are required to keep the land's agriculture exemption.[17] In the Eagle Ford Shale alone it is estimated as many as 25,000 wells will be drilled over a number of years. That level of drilling and investment is based on predictions that the Eagle Ford Shale is likely to produce more crude oil than the Alaska slope![18]

Not only does fracking use up lots of water, usually obtained from groundwater sources near the well site, but many people also believe that the hydraulic fracturing of an oil and gas well contaminates other groundwater. The *San Antonio Express-News* posed this question in an editorial on December 21, 2011: "Is fracking an environmental hazard that could endanger Texas' already strained water resources?" The answer this editorial appears to offer is yes, but not all the consequences are bad for Texans or the economy. Mentioning a study conducted by the Center for Community and Business Research at the University of Texas at San Antonio, the editorial said this study concluded that by 2020 the Eagle Ford Shale formation (the Eagle Ford Shale runs from northeast Texas around Gonzalez to the southwest all the way to the Rio Grande, including the Uvalde area and beyond) will account for close to $11.2 billion in gross state product, with $21.6 billion in total economic output supporting 68,000 full-time jobs, good news for the future of Texas.

While the university study suggested fracking does not pose the threat of groundwater contamination, my understanding from countless interviews with landmen, oil and gas operators, and environmentalists is that they concur on one thing: if the well casing leaks where the drill pipe crosses a groundwater table, then, yes, the groundwater can be contaminated. Why? Because the water used to frack wells is supplemented with a proprietary mix of chemicals. Recently the Texas Railroad Commission, regulator of the oil and gas industry, passed a mandatory rule requiring drillers to disclose the chemical ingredients of their fracking mixtures.[19]

Be careful to consult with your attorney when considering water transactions involving oil and gas operations, which have favorable water rights in Texas and have had for more than 100 years. A prudent landowner should seek legal help as soon as contacted about leasing water rights for oil and gas operations.

ENVIRONMENTAL FLOWS

The US government has some supralegal authority over state water policies in several areas, most significantly so far under the Endangered Species Act. The Edwards Aquifer maximum withdrawal of 572,000 acre-feet a year is in part based upon the flow from Comal Springs in New Braunfels and San Marcos Springs in San Marcos. Environmental flows are mandated by the federal government at levels to protect many aquatic, avian, and other endangered species. On March 11, 2013, the US District Court for the Southern District of Texas issued a decision in *The Aransas Project v. Shaw,* an action relating to the TCEQ's water management policies with respect to the endangered whooping crane's winter habitat, the Aransas National Wildlife Refuge. The court found that the TCEQ violated Section 9 of the Endangered Species Act in failing to allow for sufficient freshwater flows from the San Antonio and Guadalupe Rivers into the refuge during the winter of 2008–9. The ruling was stayed on March 26, 2013, pursuant to a motion by TCEQ and the Guadalupe-Blanco River Authority as an intervenor. The question at hand is whether the science "proving" that the deaths of 23 whooping cranes were a result of water being diverted from the rivers, depleting the flow to the refuge and affecting the birds' food supply, was credible. The outcome of this case will someday set key precedents in water policies in Texas and elsewhere in the United States.

The tension between the needs of people for water and the needs of endangered species, especially in times of drought, may become the key issue in water rights of our time. Almost everyone wants to protect environmental flows for all species. How to allocate scarce water resources to enable all species to survive, including humans, is a question we will grapple with for years to come, especially in rapidly growing, drought-prone Texas.

WHO REGULATES WATER USE?

The rights to water and the conditions under which it may be used are further complicated in Texas because they are directly and indirectly subject to the jurisdiction of a myriad of governmental agencies, including these:

- Texas Commission on Environmental Quality;
- Texas Parks and Wildlife Department;
- one or more of the 99 groundwater conservation districts across the state;
- other special districts, such as the Edwards Aquifer Authority and the Houston-Galveston Subsidence District;
- municipalities, some of which are very powerful and influential, such as the San Antonio Water System (SAWS);
- river authorities, such as the Lower Colorado River Authority (LCRA)
- US Fish and Wildlife Service;
- US Environmental Protection Agency;
- rules of the Watermaster Program in Texas;
- rules and regulations of irrigation districts around Texas; and
- Texas Water Development Board.

This chapter, for the purposes of clarity and space, discusses in detail GCDs, the Edwards Aquifer Authority, the Watermaster Program, and the river authorities, with focus on the LCRA. Keep in mind that each municipality and many counties may also exert some jurisdiction over water in their areas. Some federal agencies have supralegal authority over the state agencies, but since the federal agencies are rarely involved in the day-to-day permitting and water management, detail about their activities is not included. I do mention, where appropriate, the significant effect of the federal agencies on any one water management and allocation situation statewide. The Texas Parks and Wildlife Department has an impact on water management policies mostly through the wildlife management plans it supports statewide.

GROUNDWATER CONSERVATION DISTRICTS

Groundwater conservation districts manage most of the groundwater in Texas, and the Texas legislature has asserted on a recurring basis that it prefers that groundwater be managed by GCDs.[1] The map depicts the locations of the individual Texas GCDs. The areas in white have no GCD at this time (although Kirk Holland believes that "every square inch of ground in Texas should be in a groundwater conservation district").[2]

In the areas where no GCD exists, there is no management or protection of groundwater. Without a GCD, landowners risk a loss of their groundwater, not only to adjacent landowners with the same rights for local use but also to those who would transfer large amounts of groundwater to other areas of the state. This should cause a great deal of alarm and consternation for people living in those unprotected areas. For example, one area without a GCD is Val Verde County, the home county of the City of Del Rio. Del Rio was warned by its own consulting engineer of its impending risks in not being covered by a GCD; however, the local people I personally interviewed feel creation of a GCD in their area by local election is not probable in the near future—maybe ever.

As an example of a different anomaly in groundwater management in Texas with potential negative impact on both the aquifer and public attitude toward conservation, the City of Austin's groundwater north of the Colorado River is not covered by a GCD. The imposition of watering restrictions during drought and the increasingly high cost of lawn irrigation have spurred the installation of hundreds of private water wells within the city's service area since 2006, with essentially no re-

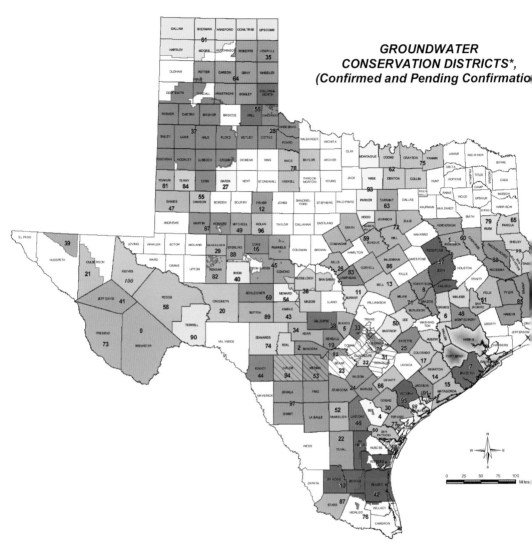

strictions on their spacing or the amount of water produced by each, in an area already adequately served by centralized water supplies.[3] The impact on the aquifer of these new wells and their interference with each other, especially during prolonged drought, are unknown at this time. But the sense of a reduced need for conservation among those generally well-heeled private well owners and the inequity perceived by other landowners without such wells make sorely needed water conservation, regardless of water source, more difficult and of concern to water managers.

How Groundwater Conservation Districts Are Created

The Groundwater Conservation District Act of 1949 provided for conservation and development of groundwater with GCDs as managers, and in 1951 High Plains Underground Water Conservation District No. 1 became the first GCD created in Texas. Chapters 35 and 36 of the Texas Water Code describe (1) the specific legal authority granted GCDs relating to the management of groundwater and (2) the administrative governance and oversight of GCDs by state agencies, primarily the rules of both the TWDB and the TCEQ. Groundwater districts are political subdivisions in Texas, and as such they are additionally obligated to abide by all state laws relating to political subdivisions, including laws related to open government and public information, ethics, and voting. Any landowner whose land lies in a GCD should review the GCD's enabling legislation as a routine practice.

There are currently 99 GCDs (and two pending at this writing) covering all or part of 173 counties. These GCDs have broad statutory authority, but their activities remain ultimately under the electorate's supervision. Each district presides over a territory described at its creation. GCDs strive to protect property owners' rights while at the same time preserving groundwater resources. Landowners may petition to create a GCD or petition an existing GCD for annexation of their land. Generally, voters approve the formation of the district and elect the governing board of directors, but in some areas county commissioners appoint the board of directors. All GCDs must develop a groundwater management plan every five years to address water supply needs, management goals, and estimates of water usage. The GCD submits the plan to the TWDB for approval, and it is subject to review by the State Auditor's Office.

Most GCDs in Texas face significant funding challenges, as they have statutorily restricted water use fee rates and low ad valorem taxation rates. Some GCDs cannot afford to open their offices more than a few days per week or even per month.[4] Many times voters express their keen desire to establish a GCD but are not willing to vote any amount of additional taxes for adequately funding it. Revenue for GCDs can also be generated from water use fees on larger, nonexempt wells and from miscellaneous other fees, such as new well permit fees. However, in some GCDs there is not enough groundwater production from larger wells and not enough applications for new well permits or other fee-based activities to generate adequate revenue for full-time operations.

How Groundwater Conservation Districts Work

According to the Texas Water Code, Section 36.0015, "[GCDs] created as provided by this chapter are the state's preferred method of groundwater management through rules developed, adopted, and promulgated by a district in accordance with the provisions of this chapter." Section 36.113 provides that GCDs must "require a permit for the drilling, equipping, operating, or completing of wells or for substantially altering the size of wells or well pumps." It also states that when acting on permit requests, a district must consider whether "the proposed use of water unreasonably affects existing groundwater and surface water resources or existing permit holders," whether "the proposed use of water is consistent with the district's approved management plan," and whether "the proposed use of water is dedicated to any beneficial use." GCDs formulate and are guided by groundwater management plans that

- provide for the most efficient use of groundwater;
- control and prevent waste of groundwater;
- control and prevent subsidence;
- address conjunctive surface water issues;
- address natural resource issues;
- address drought conditions; and
- address conservation.

The rules of most GCDs include the registration of all water wells, even those exempted from permitting by the Texas Water Code. The primary exemptions are (1) domestic and livestock use of water from a well on tracts larger than 10 acres and that is capable of producing no more than 25,000 gallons per day;[5] and (2) water wells used in oil and gas exploration (excluding production).

Section 36.116 (a) of the Texas Water Code outlines broad regulatory authority for GCDs. Here is an outline of their authority.

In order to minimize as far as practicable the drawdown of the water table or the reduction of artesian pressure, to control subsidence, to prevent interference between wells, to prevent degradation of water quality, or to prevent waste, a district may regulate:

(1) the spacing of water wells by:

(A) requiring all water wells to be spaced a certain distance from property or adjoining wells;

(B) requiring wells with a certain production capacity, pump size, or other characteristic related to the construction or operation of and production from a well to be spaced a certain distance from property lines or adjoining wells; or

(C) imposing spacing requirements adopted by the board; and

(2) the production of groundwater by:

(A) setting production limits on wells;

(B) limiting the amount of water produced based on acreage or tract size;

(C) limiting the amount of water that may be produced from a defined number of acres assigned to an authorized well site;

(D) limiting the maximum amount of water that may be produced on the basis of acre-feet per acre or gallons per minute per well site per acre;

(E) managed depletion; or

(F) any combination of the methods listed above in Paragraphs (A) through (E).

As provided in the same section of the Water Code, some GCDs also have the power of eminent domain. The Water Code allows GCDs to consider how granting new permits will affect existing permit holders and surface water resources. The rights of historic users may be protected in considering permitting of new users. Since there is a real possibility that drought or other scarcity may force GCDs and other Texas agencies to enact increased limitations on groundwater withdrawals, it may be wise for landowners to meter any well, including exempt wells, and document the amount of water used historically.

The most controversial GCD rules involve restrictions on withdrawals. Historically, districts have sought to protect groundwater by regulating the spacing of wells, the rate of pumping, the amount of pumping each year, or a combination of these measures. There are high limits to the fines associated with violation of GCD rules, up to $10,000 per day for each violation. Those neighbors who own land adjacent to a well in violation of GCD rules may sue the well owner for damages to stop the violation and to recover damages. Outside a GCD, no such lawsuit could be brought, as the rule of capture prevails.

Can GCDs generally prohibit landowners from access to water under their own land? GCDs are barred from prohibiting landowners from drilling wells that meet exempt criteria, but they can regulate amounts of water withdrawn for municipal, industrial, and agricultural irrigation use. GCDs often regulate spacing between wells. Will most districts eventually require meters on existing wells? Considering the forecasts for Texas growth and future droughts, it may be a prudent practice of GCDs to require meters on all wells since the more accuracy in determining the actual amounts of groundwater used protects not only the resource but all users in the district. According to a study conducted in May 2012 by Stacey Steinbach, executive director of the Texas Alliance of Groundwater Districts, 60 percent of GCDs require meters on at least some of their permitted wells.

Groundwater Management Areas and "Desired Future Conditions"

Since 2005, all GCDs participate in joint planning within groundwater management areas (GMAs) as part of the regional water planning process (see map). The logic behind the formation of GMAs was simple. Since many of the 99 GCDs are defined more or less by county boundaries and many share the same aquifer and underground water sources, the GMAs give long-term water planners a chance to consider on a more regional basis the impact the GCDs have in total over an aquifer or underground water source. In other words, GMAs were created for the same reason as the answer to my favorite question in my water classes, "What does water ignore?" The correct answer is, "Political boundaries." The boundaries of GMAs were set to better outline the "pool" of groundwater in the overall area and to help generate groundwater policies that considered the shared groundwater sources among the GCDs.

As required by statute, in 2010 the GMAs used a defined joint planning process among their member GCDs to develop desired future conditions (DFCs) for their aquifers, which they delivered to the Texas Water Development Board. According to a memorandum to board members dated September 9, 2009, "a desired future condition is essentially a management goal that defines the philosophy and policy of groundwater management in a defined area." In other words, DFCs are a policy statement of what the GMAs would like to see their groundwater conditions be in 50 years, so that each of its member GCDs can begin to establish its own mandatory groundwater management objectives. In order to establish the DFC for the groundwater management area, the member districts

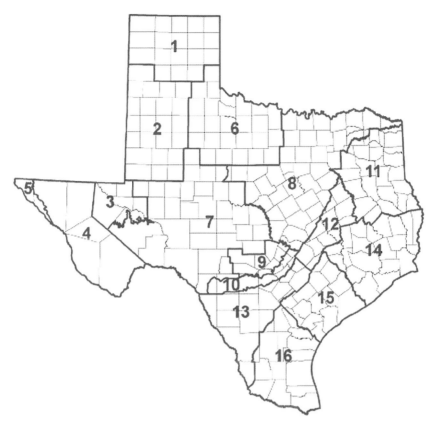

Groundwater management areas. Courtesy Texas Water Development Board.

must adopt the DFCs by at least a two-thirds majority vote. When the DFCs are submitted to the TWDB for review, the board can only recommend changes, not mandate the districts or GMAs to make the changes.

DFCs may be revised at any time and must be updated at least every five years. After the DFCs are generated, each GMA presents them in local hearings to receive public comments. A few of these hearings have been thorny, as members of the public have disagreed with the DFCs in some areas. The public has the right to appeal the decisions of the GMA and has used the right several times across the state, some of which are still pending in the courts.

DFCs are critical for planning in each GCD. The 82nd Texas Legislature added a definition for DFCs to Chapter 36 of the Water Code in SB 660, which requires GCDs to ensure that management plan goals and objectives are consistent with achieving applicable DFCs. The bill added nine new factors that districts must consider when renewing or establishing DFCs:

1. aquifer uses or conditions within the management area, including conditions that differ substantially from one geographic area to another;
2. the water supply needs and water management strategies included in the state water plan;
3. hydrological conditions, including for each aquifer in the management area the total estimated recoverable storage as provided by the executive administrator, and the average annual recharge, inflows, and discharge;
4. other environmental impacts, including impacts on spring flow and other interactions between groundwater and surface water;
5. the impact on subsidence;
6. socioeconomic impacts reasonably expected to occur;
7. the impact on the interests and rights in private property, including ownership and the rights of landowners and their lessees and assigns in groundwater;
8. the feasibility of achieving the DFC; and
9. any other information relevant to the specific DFCs.

Pursuant to the act, DFCs must also "provide a balance between the highest practicable level of groundwater production and the conservation, preservation, protection, recharging, and prevention of waste of groundwater and control of subsidence in the management area."[6]

Modeled Available Groundwater

After the DFCs are delivered to the Texas Water Development Board, the board then generates modeled available groundwater (MAG) reports for each DFC on the basis of groundwater models and the best science available. Formerly called managed available groundwater, in 2011, under SB 737 the 82nd Legislature changed the term "managed" to "modeled" and modified its definition for clarity.[7] A MAG is now defined as "the amount of water that the [TWDB] executive administrator determines may be produced on an average annual basis to achieve a desired future condition established under [the joint planning process of] Section 36.108." The MAG includes water produced from both exempt and nonexempt wells. The TWDB then apportions the MAG among the individual districts through the GMAs and also as warranted among the relevant regional water planning areas (RWPAs), which overlay GMAs with surface water jurisdictions. Essentially, GMAs and RWPAs are interlinked planning areas attempting to recognize the true relationships of groundwater to the surface districts and groundwater's conjunctive relationship with surface water.

The MAGs are used as the mandatory basis for groundwater availability in regional water planning. But they are also a major consideration in permitting decisions and other groundwater management activities by individual districts. Their use and significance are best judged at the individual district level. For example, after reviewing the Hays-Trinity Groundwater Conservation District MAG for the Trinity Aquifer in the fall of 2011, I discovered that taking into consideration only the statutory exemptions for domestic and livestock use and no others, the current amount of exempt use and permitted use may mean groundwater is almost or soon could be fully allocated in this district. Of course, that assumes that the current domestic and livestock exemption amount of 25,000 gallons per day on a 10-acre tract remains in effect. I have asked many Texans, considering most have never come close to using 25,000 gallons a month, much less in a day, for domestic and livestock use, if they would be willing to support a move in their district to lower the daily amount of domestic and livestock exemption. To a person they said no—some added that they might consider it but with financial compensation only. They see the exemption as a property right. In their mind the exemption has value, again even though they never used it fully, and even though I discussed with them the risk to their area's future growth prospects when all the groundwater is fully allocated.

What does this particular MAG mean for the future of Hays County? Does it follow that the district will not allow any new water wells? What if a new crop is economically feasible and requires irrigation? Does this indicate that no new irrigation permits can be issued? If an existing landowner wants to change the use of the property to some use requiring irrigation, is that landowner going to be denied the request? Will the existing landowner have priority over the new landowner if they request irrigation permits at the same time? Did this create two classes of landowners? I do not have the answers, but assuming that the model accurately considers the consequence of growth in its jurisdiction and the GCD maintains its current definition of exempt wells, the district's ability to "manage" its groundwater production with the large number of exempt wells is effectively eliminated.

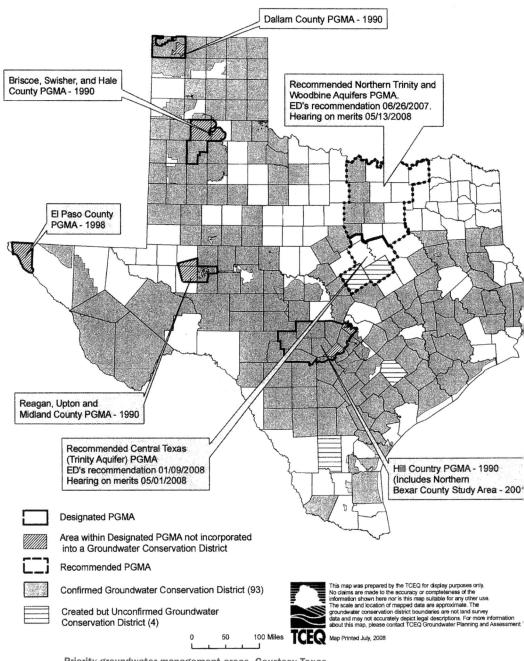

Priority groundwater management areas. Courtesy Texas
Commission on Environmental Quality.

The Texas Water Development Board website publishes the MAGs for all of the districts in the state.[8] They are interesting to review for the various areas of the state. What will land values do in the future in the case that the full effect of exempt domestic and livestock use is considered? If history tells us anything, declines in population and their supported economy occur when in prolonged drought or when a permanent loss of water rights occurs.

In addition to GMAs, Texas has currently designated six priority groundwater management areas (PGMAs). These are areas in which critical issues associated with quantity or quality of groundwater either already are occurring or may reasonably be expected to occur in the next 50 years. For areas not covered by GCD protections inside any of these priority management areas, if the local population has not created a GCD on its own, the TCEQ has an obligation to create one even without local voters' approval, although any new tax rate associated with the new GCD must be voter approved.

Counties in PGMAs may impose groundwater availability requirements on new developments dependent on groundwater. A recent controversy in Travis County formed the basis of a request for an opinion to Attorney General Greg Abbott from the Texas House of Representatives Committee on Natural Resources. The question presented was whether a county that is *partially* designated as a PGMA may adopt a groundwater availability ordinance in the *entire* county or only apply in the *portion of the county* designated as a PGMA.[9] The attorney general's opinion indicated that the county could adopt the groundwater availability ordinance on a county-wide basis, even though only part of the county was in the PGMA.[10] This could have far-reaching impacts inasmuch as the areas of the state that are likely to experience groundwater problems over the next 50 years will grow, and the number of PGMAs, defined by aquifers and not county boundaries, will increase.

GCDs and Everyday Lives

GCDs protect everyone's interests in groundwater. Yet not all of Texas is protected by a GCD. When searching for a place to live in Texas or selling an existing one, be sure to find out if your property is in the jurisdiction of a GCD. If so, seek guidance from the staff there to determine your rights and obligations. GCDs hold public hearings often; please take the time to attend and offer your opinions. Your comments and opinions help the GCD leadership make better decisions for everyone.

"The Edwards Aquifer is the sole source of water for San Antonio, Texas. The Aquifer contributes surface water flow in the Guadalupe River through Comal and San Marcos Springs, both of which are home to endangered aquatic species, including the fountain darter. In 1993, a U.S. district court ruled that the Secretary of the Interior allowed takings under the Endangered Species Act (ESA) by not ensuring adequate flows from the Springs. The Texas legislature responded to a court mandated deadline to protect springflow by establishing the Edwards Aquifer Authority (EAA) to regulate groundwater withdrawals."[11]

The Edwards Aquifer Authority is a conservation and reclamation district created under the Conservation Amendment to the Texas Constitution; its powers and duties are governed by the Edwards Aquifer Authority Act, not by Chapter 36 of the Texas Water Code. The EAA has broad powers, and any seller of land, potential purchaser of land, or real estate agent dealing in land within the jurisdiction of the authority must become aware of its rules and regulations. According to the Edwards Aquifer Authority:

> The Edwards Aquifer Authority (EAA) is a regulatory agency established by the 73rd Legislature in May 1993 with the passage of the Edwards Aquifer Authority Act to preserve and protect this unique groundwater resource. However, legal challenges prevented the EAA from operating until June 28, 1996. Today, a 17-member board of directors representing Atascosa, Bexar, Caldwell, Comal, Guadalupe, Hays, Medina, and Uvalde counties continues its mission. Teams of geologists, hydro-geologists, environmental scientists, environmental technicians, educators, and administrative staff collaborate daily to manage, enhance, and protect the Edwards Aquifer for the approximately 2 million South Texans who rely on the aquifer as their primary source of water.[12]

When the Texas legislature created the Edwards Aquifer Authority in 1996, the EAA was directed to

- protect the quality of the aquifer;
- protect the water quality of the surface streams to which the aquifer provides streamflow;
- achieve water conservation;
- maximize the beneficial use of water available for withdrawal from

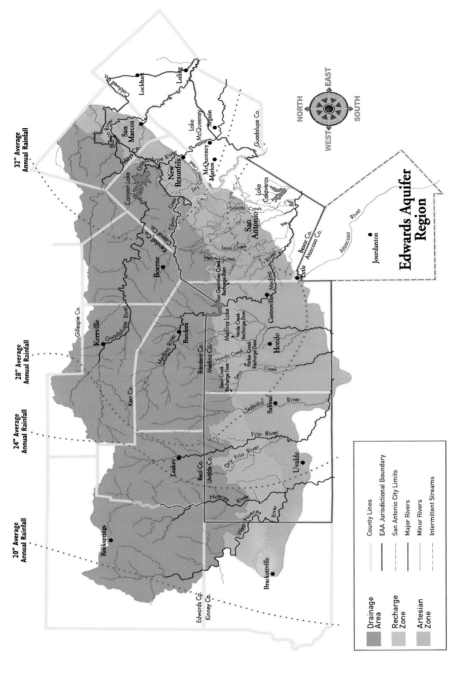

Edwards Aquifer Authority region. Courtesy Edwards Aquifer Authority.

the aquifer; recognize the extent of the hydro-geologic connection and interaction between surface water and groundwater;

- protect aquatic and wildlife habitat;
- protect species that are designated as threatened or endangered under state or federal law;
- provide for instream uses, bays and estuaries;
- protect domestic and municipal water supplies;
- protect the operation of existing industries;
- protect the economic development of the State;
- prevent the waste of water from the aquifer; and
- increase recharge of water to the aquifer.

The establishment of the EAA added not only protection to the critical aquifer but required the real estate industry to become conversant with its rules and regulations as they impact property values and transactions. Sellers, buyers, and real estate agents who operate within the jurisdiction of this specially created agency must be familiar with the role of the EAA. While a real estate agent does not have a duty to become a water expert, the agent must warn buyers and sellers that the agency's policies could impact their property. A prudent agent will have contact numbers for buyers to use in their decisions to purchase property and sellers to use to accurately represent the attributes or defects of their property if it is in the jurisdiction of the agency. Key impacts on real estate include impervious cover restrictions, water well regulations, the designation of "Karst" zones,[13] and the presence or absence of drainage fields and detention ponds.

The Edwards Aquifer spans 1,560 square miles in 13 counties and includes 2,314 square miles of subsurface area; 90 percent of the aquifer's area is subject to management by GCDs. The aquifer feeds several well-known springs, including the headwater springs of the San Antonio River (Worth's Spring or "Blue Hole" and San Pedro Springs); Comal Springs in New Braunfels, which is the largest spring in the state; San Marcos Springs in Hays County; and Barton Springs in Austin.

In 2007 the Texas legislature, in SB 3, increased the allowable withdrawals from the Edwards Aquifer in the EAA's jurisdiction during non-drought conditions to 572,000 acre-feet per year. This amount of withdrawal may have to change in a downward direction due at least to the March 2013 federal court ruling to protect the habitat of the endangered whooping crane. As mentioned earlier, that ruling, now under appeal, found that the TCEQ failed to allow sufficient freshwater flows from the San Antonio and Guadalupe Rivers into the Aransas National Wildlife Refuge in the winter of 2008–9, which resulted in the negligent death of 23 whooping cranes.

Whether or not there is more water in the Edwards Aquifer is moot— the EAA must be cognizant of the impact the flow from Comal Springs and San Marcos Springs has on the habitat of endangered species. The initial ruling in the whooping crane lawsuit would require additional flow from these springs to the rivers to in turn provide adequate flow to the coast to protect the cranes and other species.[14] Another possible lawsuit concerns our creeks' freshwater mussels and the need to further protect their habitat by increasing flow. This issue could possibly place downward pressure on the allowable withdrawal from the Edwards and other aquifers across the state.

A great deal of cooperation among those who have a stake in these issues is important. In the case of the Edwards Aquifer, a group of stake-holders has emerged who refer to themselves as partners and are known collectively as the Edwards Aquifer Recovery and Implementation Program (EARIP). They include the Edwards Aquifer Authority, City of New Braunfels, City of San Marcos, City of San Antonio acting by and through its San Antonio Water System Board of Trustees, Guadalupe-Blanco River Authority, Texas State University, Texas Parks and Wildlife Department, and US Fish and Wildlife Service. Together, they are trying to find ways to improve overall habitat for endangered species, which involves more than just increased environmental flows from the springs and rivers.

Habitat for endangered species is as much dependent upon water quality as quantity. Karl Dreher, speaking at a gathering of the San Marcos Board of Realtors, mentioned the EAA's efforts along with others in a study to find all the elements that will be needed to improve the habitat of all endangered species, including a salamander in San Marcos Springs, the native wild Texas rice that also grows there, and many other protected species. The following table indicates the EAA's projections for water demand in their area through 2030.

Many people in the San Antonio area are concerned that the legisla-ture's authorization of 572,000 acre-feet approved withdrawal will be inadequate by 2020. While conservative when prepared in 2006, the pro-jections indicated a withdrawal from the aquifer of more than 620,000 acre-feet by 2030. Demand in Bexar County alone, home to the nation's seventh-largest city, San Antonio, is projected to increase more than

Table 2.1: Total Water Demand Projections for the Planning Area

Edwards Aquifer Area County	Total Project Water Demand (ac-ft/yr)				Percent Change** (%)
	2000	2010	2020	2030	
Atascosa*	1,437	1,612	1,607	1,598	11.20
Bexar	288,431	325,540	356,724	388,873	34.82
Caldwell*	3,774	5,035	6,268	7,365	95.15
Comal*	17,891	23,761	28,881	34,456	92.59
Guadalupe*	9,100	20,642	26,906	31,581	247.04
Hays*	9,001	19,320	27,381	33,248	269.39
Medina	64,510	63,521	62,347	61,178	−5.17
Uvalde	67,741	65,886	64,087	62,286	−8.05
Edwards Aquifer Area***					
Total	461,885	525,419	574,298	620,713	34.39

* denotes portion of county within Edwards Aquifer Authority boundaries
** percent increase is calculated from the total projected change in water demand between 2000 and 2030
*** Edwards Aquifer area as specified in Senate Bill 1477, Texas Legislature, 73rd Session, 1993, as amended
Source: 2006 SCTRWPG Revisions to Population and Water Demand Projections: Water Demand Scenario: most likely case, below normal rainfall, advanced water conservation

Edwards Aquifer future demands. Courtesy Edwards Aquifer Authority.

100,000 acre-feet in 2030 over demand in 2000. Again, remember that San Antonio is the only major city in the United States whose water supply comes solely from groundwater sources.

The EAA is aware of water-marketing activity in its area, which includes sales of water rights between rights holders across its jurisdiction, and has established a groundwater trust to facilitate the sale or lease of water by holders of EAA initial regular permits (IRPs). This is a prudent and appropriate approach to help ensure the establishment of a stable market for groundwater withdrawal rights. It is a logical outcome of the EAA permitting process, helping to ensure that the water authorized under the IRPs will be put to use.

Water wells have to be permitted prior to drilling in the EAA jurisdiction. Normally the driller obtains the permit for domestic and livestock wells incapable of producing more than 25,000 gallons per day or 17.36 gallons per minute. Although domestic and livestock wells do not have to be metered, all wells that produce more than 25,000 gallons per day must be metered.

An EAA official described to me the process of metering water wells. Records of the production must be kept monthly and reported to the EAA annually. The EAA rules contain the procedure for record keeping and also include specifications for an acceptable meter. The official said EAA staff visit in person once per year to check each and every metered well. They have available a portable meter to check the accuracy of the meter at the site. The EAA owns meters on agricultural irrigation wells and closely monitors them. Domestic and livestock wells are checked as well for permits and periodically monitored to be sure they comply with the rules. Since these wells must not be capable of producing more than 25,000 gallons per day, I asked how a well is made "incapable." The official said the pump capacity is the best way to be sure of compliance with the limitation. "Be sure the submersible or other type pump simply cannot produce more than the allowable."[15]

The lawsuit *Day McDaniel v. Edwards Aquifer Authority* demonstrated the importance of water meters when historic use is a key issue, as it was in this case, which involved a challenge to EAA over an amount of irrigation water that was requested and denied.[16] While testimony of witnesses was admissible, it appears the only evidence that was considered convincing was the written record of historic use based upon the meter on the water well in question. Of course, this creates a conundrum for the water user. Most farmers and ranchers are worried about placing a meter on their well for fear that the water agency with jurisdiction will charge more for their usage or cut back potential amounts based upon their current use. However, if those same farmers or ranchers had to prove their historic use, then a meter is probably the only acceptable proof of use for the regulatory agency. The legislature would be well served someday to address these issues statewide.

WATERMASTERS

"The rules of surface water rights and use are relatively well settled; the demand and accounting for surface water are not. Senior rights holders, from farmers to municipalities, may seek watermaster programs to protect their interests and address their legal, political, economic, and environmental concerns."[17] Almost one-third of Texas is covered by one of three Watermaster Programs, which are administered by the TCEQ: the South Texas Watermaster; Rio Grande Watermaster, which covers most of the Rio Grande; and Concho River Watermaster in the San Angelo area. According to the Texas Water Code 11.327(a)–(c),

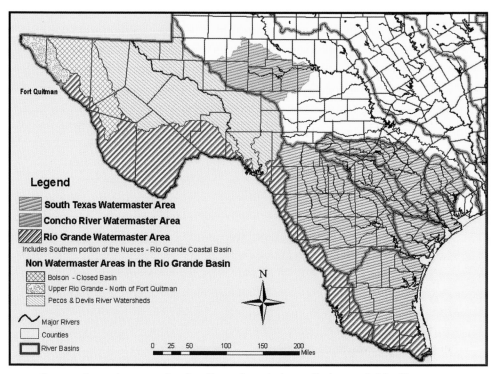

Texas watermaster areas. Courtesy Texas Commission on Environmental Quality.

(a) A watermaster shall divide the water of the streams or other sources of supply of his division in accordance with the adjudicated water rights.

(b) A watermaster shall regulate or cause to be regulated the controlling works of reservoirs or diversion works in time of water shortage as is necessary because of the rights existing in the streams of his division; or as is necessary to prevent the waste of water or its diversion, taking, storage, or use in excess of the quantities to which the holders of water rights are lawfully entitled.

(c) A watermaster may regulate the distribution of water from any system of works that serves users whose rights have been separately determined.

The idea of "watermasters" has been at work in Texas from the time of the Spaniards in earliest San Antonio and at that time were called *mayordomos*. The first *mayordomo* of Villa de San Fernando, Geronimo Flores, only 18 at the time, was from the Canary Islands. He supervised the sharing of the waters in the *acequias* (canals or ditches) and also was in charge of leasing the *aqua de propios,* or water rights owned by the villa, to settlers from time to time.[18] The leasing of the waters was one of the only sources of revenue for the villa. Today's watermasters, much like *mayordomos* of old, monitor, supervise, and control irrigation activities along the streams in which they have jurisdiction so as to protect the interests of all the rights holders; they also have the authority to regulate water volumes in times of drought.

The only duty they no longer have is to lease municipal waters, although all three watermasters assist in leasing and selling water rights in their jurisdictions and are the "go to" source for information about availability of water on the open market. For example, on December 7, 2009, the Rio Grande Watermaster posted the Cameron County Irrigation District 2's offer to sell 2,400 acre-feet of water for industrial use.

The first watermaster, appointed by the State of Texas through the 107th District Court of Cameron County in 1952, as the effect of the 1950s drought was bearing down on all Texans, was called the "master in chancery." According to Augustus L. Campbell, who wrote the legal history of the watermaster program, "The master in chancery oversaw initial water disputes and preliminary hearings, made reports and recommendations to the court, and enforced court rules and regulations." In a footnote, Campbell illuminates the "enforcing tool" of the master: "The enforcing tool, and the only tool mentioned in the order [establishing the master in chancery], from beginning to end, is the judicial power of injunction permitting and restraining the use of water, the amount of which would be variable and would require the services of a Master."[19]

There was great controversy surrounding the master in chancery among the water users in the area at the time, but in 1957 the master in chancery's position was codified by the Texas legislature. Then, as a consequence of the Water Rights Adjudication Act of 1967, the system of watermasters we know today was born when the Texas Water Commission, one of the predecessor agencies to the TCEQ, was empowered to determine or adjudicate the rights to surface water claimed by individuals and corporations in Texas. Watermasters would be appointed by the Texas Water Commission but would be allowed to administer only *adjudicated* rights; hence, all the water rights in the water district had to be determined before the watermaster had true authority over the allocation of water. The adjudication process that started in 1967 took many years to complete and survived several court challenges.

The legislature explicitly defined the commission-appointed water-master's duties:

1. Dividing the waters within the "division in accordance with the adjudicated water rights";
2. Monitoring and regulating water control and diversion works on reservoirs and streams;
3. Preventing the waste of water;
4. Giving parties notice of state water law and Commission regulations; and
5. Enforcing Commission orders to adjust, limit, or withhold water diversion by violators of water laws or Commission orders.[20]

Today the Rio Grande, South Texas, and Concho River Watermasters are best described as "compliance officers" with a wide range of authority over water rights in their jurisdictions. Their duties include

- monitoring stream flows;
- monitoring reservoir levels;
- monitoring water use;
- coordinating diversions in the basins in their jurisdictions;
- regulating reservoirs to prevent waste of water; and
- overseeing the quantities used to ensure users do not exceed their rightful share.

The users in the jurisdiction pay two fees to cover the expenses of administration of the watermaster's duties. One fee is based on use or on the number of acre-feet the owner of the water right is authorized to divert per year for each authorized use. The other fee is referred to as a "base" fee per account, which currently is $50 per year. The base fee generally does not change from year to year, but the use fee is determined each year from the proposed operating budget for each Watermaster Program.

"One of the most challenging and necessary duties of watermasters," wrote Campbell, "is to divide and allocate water rights, especially during times of drought." A water right holder must follow this process:

1. File a declaration of intent to divert water with the watermaster;
2. Declare the amount of water proposed to be diverted including diversion rate at each point of diversion;
3. State the intended purpose of the diversion of the water; and

4. Declare starting and ending times of opening their respective gates.[21]

This process sounds remarkably like the old irrigation process of water diversion based upon time periods, or *dulas,* in old Spanish colonial San Antonio. In the eighteenth century, the *mayordomo* would observe each gate opening whenever possible; the gates were handmade and opened by hand. The modern watermaster verifies that the amount requested is within the individual's water right, again similar to the *mayordomo* of old. But today's technology has allowed for a more thorough and accurate process. According to Campbell, today's water right holders and users must meter their diversion works and lock their gates at all times. The deputy watermasters "continually" monitor the diversions and keep records of all water volume that passes through the right holder's gate.

The watermaster of today, again as of old, is a critical manager in times of drought. The watermaster has absolute control of the water flow to each user based upon the watermaster's assessment of water flow, consumption, and weather conditions that relate to river or stream flow. The prior appropriation concept, or "first in time, first in right," makes the watermaster's job all the more complicated and significant. The watermaster must honor the downstream demands and rights of the senior appropriators even when it is obvious that the denial of flow to the upstream user could cause crops to fail. Imagine the frustrating position drought places the watermaster in as he or she witnesses the suffering caused by the lack of water to junior upstream appropriators.

Controversy is ever present in the watermaster's office, and much of this controversy is based upon the conflict between urban and rural interests. According to Campbell,

Cities in particular oppose these [watermaster] programs because they have relatively junior rights in comparison to farmers and ranchers. Consequently, current law requires watermasters to restrict cities' consumption of water before most agricultural users. D[omestic] and L[ivestock] users are entitled to 200 acre-feet of water without a permit or charge, and have senior rights to all other users. Many irrigators obtained their rights before or shortly after the Irrigation Act of 1913, which required individual, but not municipal water users to acquire permits for water rights. . . . Municipal and industrial users are charged more per acre-foot than irrigators, while D & L users are not charged at all. While irrigation constitutes a majority of water use, municipal and industrial water users are the largest single consumers and pay the largest individual bills for watermaster services.[22]

Why do cities have junior rights? One reason is that Texas has always honored colonial Spanish land and water grants. In fact, the strongest water right claim during the adjudication process of the 1960s and 1970s was to trace the right to a Spanish irrigation grant. The cities of today did not exist when representatives of the king of Spain made these grants; hence, these grants are senior.

As amazing as the volume of work and outcome of the Water Rights Adjudication Act of 1967 were in settlement of the continual stream of water rights lawsuits throughout Texas history, controversy over surface water still exists. It is a well-known fact that our surface waters are over-allocated when all the volume rights detailed in the filed documents of record are considered, even in nondrought times.

The Rio Grande Watermaster

The Rio Grande Watermaster has additional duties that affect his or her work due to the shared nature of the Rio Grande with Mexico based upon treaties and the rulings subsequent to those treaties. The Texas Water Code, Section 11.3271(h), formally recognizes that any rule the watermaster promulgates "must be consistent with the Treaty Relating to the Utilization of the Waters of the Colorado and Tijuana Rivers, and of the Rio Grande (Rio Bravo) from Fort Quitman, Texas to the Gulf of Mexico, concluded by the United States and the United Mexican States on February 3, 1944, and with any minute order adopted by the International Boundary Water Commission."

The Rio Grande Watermaster's jurisdiction is in the Rio Grande River basin and includes Brewster, Cameron, Dimmit, Hidalgo, Hudspeth, Jeff Davis, Jim Hogg, Kinney, Maverick, Presidio, Starr, Terrell, Val Verde, Webb, Willacy, and Zapata Counties. Above Amistad Dam, located on the Rio Grande a few miles north and west of Del Rio, water rights to the river water are managed following the prior appropriation concept as they are in other parts of Texas. Below Amistad Dam the water is allocated on an "account basis," which is described by the TCEQ as "much like having a bank account with a constantly changing balance. Priority is given to municipal accounts so, at the beginning of each year, each municipal account's storage balance is set to the authorized water-

The major irrigation canal in McAllen within 100 yards of new subdivisions.
Photo by author.

right amount. The municipal priority is guaranteed by the monthly re-establishment of a muncipal reserve in the system of 225,000 acre-feet. This is equivalent to one year's average diversions for all municipal demands below Amistad for Texas users."[23] Water rights are "served" in the Middle Rio Grande and Lower Rio Grande by both Amistad Dam and Falcon Dam, which is located just below Laredo close to Rio Grande City in the Valley.

Unlike municipal accounts, irrigation accounts are not reset each year and rely instead on "balances forward." The Rio Grande Watermaster must keep a strict accounting of irrigation water under international treaties and agreements with Mexico. Each month, the watermaster determines how much unallocated water from the waters of the Rio Grande below Amistad Dam is assigned to the United States. If and when surplus water is identified, it is allocated to the irrigation accounts on a monthly basis and adjusted per account as it is used by subtracting used water from the individual account balance.

Irrigation from the Rio Grande has sustained the agricultural interests of the fertile valley for decades. The irrigation systems, even around fast-growing areas such as McAllen, are still in use directly adjacent to

Another view of the major irrigation canal in McAllen. Photo by author.

new home subdivisions similar to those of larger cities like Houston or Dallas. This creates a stark contrast between rural and urban lifestyles.

South Texas Watermaster

The South Texas Watermaster's jurisdiction encompasses 50 counties in south-central Texas. This area covers the basins of the Guadalupe, Lavaca, Nueces, and San Antonio Rivers, as well as the "Lavaca-Guadalupe Coastal" and "San Antonio Coastal" basins. The area is patrolled by five field deputies who are constantly on the road due to the nature of their duties and the size of their territories. Water right management is based upon "run-of-the-river rights,"[24] according to the TCEQ, and their jobs are further complicated by the "constantly changing, dynamic surface-water system of rivers and tributaries that allow diversions as water is available and as it passes through individual diversion points."[25] The South Texas Watermaster also updates and maintains water right ownership databases and assesses the fees due on each water right account.

Concho River Watermaster

The Concho River Watermaster Program was established by the legislature in 2005. Its jurisdiction is the Concho segment of the Colorado River basin and includes Coke, Concho, Irion, Reagan, Runnels, Schleicher, Sterling, and Tom Green Counties. Two field deputies patrol the area, assist surface water right holders to comply with all guidelines, maintain and update water right ownerships, and assess the fees due from each water right account. As it is for the South Texas Watermaster, water right management in the Concho River Watermaster jurisdiction is based on "run-of-the-river rights."

When I met with watermaster specialist Molly Mohler in the San Angelo office in 2010, the first point that really hit home was that even irrigators with senior appropriative rights to the Concho River water rarely receive their full amount of water. The watermaster allocates the water based upon the seniority of rights, but these rights are also based upon a sufficient flow in the entire system. Since she started in 2005, Mohler has always had to restrict requests for water due to scarcity of flow, which is determined by USGS gauges that provide data for a system spreadsheet.

Mohler explained that to receive water, irrigators send in a request for an amount stating their permit number, the amount of acre-feet requested, their priority date (indicating their seniority), and the gallons per minute they expect to need. Irrigators call in and typically ask for seven days at "X" volume per minute.

Mohler said the water right holders date from as far back as 1898 up to 1970 (after the Water Rights Adjudication Act of 1967, all water rights to the Concho River were fully allocated). She said the community of irrigators in her area is very conscious of the rights of neighbors and respectful of both the river and the watermaster's role. It was my understanding that at the time of my visit, more than half of the irrigators were not active.

Watermaster Advisory Committees

In 1997 the Texas Water Code was amended to require the executive director of the TCEQ to establish Watermaster Advisory Committees for each program. The committees are made up of holders of water rights or their representatives. According to the TCEQ, the members of the advisory committees are appointed from "different types of holders of water rights and users such as water districts, municipal suppliers, irrigators, and industrial users who have experience and knowledge in water management practices."[26] Their duties include

- providing recommendations to the TCEQ executive director about activities beneficial to water rights holders in the adminstration and distribution of water;
- review and comment of watermaster budgets; and
- other duties as to the administration and operations of the water distribution system.

The advisory committees are very helpful to the TCEQ and the watermasters in their areas and are indicative of the spirit of community in which the water is administered under this program.

Watermasters and Real Estate Transactions

How does the watermaster's authority impact real estate transactions? Since disclosure of all known facts to any potential buyer is a duty of the seller and real estate agent, a known fact in the case of the sale of a property that is under the jurisdiction of a watermaster is the true amount of diversions allowed for irrigation in the past. If, as in the case of the Concho River, the full right is usually curtailed due to lack of flow in the river, then the seller and the agents must represent the true amount of water that has been allowed to be taken, not only the basic amount of acre-feet in the water right or permit itself.

For example, if my senior appropriative right is 130 acre-feet annually but I have only been able to take 50 acre-feet in any one year over the past 10 years, I must disclose to any potential purchaser the facts of my relationship with the watermaster and any curtailment of the amounts of water I request or am entitled to by my permit.

〰〰〰 **THE RIVER AUTHORITIES**

Over the years, the legislature has set up 17 river authorities to conserve, store, and manage the state's rivers in specific geographic regions. Their duty is basic—manage the waters of their jurisdiction for the benefit of the public. These are the Texas river authorities:

- Angelina-Neches River Authority
- Brazos River Authority
- Central Colorado River Authority
- Guadalupe-Blanco River Authority

- Lavaca-Navidad River Authority
- Lower Colorado River Authority
- Lower Neches Valley Authority
- Nueces River Authority
- Palo Duro River Authority
- Red River Authority
- Sabine River Authority
- San Antonio River Authority
- San Jacinto River Authority
- Sulphur River Basin Authority
- Trinity River Authority
- Upper Colorado River Authority
- Upper Guadalupe River Authority

Each of the river authorities has a unique structure of management with similar but locally designed duties to best manage the diverse river basins around the state. For the purposes of this book, I discuss in detail the Lower Colorado River Authority (LCRA), which is one of the most influential and manages the largest system of lakes in the state, generally known as the Highland Lakes.

The LCRA summarizes its role this way: "LCRA is a conservation and reclamation district created by the Texas Legislature in 1934. It has no taxing authority and operates solely on utility revenues and fees generated from supplying energy, water and community services."[27] Its "By the Numbers" chart on the LCRA website best describes the significance of its activities.

- LCRA owns or operates 16,440 acres of parks and recreational areas.
- With six hydroelectric dams and wind power purchased from West Texas wind farms, LCRA ranks as the largest publicly owned supplier of renewable energy in Texas.
- LCRA's electric service area stretches 29,812 square miles, covering all or part of 55 counties.

To say the least, the LCRA is an exceptionally important water manager, electricity provider, and protector of the lower Colorado River. The LCRA manages water supplies for cities, farmers, and industries along a 600-mile stretch of the Texas Colorado River between San Saba and the Gulf Coast. It operates six dams on the Colorado River that form the scenic

Highland Lakes: Buchanan, Inks, LBJ, Marble Falls, Travis, and Lake Austin. It regulates water discharges to manage floods and releases water for sale to municipal, agricultural, and industrial users. The organization helps communities plan and coordinate their water and wastewater needs. It also operates an environmental laboratory and monitors the water quality of the lower Colorado River. More critically, it enforces ordinances that control illegal dumps, regulates on-site sewage systems, and reduces the impact of major new construction along and near the lakes.

Its work in on-site sewage systems hit home a few years ago. My daughter was severely injured in a boating accident on Lake Travis in 1996; her leg was broken very badly by a propeller of a fishing boat after she fell down while skiing. Of our many worries, the most significant was bacterial infection because of the water quality of Lake Travis. The conventional wisdom among those of us who grew up in Austin was that many older homes on Lake Travis dumped raw sewage into the lake either from poorly maintained septic systems or in other ways too horrific to imagine. We had a special bacteriologist oversee her progress in the hospital for 16 days because of this threat. The LCRA's work to clean up the impact of human sewage systems on the Highland Lakes, while successful, is ongoing.

One of the most controversial issues faced by the LCRA concerns its management of Colorado River waters to irrigation users in the lower reaches of the river, commonly referred to collectively as the "rice farmers." In the 1950s, and through each successive drought experienced by those watching the 80-mile-long Lake Travis drastically and so visibly fall, the topic of complaint always seemed to be about the "rice farmers" taking all of "our" water. (For the LCRA's description of why and how water is supplied to rice farmers, see the LCRA website.)

Downstream rice farmers hold a prior appropriative right, or senior right, to the LCRA's rights. However, the LCRA has the right to curtail downstream irrigators in times of water shortages. In January 2012 the LCRA promulgated a new water management plan that, according to an article in the *Austin American-Statesman,* "would place an annual limit on water for farmers and use separate triggers for providing water for rice farmers' first and second crops, among other changes from current planning strategies. . . . LCRA board members and staffers discussed water management exceptions that would allow more strict curtailment to farmers in dry years and release more water downstream in wet years."[28]

On March 1, 2013, the LCRA board of directors, following the new plan, curtailed Highland Lakes water to downstream users, including the rice farmers, because the combined storage in the lakes failed to exceed 850,000 acre-feet. At 11:59 p.m. on March 1, 2013, the Highland Lakes had a combined storage of 822,782 acre-feet, well short of the minimum threshold needed to allow water downstream. One of the most significant changes in the LCRA plan of 2012 was that the rice farmers would no longer enjoy "open amounts" of water use during nondrought periods, but their maximum water use would be prescribed annually ("closed amounts") regardless of drought conditions. Here is yet another "battleground" between urban and rural interests. Not only do the rice farmers suffer under this plan; so do the many businesses that supply their activities. Yet they agreed to give the LCRA the right of curtailment in the 1930s to support the control of flooding on the Colorado River by the Highland Lake system of dams.

Keep in mind the long history of rice farming on the lower Colorado River. According to the LCRA, irrigated rice farming in the lower Colorado River valley began in 1885. Farmers used manual labor, mules, and horses to move the water from the river into their fields. Until the creation of the Highland Lakes, starting in the 1930s, rice farming was a high-risk business easily wiped out by flood or drought. Since the LCRA's inception in 1934, providing reliable water supplies for rice farming has been one of its principal functions.[29] The rice farmers have enjoyed the stability of the LCRA water and the protection from flooding.

Kate Galbraith wrote in her *New York Times* article, "Amid Texas Drought, High-Stakes Battle over Water," on June 18, 2011:

Rice farmers used the Colorado River water long before the L.C.R.A.'s creation, and thanks partly to this history, they get the water far cheaper: the L.C.R.A.'s city customers pay over 20 times more for their water than do rice farmers, although rice farmers pay hefty additional fees to cover the cost of delivering water to their fields, often via canals.

In exchange for cheaper water, rice farmers agree to allow their supply to be cut off or reduced in times of drought. In the past, however, they have never had their supplies reduced, to the frustration of lake residents and other water users.

This will most likely change. If the current drought does not abate soon—and the L.C.R.A.'s meteorologist is not forecasting substantial rainfall at least until the fall—rice farmers could lose one of their two annual crops next year, said Suzanne Zarling, the L.C.R.A.'s executive manager of water services.

For the local rice grower's perspective come these comments from various publications around the state. According to Dick Ottis, president of Rice Belt Warehouse in El Campo, "Rice farmers in the region have greatly reduced rice acreage in recent years largely because of water problems. But more is going to be needed if rice farming is to survive this and future water problems in Texas." Ottis added, "But there is still not enough water coming down the river to support that, and under terms of the new (LCRA) water plan, the water would be cut off anytime lake levels fall below a certain level. These triggers in the new plan make it difficult for farmers to plan their crop and impossible to sustain it in times of drought."[30]

Justin Ellison, staff writer for *Farm Plus Financial,* a Colorado-based lender in Fort Collins specializing in agricultural loans said, "Without irrigation from the Colorado River, many rice farms, and other farms in the region, risk bankruptcy."[31] Without doubt, especially with the probability of drought continuing in the near future, lower Colorado River rice farmers are facing a tough challenge, and without rain in their area, a challenge that may be impossible to overcome. Here is yet another example of the tough choices Texan water policymakers face, a choice between rural and urban interests, especially with Austin growing by leaps and bounds, even during the economic slowdown of 2008 and after. The significance of water to life in Texas may be no better illustrated than the example of the LCRA and the rice farmers.

Part Four

HOW DO WATER RIGHTS AFFECT REAL ESTATE TRANSACTIONS?

9

WATER AND EVERYDAY REAL ESTATE TRANSACTIONS

Water rights and everyday real estate transactions set the market value of land and have far-reaching consequences for every Texan. Today, assessing the water characteristics of property presents unique challenges to buyers, sellers, lessors, lessees, and real estate agents. The water scarcity predicted in our future requires potential buyers to consider a variety of heretofore less-often-considered assessment criteria. Likewise, the potential of future water scarcity requires sellers and their real estate agents to exercise extreme caution and prudence in their duties of disclosure of the water situation of any property being offered for sale.

 LOOKING TO THE FUTURE

The TWDB's State Water Plan for 2012 posed this primary question: "Do we have enough water for the future?" The answer was unequivocally that we did not. According to the plan's executive summary, "We do not have enough existing water supplies today to meet the demand for water during times of drought. In the event of severe drought conditions, the state would face an immediate need for additional water supplies of 3.6 million acre-feet per year with 86 percent of that need in irrigation and about 9 percent associated directly with municipal water users. Total needs are projected to increase by 130 percent between 2010 and 2060 to 8.3 million acre-feet per year. In 2060, irrigation represents 45 percent of the total and municipal users account for 41 percent of needs."[1]

This startlingly blunt answer leads to a follow-up question. How much water do we have today? The TWDB's latest estimates were made in 2010 and indicated 17 million acre-feet in total statewide water supplies of surface water, groundwater, and reused water.[2] After the terrible drought of 2011, surely we have less water in 2012 than in 2010. The 2012 State Water Plan projected a decrease from 2010's estimate of 17 million acre-feet to about 15.3 million acre-feet in 2060. Groundwater supplies alone are projected to decrease by 30 percent by 2060, mostly due to depletion of the Ogallala Aquifer and mandatory reductions in the Gulf Coast Aquifer to prevent land subsidence. To supply our population projections, which predict growth from 25,388,403 people in 2010 to 46,323,725 by 2060,[3] we will need 50 percent more water over the next 50 years! According to the TWDB, if we do not make prudent long-term plans to provide for our future water needs, Texas businesses and workers could lose as much as $116 billion in income and 1.1 million jobs by 2060.[4]

Competition for water between individual, corporate, municipal, industrial, agricultural, and environmental interests will surely increase. Fair water management practices, conservation, and visionary policies undertaken by individuals and government agencies led by a responsible legislature will reduce our water risks. Prudently funded and implemented long-term water planning must begin *now*. New water infrastructure takes years to complete; the right-of-way acquisition for pipelines could take decades. Water more than ever before will dictate the market value of land in our state, and land values are crucial to all private and public economic activities.

WATER, WATER RIGHTS, AND THE MARKET VALUE OF LAND

Land adjacent to flowing water is generally some of the most valuable land in the state, whether rural or urban; the better the water and, in the case of rural property, the more permanent the water right, the more valuable the land. An illustration of this statement can be found in the historical record.[5] On November 19, 1879, George W.

Brackenridge—pioneer San Antonio banker, University of Texas regent, and donor of the "Brackenridge" tracts in Austin and San Antonio[6]—completed an inspection of several sections of land in Kimble County owned by his land-speculating brother, Thomas. His enthusiasm about the land was based upon its water: "We arrived on this place last evening from a survey of the Seventeen Sections [10,880 acres] of your land in the northern portion of this County and I found it to far exceed my expectations. [He described] . . . an abundance of water [on several of the tracts, and he said tract 19 had] . . . all the water there is in that section in [a] splendid spring." Toward the end of the letter, Brackenridge made a prophetic statement: "You must be careful not to dispose of those sections on which the water is unless the other goes with it, as the water renders the land valuable."[7] Nothing was truer then, and nothing is truer now.

Considering that the "norm" for Texas is drought or "soon to be back in drought," the troublesome consequence of water scarcity, outside the most obvious—the ability of an area to sustain life—will be a decrease of land values leading to a weakened ad valorem tax base, inevitably making Texas a less attractive home for new people and industry. Our ad valorem tax base across the state underlies the funding of our most cherished public services, like education and health care, and affects how we view two basic ways of life in Texas, rural and urban. The state's cities are thirsty for water, and the source they seek to quench this thirst is, in many cases, the groundwater held by rural neighbors.

If an urban area pumps away a rural neighbor's groundwater, land values in the rural area drop, subsequently diminishing its ad valorem tax base and affecting how the community can support public services. Since almost 90 percent of Texans now live in urban areas,[8] we simply cannot and likely will not allow any urban area to decline even if that urban area's only available new water resource comes from adjacent rural groundwater. Competition over water is a zero-sum game. The choice between urban and rural life is one no legislature or court should have to make, but without fully funded, comprehensive, long-term, statewide water planning that respects all the stakeholders' needs, there could very well be winners and losers. The cities will rightly do their duty and act to protect their citizens by gathering rural groundwater in any manner legally possible.

The market value of water at the everyday level is easily determined. We quickly understand the price of water when we read and pay our water bills or buy bottled water. The market value of a water right is not as obvious. The fair market value of a water right, what a willing buyer and a willing seller will agree to in price when neither is under duress, is based upon comparable sales of existing water rights, judicial rulings, and government contracts. Over the years, a tepid marketplace has developed for the sale of surface and groundwater rights.

Beginning around 1742 in Spanish colonial Texas, water rights were severed from land and have been ever since in the normal course of business.[9] Comparable sales and leases of today's water rights are discoverable; some of the groundwater conservation districts, and the Edwards Aquifer Authority in particular, post sale or lease notices by holders of water rights in their jurisdictions. Some real estate appraisers recently have been willing to give reasonably well-supported valuations of water rights based upon a larger pool of confirmed comparable sales, always the best indicator of fair market value.

Yet many buyers and sellers of water rights keep the actual transaction confidential, leading to difficulty in confirming actual prices paid. And due to the tremendous variety of aquifers and the differences in regulations across the state, credible comparable sales, when confirmed, still cannot be relied upon outside the immediate regulatory jurisdiction area of the transaction. For example, a water right in the EAA sold for around $7,500 per acre-foot in 2013. However, because of the vast differences in aquifers and regulations, that value may not necessarily apply in the Panhandle.

A notable indication of the nuanced nature of the valuation of water rights came in a court ruling in 2010, the "cat case," or the "case with nine lives." The judge considered the market value not only of groundwater rights per acre-foot but also of the added incremental value of market classification of the land in the matter as an irrigated farm rather than a nonirrigated farm.

JoLynn and Glenn Bragg operated two farms in the Medina County area that required irrigation to be productive: the D'Hanis Orchard and the Home Place Orchard.[10] The irrigation wells for these farms required permits from the EAA. When the Braggs requested more groundwater than the EAA granted, long years of litigation resulted in decisions generally in favor of the EAA. However, the Braggs persisted in the face of these unfavorable rulings and filed another lawsuit under a "takings"[11] claim against the EAA after an appeals court ruling in a similar and more famous case, *Day and McDaniel v. the Edwards Aquifer Authority,*[12] brought up the possibility that the EAA owed landowners just compensation for their regulatory actions. The Braggs' new lawsuit sought just compensation from the EAA for the amount of groundwater they were denied. Judge Thomas Lee of Hondo ruled favorably for the Braggs on May 7, 2010, with language that should awaken everyone concerned about groundwater in Texas: "The implementation of the Edwards Aquifer Act, and the denial of an Initial Regular Permit (IRP) on February 8, 2005, for an amount less than requested or needed by the Plaintiffs to operate their Home Place Orchard, unreasonably impeded the Plaintiffs' use of the Home Place Orchard as a pecan farm, causing them severe economic impact; interfered with their investment-backed expectations, and constituted a regulatory taking of the Plaintiffs' property. . . . [T]he Plaintiffs are entitled to be compensated for their loss."[13]

The difference in the amount requested by the Braggs and the amount the EAA granted them was 108.65 acre-feet of water. The Plaintiffs requested that their compensation for this water would be based upon $7,500 per acre-foot for a total of $814,875. Judge Lee determined that the water was worth $5,500 per acre-foot for a total award on this portion of the damage claim of $597,575. Further language he chose seemed to be written to meet the requirements that the actions of the EAA constituted a "taking." All Texans should take close notice of this section of Judge Lee's ruling: "I believe this is as much about the taking away of a lifestyle as it is about the decrease in the value of land. The Braggs invested their lives, labor and money in a good family farm that could be passed on to their heirs. That life plan has been undermined, and their investment severely damaged." Judge Lee assigned additional damages to the other tract of land, the D'Hanis Orchard, on different grounds. The denial of the water for this orchard no longer allowed it to be considered an "irrigated" farm. He determined that the difference between the value of a dryland farm and an irrigated farm was $3,200 per acre. Judge Lee's total compensation award to the Braggs for both elements of damage was $732,493.40.[14] The total acreage of the two orchards is 100.67 acres, making this award $7,276 per acre.

This ruling is one cornerstone that can be used in determining the market value of both groundwater and of irrigated land. It may not reflect a fair market valuation at any one time in the future, but at the time of his finding, it was a strong indication of the value of water and the incremental value of an irrigated farm over a nonirrigated farm. The incremental value of an irrigated farm was a significant though highly subjective new consideration in land valuation.[15] His award of $5,500 per acre-foot of water for the Home Place Orchard reconfirms another well-known, acceptable, and reliable comparable valuation. Considering that both tracts of land were valued by the appraisal district at $4,000 per acre, apparently without adjustment for the irrigated value found by Judge Lee, the fact the farm was considered "irrigated" at a premium of $3,200 per acre almost doubled the land value. The water rights, therefore, could also be said to *more than double the value* of the land.

This ruling was yet another confirmation that water availability and adequate water rights strongly enhance the value of land. The judge's findings also assumed the Braggs' interest in groundwater was a "vested" property right,[16] a right that government has a primary duty to protect. Since water rights, or the lack thereof, so significantly affect land values, the terms of, and especially any defects in those rights, must be disclosed by sellers and their real estate agents to any potential purchasers of property.

≈≈≈ DISCLOSURE DUTIES OWED BY SELLERS TO BUYERS

The land-buying public statewide is becoming more cognizant about defects in water rights and water sources. For almost two decades, any defect actually known to the seller and the real estate agents has had to be disclosed to potential purchasers of single-family homes, and their duties concerning disclosure are similar. Nondisclosure of defects involving access to water and water rights by the sellers and/or their real estate agents potentially creates substantial liability for civil damages in lawsuits.

Since 1993 in Texas, the concept of "caveat emptor" or "let the buyer beware" has disappeared in single-family residential transactions, where the sellers, whether represented by a real estate agent or not, are now required to disclose *known* defects to any potential buyer while the buyer is making the decision to purchase the property. The 73rd Texas Legislature added Section 5.008 (a), Seller's Disclosure of Property Condition, to the Texas Property Code effective January 1, 1994: "A seller of residential real property comprising not more than one dwelling unit located in this state shall give to the purchaser of the property a written notice as prescribed by this section." From this revision to the property code came a myriad of locally developed seller's disclosure notices, the birth of the home inspection industry, and of course, hundreds of lawsuits.[17]

Seller's disclosure notice forms are required, at a minimum, to include this line to disclose information about the water source of the property for sale: "Water Supply: ___ City ___Well ___ MUD ___ Co-op." Not all farms and ranches include single-family residences, but if a single-family residence is on the property, any defect in the water system or any well's water quality or working status, permit status, or any other known defect must be disclosed to a potential purchaser. Typical plaintiff's petitions involving nondisclosure of defects include claims under the Texas Deceptive Trade Practices Act and claims of common law fraud or fraud in the inducement, negligent misrepresentation, and civil conspiracy, even in situations where there is no single-family home on the property. A prudent seller, agent, or buyer keeps in mind that the source and availability of water to any property are absolutely critical items that must be fully and truthfully disclosed.

These are other questions on the minimum statutory seller's disclosure notice form that could involve water conditions:

- Are you (Seller) aware of any item, equipment, or system in or on the property that is in need of repair?
- Are you (Seller) aware of . . . any notices of violations of deed restrictions or governmental ordinances affecting the condition or use of the Property?
- Are you (Seller) aware of . . . any condition on the Property which materially affects the physical health or safety of an individual?[18]

Any pertinent water-related issues must be disclosed in the answer to any or all of these questions, and supporting documents should be provided to the purchaser prior to making a commitment to buy.

〜〜〜 **DISCLOSURE DUTIES OWED BY REAL ESTATE AGENTS**
The duties of disclosure of defects for real estate agents are even broader in some ways than those for sellers. Real estate agents' duties of disclosure are outlined in the Texas Occupations Code; the Rules of the Texas Real Estate Commission (TREC); and, if the agent chooses to join the National Association of Realtors (NAR), in NAR's Code of Ethics.

A real estate licensee's duty to disclose defects is found in the Texas Occupations Code, Chapter 1101, Sections 1101.652 (b) (3) and (4), also known as the Real Estate License Act. Any and all actually known defects must be disclosed by the agent even if the seller has not disclosed them.

Knowledge of latent (hidden) defects is not considered confidential information in Texas or elsewhere in the United States, and an agent does not violate any obligation to the client by disclosing them.

The TREC may revoke an agent's license if the agent fails to disclose to a potential purchaser structural or other latent defects *known* to the agent. In fact, this duty to disclose applies to all types of real estate, not just single-family homes, a fact many agents in Texas still fail to recognize. Note the key word *known*. Most attorneys who defend agents in disclosure lawsuits correctly demand proof of the accused agent's *actual knowledge* of any alleged defect. Plaintiff attorneys, on the other hand, feel the agent's conduct should be judged not only upon what the agent knew but also what the agent heard, thought, said, did, decided, and failed to do. Many plaintiff attorneys would also like to see "known" changed to "should have known." "Should have known" is considered "constructive" knowledge, which is deemed to be actual knowledge in Texas.[19]

The Rules of the Texas Real Estate Commission, codified as Title 22, Chapter 531, of the Texas Administrative Code (TAC) and titled "Canons of Professional Ethics and Conduct for Real Estate Licensees," organizes these duties under the general headings of fidelity, integrity, and competence. Under this code of ethics, effective since 1976, an agent is deemed to be a fiduciary for the client.[20] Fiduciary duty, per the code of ethics, means that the agent must place his or her clients' interests above those of the agent and that the agent be *scrupulous and meticulous* when performing the work.[21] The agent must also avoid misrepresentation by acts of commission or omission; must be informed on market conditions affecting the real estate business; must be informed on national, state, and local issues and developments in the real estate industry; and must exercise judgment and skill in the performance of the work.[22] If the real estate agent fails to inquire about the water rights and conditions of a property, the agent may violate some or all of these duties in the statutory code of ethics.

Additional Duties Owed by Real Estate Agents

The fiduciary duty is greater for those holding the status of broker according to the TREC rules in Section 535.2 (b): "A real estate broker has the very highest fiduciary obligation to the agent's principal and is obliged to convey to the principal all information of which the agent has knowledge and which may affect the principal's decision."[23] The significance of this fiduciary duty is further mentioned under Section 535.156, Dishonesty; Bad Faith; Untrustworthiness:

(a) A licensee's relationship with the licensee's principal is that of a fiduciary. A licensee shall convey to the principal all known information which would affect the principal's decision on whether or not to make, accept or reject offers; however, if the principal has agreed in writing that offers are not to be submitted after the principal has entered into a contract to buy, sell, rent, or lease property, the licensee shall have no duty to submit offers to the principal after the principal has accepted an offer.

(b) The licensee must put the interest of the licensee's principal above the licensee's own interest. A licensee must deal honestly and fairly with all parties; however, the licensee represents only the principal and owes a duty of fidelity to such principal.

(c) A licensee has an affirmative duty to keep the principal informed at all times of significant information applicable to the transaction or transactions in which the licensee is acting as agent for the principal.

(d) A licensee has a duty to convey accurate information to members of the public with whom the licensee deals.

All of these additional duties definitely apply to the water circumstances of any property. Section 535.156 is especially applicable to water rights; agents must make an effort to provide their clients with "significant information," and what is more significant than information about water rights?

The National Association of Realtors Code of Ethics

Real estate agents who choose to join the National Association of Realtors pledge themselves to honor NAR's Code of Ethics. This Code of Ethics also recognizes the obligation of agents to disclose defects in properties, which of course includes the circumstances of water. In 2001, NAR added a sentence to Article 1 of its Code of Ethics and Standards of Practice for Realtors, clearly stating that information about defects is *not* considered confidential information. This provision makes it clear that the agent is not at risk of violating loyalty to his or her client under NAR's Code of Ethics when the agent discloses defects. Disclosure of defects is a nationally recognized duty of NAR members. Agents may owe fiduciary duty to their client, but Article 1 still requires the agent to treat all parties to the transaction honestly. Therefore, NAR agrees with Texas law that all defects such as those pertaining to water on a property must be disclosed.

Civil Liability for Nondisclosure of Known Defects

The only safe and prudent practice for sellers and real estate agents is to disclose anything and everything actually known about any defect in a single-family residence or any other property for sale or lease, including defects related to water and water rights. The potential monetary damage to unwitting sellers and agents who fail to disclose known defects can be and are many times quite substantial. Agents who conspire with sellers to hide defects should be held especially liable for damages and severely sanctioned by the TREC.

The path to civil damages against a real estate agent follows from how an agent can lose his or her license by negligent behavior and failing to meet duties owed under the statutes.[24] However, real estate agents have duties that exceed the ordinary standard of care as outlined in the statutes. The Texas Occupations Code, Chapter 1101, Section 1101.652 (b) (1), states that an agent who acts negligently or incompetently could have his or her license suspended or revoked by TREC. Since civil damages stem from negligence, if the agent is negligent under the license act, then the agent is or could be liable for monetary damages.

There is a fundamental value and ethical concept we hold dear in the United States: *The public has a right to rely upon the representations of agents, and these representations must be accurate and true.* Prudent agents and sellers disclose all defects in writing prior to offering the home for sale to help purchasers assess their risk while they are making their decision to purchase. In Texas, amazingly, verbal disclosure is still allowed, but it is more correct behavior to keep everything in writing. Remember, new purchasers will have to disclose defects when they sell the home in the future, so buyers' agents acting dutifully will assist their buyers in careful review of the disclosures before committing to purchase the property. Buyers' agents should always recommend to their clients that they *consult an attorney,* which appears in bold print in every TREC-promulgated contractual document, or a licensed inspector, engineer, or any other appropriate consultant.

Understanding the complex issues regarding water on a property, whether the agent represents the buyer or the seller, is a clear duty owed by the agent. Does this mean the agent and seller must know the law like an attorney does or the science of water like a hydrologic engineer does? No, but the agent must be *cognizant of the water circumstances* on any property and advise the client, whether buyer or seller, to seek the help of appropriate professionals to assess water rights, access, availability, quality—all the water features and issues of a property. In the case of most rural properties, water is so critical to the value of the land that any prudent agent will first seek to understand what water rights exist so as to fully inform the potential buying public of the property's features. A property with verifiable water rights will be easier to market and of course will likely bring the highest price to the seller. Water status should be one of the first of a property's features to be investigated by real estate agents, sellers, and buyers.

≈≈≈≈ **EXAMPLES OF UNIQUE DISCLOSURES**
       ABOUT WATER AND WATER RIGHTS

If the property is located in the jurisdiction of a GCD, the seller must disclose, for example, that a water well does not have a required permit. Other examples of required disclosures are a well in which the pump is not working properly, a well dug too close to a septic field, or a well in which the water is salty or brackish.

Another more subtle example occurs when a home is located adjacent to a running creek and a well serves this home. One would think the source of the water is groundwater, but the source might be from the unseen underflow of the running, or at times "dried-up," creek. "Dried-up" creeks and streams many times have underflow, sometimes very shallow underflow. If the source of the well water is the underflow of the creek, then the water is owned by the state; the landowner would own the well water if it were groundwater. Even if the well is used for domestic and livestock purposes, which could be exempt from permit, this fact must be disclosed. The TCEQ is the agency of jurisdiction for surface water and any water *flowing* underground in a defined channel.[25] A prudent buyer, seller, and/or real estate agent should seek assistance from the TCEQ to be sure the well complies with all regulations and is not in the underflow because of the close proximity of the well to the creek.

The photograph of a historic well near Leon Creek shows the well in the underflow of the creek; it is basically in the creek bed itself. More than likely, homesteaders used this well to find water when their other wells dried up, probably only on a seasonable basis. The state owns the *underflow* of this creek and the water in this well. This must be disclosed

Nineteenth-century well found 3 feet from the bed of Leon Creek. Photo by author.

to a potential purchaser, along with the hazard the open hole creates. Is the fact that the source of the water in this well is actually from state-owned water drawn without a permit a potential defect that must be disclosed to a potential purchaser? Yes. Is it a defect that might cause liability to fall upon the seller if not disclosed? Yes. Will a purchaser sue for damages based upon the nondisclosure of this water well's true source? It depends, but the purchaser may have a strong cause of action.

As the price of real property increases, and along with it the costs of ownership such as ad valorem taxes, insurance, and normal maintenance costs, consider this question: Would you want to buy a home on that bubbling creek and take the risk that the TCEQ might put you on notice that you have no right to use the water from the well serving your home? Worse still, would you want to risk the high fines applicable for using the underflow state water without a permit or water right? Of course not. The scenario just described indicates clearly that modern real estate investment requires more in-depth research than ever before in order to adequately assess the risk of purchase and ownership.

As technology improves in the science of hydrology, enabling us to better understand groundwater and the underflow of streams, creeks, and rivers, it is reasonable to predict that more claims for defects involving water will be pursued under the statutes. Why? Because defects concerning water have the potential to severely diminish real property value. Of equal importance, once a defect is known by the new owner, disclosure of the defect will continue to be an obligation in future sales until cured. Even then, it is advisable to disclose the defect and take corrective actions.

Another example of a potential defect that is not normally considered occurs when a seller has rights to divert water from a stream or river for irrigation. The seller may very well have a senior appropriative right to divert and use the water, but the amount of water permitted could be curtailed by acts of the river authorities or watermasters. For example, assume the seller has a 30-acre-foot appropriative right to divert water from the Concho River for irrigation, but the Concho River Watermaster has not approved the full volume, which has been the case along this river for many years. If the approved volume is only 15 acre-feet, then this should be disclosed to a potential purchaser. Offering the property by marketing the full right of 30 acre-feet must be modified with a statement of actual allowed diversions. The potential damage in a subsequent lawsuit could be $82,500, the result of 15 acre-feet (30 acre-feet in right less 15 acre-feet actually granted) at the market rate of $5,500. Add in the possibility that the property could no longer be considered "an irrigated farm" as in the Bragg case, and the damages could increase. Certainly, there are many other unique water issues that require disclosure.

Just as water is essential to life, water rights are essential in the everyday real estate transactions of Texans. As Texas grows and water becomes an even more valuable commodity, the need for sophistication in the understanding of water rights will become increasingly critical for everyone.

~~~~ TRANSFER OF WATER RIGHTS

In Texas, water rights can be severed from the land, sold, leased, or reserved by the seller just like any mineral interest. This practice can be considered an everyday part of our lives, especially in the drier areas of the state. The water rights for a piece of land will become an even more important aspect of negotiations in transactions as water becomes scarcer and more valuable. Water marketing and transfer of water from one area of the state to another have attracted a lot of attention in the past few years.[26] But the practice of transferring water rights has been in place since early Spanish colonial times in Texas.[27]

The TWBD has published a good resource to begin to understand water marketing in Texas called *A Texan's Guide to Water and Water Rights Marketing,* hereafter referred to as *Texan's Guide.* A strong word of caution—if you are considering marketing your water rights or groundwater or someone has contacted you about the purchase or lease of your rights, *seek counsel from a qualified attorney from the very begin-*

ning before making any final decisions or commitments! This point cannot be more stridently stressed. *The complexities of the transactions make it absolutely impossible to participate without legal counsel.*

In Texas, water rights can be transferred by sale or lease within your river basin or outside your basin. Groundwater transfers with permit in hand from a GCD are also allowable. Even a cursory search on the Internet will discover a large number of articles about water transfer in Texas.

According to the *Texan's Guide,* there are several forms of water transfer in the state:

- Sale of a Surface Water Right—a sale between a willing buyer and willing seller or other type of mechanism such as condemnation through the right of eminent domain which may not only rest in the authority of governments, but also may rest in the authority of other private entities;
- Contract Sale of Surface Water—water is sold by way of wholesale contract apart from the transfer of any interest in the water right itself;
- Lease of a Surface Water Right—a lease, just like a sale, is made between willing parties based upon agreed terms;
- Interbasin Transfer of Surface Water—Senate Bill 1 enacted by the Legislature in 1997 imposed strict standards on new interbasin transfers of surface water hence it is a tough proposition to gain TCEQ approval;
- Dry-Year Option Contracts—Surface Water—generally used by cities to augment their water needs during times of drought;
- Transfers of Conserved Water—Surface Water or Groundwater— in some parts of the state, water conserved can be marketed and transferred; and
- Sale/Lease of Groundwater—rights to groundwater may be severed from the land in Texas and made available for sale.[28]

Water transactions that fall within one of the above-mentioned general types close as a matter of course every day in Texas and have done so for many years. There can be a "substantive review process" to modify an existing permit or water right if any alteration to a change of use, location, or amount of water diverted is contemplated. The TCEQ is always involved in surface water transactions, and many times GCDs and other special districts such as the EAA require a "substantive review process" in order to obtain the proper permits. A party to any contemplated transaction must also spend time with professional experts such as attorneys, engineers, and contractors to develop a budget of all the potential associated costs.

Each water transfer transaction occurs under such unique circumstances in terms of the contracts and permits that it is difficult to determine market-value true comparables. Comparable prices in water transfer transactions must be adjusted to consider all the terms of each transaction, most of which are very confidential in nature. Suffice it to say, these transactions are so unique that each and every contemplated transaction must be considered on its own merits and based upon the negotiated terms between the parties.

Water rights attorney Russ Johnson has discussed the problems with water marketing in a publication for the Texas Real Estate Center. Written in May 2001, it is a fine resource for gaining an in-the-daily-fray professional opinion of water marketing's history and future. Johnson confirms my opinion about why it is so difficult to quote prices: "The burning question on everyone's mind is: What is water worth? While it seems a simple question, the answer depends on so many variables that it cannot be answered without a frame of reference. Examination of other areas of the country where the water market has operated historically provides little guidance in valuing water resources in Texas. . . . The current state of Texas law prevents any kind of statewide analysis of unit value of water."[29]

These headaches of valuation have not stopped water marketing in Texas. There are many projects in various stages of planning ongoing as this book is being written. Most of the major projects are overwhelmed with controversy, and the outcomes of these various proposed projects, some of which are enormous in cost and scope, are yet to be fully determined. According to Johnson,

> Recognition by the state and its citizens of the value of water will propel and fuel an emerging market in water resources. Governmental limitations on this market generally will frustrate, impair or artificially inflate the cost or value of water and must, over time, be reduced or eliminated. . . . Land owners' ability to participate in the market will be highly variable depending upon numerous factors, including whether the water has been produced by the land owner historically, the size of the area, the productivity of the resource, and proximity

to demand. Texas is decades away from a commodity-priced water market. Transactions and projects will help alleviate future demands, but organized, centralized or commodity-based selling and buying of water is impossible to achieve in the current regulatory and legal environment.[30]

The trend in future water policy appears to encourage support for long-distance transfers of water, but the jury is still out on the successful and profitable implementation of long water pipelines serving faraway cities and people. Why? Right-of-way acquisition is the expensive and delaying factor. Water cannot be compressed and has to be pumped all along the way. The end users of the water, which will often be the cities of Texas, will hold tight to the lowest water rate possible due to political pressure. Only the boldest entrepreneurs and investors who take the time to fully assess all the risks of water transactions, especially with cities, will have success in the long-distance transfers by pipeline.

Another consideration for property owners who lease their water rights to marketers is the power the leaseholder gains over the surface of the land. As in oil and gas and other mineral rights leases, the lessee's estate becomes the dominant estate and the surface owner's estate becomes servient to it. A competent attorney should be consulted by the landowner prior to executing any water rights lease. If not, the landowner may lose some control of roads, access, and other normal rights to the enjoyment of the surface of his or her land.

Part Five

WHAT SHOULD GUIDE
WATER POLICY
"THE COMMON GOOD"
OR PRIVATE RIGHTS?

PUBLIC POLICY DEBATES
IN THE RECENT PAST

Difficult public policy issues relating to water have faced Texans for many generations. The challenging choices have not necessarily been between right and wrong; typically, the positions and arguments of all the parties involved in water disputes could be considered reasonable.

 FOUR TALES FROM THE COMMON POOL

The resolutions to those disputes have most often involved questions about who owns the water, who can use the water, and who is liable when one party uses up the water available to another party. Some of the legislative decisions and court rulings in the past seem to make common sense and create good public policy, while other decisions and rulings seem to defy all logic.

Tale #1: The Case of the Biggest Pump

Who could have known that an obscure lawsuit over rights to underground water in a small town in north Texas at the start of the twentieth century would begin a cascade of events that is still unfolding today in the

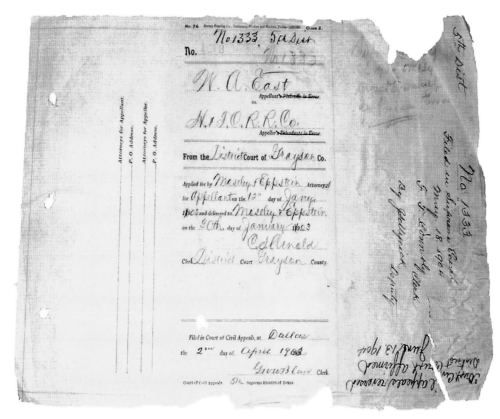

The original court file coversheet for *W. A. East v. Houston & Texas Central Railroad Company*. Courtesy Texas Water Development Board.

courts, in state government, and in people's daily lives?[1] The ultimate ruling in this lawsuit, a lawsuit that did not merit even a single word in the local newspaper,[2] is infamously known as the "rule of capture," or "he who has the biggest pump gets the most or all of the water." The rule of capture is one of the most confusing, and for some the most reviled, concepts in Texas water law today.

The roots of the rule of capture are found in the ancient idea that the ownership of wild game could not be claimed until possession was actually taken.[3] The rule of capture as it pertains to groundwater states that, unless water rights have been severed, a landowner who drills water wells can pump all the water that can be "captured" without any liability for damage to any neighboring property owner. If the landowner does not waste the water from the well, dig the water well to intentionally harm a neighbor, or cause subsidence, even if the neighbor's water well dries up completely as a result, the neighbor has no claim for compensation or damages against the landowner.

The rule of capture does not recognize correlative rights—the concept that one person's right to use a common resource impacts another person's equal right to use the same resource; hence, each needs to be cognizant of his or her shared responsibilities[4]—between landowners in pumping groundwater. Although Texas courts have consistently upheld this rule for more than 100 years, a dissenting justice wrote in the case of *Corpus Christi v. Pleasanton* in 1955: "In the field of water law there is no consolation in the rule of capture. . . . If the law of capture has any true application to underground water, it is an extremely limited one. No one can live in a vacuum. Therefore, all property rights are to a certain extent correlative." The perplexing question is, why are groundwater rights not considered correlative in Texas?

Many Texans, when asked about the origin of the rule of capture, believe that its roots are found in the oil and gas industry. Rarely is anyone aware that the rule stemmed from a water dispute and originated early in the last century as a ruling in a lawsuit in Denison, Texas, between a local property owner and a major railroad.

Denison is located about 75 miles north of Dallas and was laid out in the summer of 1872 by William Munson and R. S. Stevens on the route of the Missouri, Kansas and Texas Railroad (Katy); it was named for George Denison, the railroad's vice president. The first train arrived on Christmas Eve in 1872. By the following year the city had 3,000 residents, and in 1890 the thirty-fourth president of the United States, Dwight David Eisenhower, was born there. By 1900 the city had grown to 10,000 inhabitants, and in 1901 at least 10 railroads stopped there, making it a "bustling" business center.[5] The *Sunday Gazetteer,* a local newspaper, contained a weekly column called "Railroad Roundup." Indicative of the attitude shown toward the railroad industry bv the people of Denison, on October 2, 1904, the *Gazetteer* reported in "Railroad Roundup": "The railroads are making unusually low homeseeker's rates to Texas, and within the next thirty (30) days thousands of people will come from the North and East to this state. The railway companies are doing their share, and if the citizens of Texas will do one-half as much, Texas will grow this coming year as it never has."

Advertised as the Gateway to Texas, Katy's first stop in Texas was Denison. Joining George Denison in the Katy railway company were such notable investors as John D. Rockefeller and J. Pierpont Morgan.

Eventually, the Katy was acquired by Jay Gould. The Texas legislature gave Katy the same rights as a Texas corporation for almost 20 years before the railway officially incorporated in Austin, another indication of the favor the railroads were shown during this era. By January 1, 1904, the Katy owned and operated 1,119 miles of track in Texas. It was the first continuous railroad to St. Louis from Texas, and in the beginning, the Houston & Texas Central Railway (H&TC) was its key connector to Houston, Austin, and through acquisitions, New Orleans. In 1892 the H&TC owned 115 locomotives and 2,271 cars, generating passenger earnings of $1.0 million and freight earnings of $2.5 million. The Katy, by comparison, had passenger earnings of $1.2 million and freight earnings of $3.0 million in 1895 and owned 133 locomotives and 163 cars. By meeting in Denison, these two railways made the city grow quickly and heavily influenced the economy and citizenry.[6]

In 1903 the H&TC Railway decided to build a maintenance yard for its locomotives in Denison.[7] Steam-powered locomotives used water and lots of it. H&TC representatives asked their immediately adjacent neighbors about the water table and their water wells.[8] A representative of the company visited W. A. East, whose homestead comprised several lots of land, the nearest of which was within 100 feet of the railroad land.[9] East, more than likely a Denison policeman,[10] showed the railroad man the wells on his property, which were around 33 feet deep and 5 feet wide. East's well captured his water for household use only; his wells had been in use for a number of years prior to the railroad's inquiry. The railroad dug a well on its property shortly thereafter that was 66 feet deep and 20 feet wide. When the well was completed in August 1901, a steam pump was installed "of sufficient strength to supply a three inch pipe." The railroad began pumping 25,000 gallons a day. Within a few months, East's water well went dry, as did those of several of his neighbors.[11] East and the neighbors sued the railroad company.

Odd decisions became the norm in this lawsuit from the very beginning. Today, a plaintiff who is a local homestead owner would more than likely ask a jury of his peers to judge his case against a large company such as the railroad; even then, it was East's unilateral and unquestionable decision to ask for a jury trial for a trivial fee (today the fee to have a jury trial is still only five dollars). However, even though East was represented by well-qualified local counsel, Moseley & Eppstein, he chose to try his case with the judge only.[12] Perhaps the railroad was so beloved by the people of Denison or employed so many local citizens that East and his attorneys felt their best chance to prevail was outside the peer review of the citizens of Denison. Whatever the reason, no jury was called, and the decision was left to District Judge Rice Maxey.[13]

In East's First Amended Original Petition, he claimed the water in his well was "inexhaustible . . . pure, soft water of a kind that it was almost impossible to secure in the markets," that the water was "supplied by a subterranean stream" or if incorrect, the water was "fed by percolations of water through his land." He further claimed that the railroad well's "powerful pumps and engines . . . drew all the water from under his land as well as that of all the surrounding land owners for a very large territory." He claimed the water taken from the railroad well was "an unreasonable and unnatural supply of water out of all proportion to any reasonable or legitimate use of the said land as land." He further claimed the railroad "uses the water in supplying a vast number of engines with water and for all other purposes necessary and usual in conducting a large system of railroad extending over several hundred miles."

East's attorneys set up their claim in classic terms as the little man against the big railroad company. They claimed the "reasonable use" doctrine, known as the "American rule" that limits the amount of water one can withdraw from underneath his or her own property to be what is "reasonably" necessary for the beneficial use of the surface estate. Their claim was that the water from the railroad "well was not taken for the purposes of developing or using this land for any useful, profitable or pleasurable purpose."[14] The East attorneys made a strong case and claimed damages in the amount of $1,100, but Judge Maxey on December 28, 1902, disagreed with the East claims.

Judge Maxey found all the facts true as stated in the petition by the plaintiff, found that the damages were in the total amount of $206.25 per well dried up, and found that "the use to which the defendant puts its well was not a reasonable use of their property as land, but was an artificial use of their property." He added, though, "[A]nd, if the doctrine of reasonable use is applicable to defined streams applies to such cases, this was unreasonable."[15]

His subsequent conclusion was another oddity of this case. While his findings so far appeared to be in favor of East, his final conclusion was that "under the foregoing facts no cause of action is shown in behalf of the plaintiffs in any sum whatsoever, because I do not believe any correlative rights exist between the parties as to the underground, percolating waters which do not run in any defined channel. I therefore find for the defendant." Without any evidence to the contrary, the judge assumed the water underground was "percolating" water. Therefore, even though the use by the railroad was deemed unreasonable and he agreed East was damaged, he ruled correctly, according to the Texas Supreme Court two years later, that the plaintiffs could not recover any remedy for their damages from the railroad. Judge Maxey did not refer to any other cases, such as the 1843 case in England, *Acton v. Blundell*,[16] which the Texas Supreme Court would eventually cite. It is unknown if Judge Maxey had the English case in mind, but his declaration that the parties' rights to the water were not "correlative" was a bold judicial statement.

Judge Maxey carefully worded his decision; he recognized the tension of the industrial age, human versus machine, and was sympathetic to East, his fellow citizen. One fact was unknown, the source of the water underground: was it a pool resulting from "percolating water" from East's surface or from an "underground" stream? East's lawyers did not know, hence the wording in their petition. On this fact, however, hinged the decision, since the concept of underground water ownership had existed in Spanish water law and was time and again recognized in Texas law. Because technology was not in place at the time to actually determine the source of the water, Judge Maxey chose to base his decision assuming "percolating water" as the source.

As anticipated, East appealed the case. The railroad, at the appellate level and beyond, was represented by one of the strongest and most famous law firms in Texas, Baker, Botts, Baker, and Lovett, who were included with the original attorneys for the railroad, Head & Dillard. At the appellate level, Judge Maxey's decision was reversed and the plaintiffs were awarded $1,100 and court costs.[17]

Appellate Justice Bookout ruled that based upon a New Hampshire case, the rights of the adjoining landowners were correlative, and he was of the opinion that under the facts of the case, East and the other plaintiffs were entitled to recover the $206.25 mentioned in Judge Maxey's trial court opinion. Judge Bookout also used a New York case to back up his decision, which used the following phrase to decide for the damaged landowner in similar circumstances: "unreasonable as to the plaintiff and the others whose lands are thus clandestinely sapped, and their value impaired." Judge Bookout mentioned the railroad's plea of the English case *Acton v. Blundell,* which ruled, "If a man digs a well on his own field and thereby drains his neighbor's he may do so unless he does it maliciously," but he disagreed with its application. The Baker, Botts attorneys were astute in their research. On the basis of the English case, the railroad appealed the appellate court decision to the Texas Supreme Court.

Another oddity of the case is that Baker, Botts ignored the concept of underground water ownership. In the words of Spanish water rights law expert Michael C. Meyer,

> Water that originated on a piece of land, that ran solely within its confines, or that lay *under* [emphasis added] it was automatically alienated from state ownership with the sale or grant of the land. It was appurtenant to landownership. No special water right or additional permission was required to use it, and no limits were set on the amounts that might be used. . . . The *Siete Partidas,* in fact, specified it was an obligation of all inhabitants to make their land productive, and it further indicated that "man has the power to do as he sees fit with those things that belong to him according to the laws of God and man." Hispanic groundwater law was designed to protect individual rights, to encourage private initiative and entrepreneurship, to stimulate economic development, and even to accumulate personal wealth.[18]

Meyer went on to sum up: "It [Spanish water law] combined the reasonableness of private property with the justice of serving the common good."[19] For whatever reason, the courts ignored the much older, more appropriate, and actually at that time more recognized law in Texas, that of Spanish water law. The Texas Supreme Court on June 13, 1904, reversed the decision of the appellate court and affirmed Judge Maxey's original decision.

In upholding the original trial courts decision, the Texas Supreme Court relied primarily upon two cases, the English case *Acton v. Blundell* and a case decided by the Supreme Court of Ohio, *Frazier v. Brown,* which held that,

> In the absence of express contract and a positive authorized legislation, as between proprietors of adjoining land, the law recognizes no correlative rights in respect to underground waters percolating, oozing, or filtrating through the earth; and this mainly from considerations of public policy: (1) Because the existence, origin, movement, and course of such waters, and the causes which govern and direct their movements, are so secret, occult and concealed that an attempt

to administer any set of legal rules in respect to them would be involved in hopeless uncertainty, and would be practically be impossible. (2) Because any such recognition of correlative rights would interfere, to the material detriment of the commonwealth, with the drainage of agriculture, mining, the construction of highways and railroads, with sanitary regulations, building, and the general progress of improvement in works of embellishment and utility.[20]

By upholding the district court decision and reversing the appellate court decision, the justices of the Texas Supreme Court effectively ruled out the "American rule" of reasonable use and chose the "rule of capture" as the law in Texas, beginning a journey through decades of lawsuits and rulings consistently in favor of the landowner with the larger pump.

The *East* case caused the legislature to write an amendment to the Texas Constitution in 1917, which authorized the legislature to pass all appropriate laws to preserve and conserve natural resources: "The conservation and development of all of the natural resources of this State . . . and the preservation and conservation of all such natural resources of the State are each and all hereby declared public rights and duties; and the Legislature shall pass all such laws as may be appropriate thereto."[21] From that amendment, many years later, GCDs came into existence to manage groundwater in the state. Yet, to date, the legislature has failed to adopt a law to officially end the rule of capture and probably never will. Time and again the courts have "called upon the Legislature to exercise its proper role in regulating and managing groundwater withdrawals in the State of Texas." For example, in 1973 a Texas Supreme Court ruling concluded: "The need for additional legislation for creation of districts to cover unregulated groundwater reservoirs and to solve other conflicts which may arise in this area of water law and subsidence seems to be inevitable. Providing policy and regulatory procedures in this field is a *legislative* [emphasis added] function. It is well that the Legislature has assumed its proper role, *because* our courts are not equipped to regulate groundwater uses and subsidence on a case by case basis."[22]

In 1999 a Texas Supreme Court justice similarly expressed his frustration with the legislature's inaction in a case in which the court upheld the rule of capture and that was similar to the *East* case.[23] A large company, Ozarka, which pumped huge amounts of groundwater from wells on its property for bottling and sale to consumers, caused the water well of a neighbor, Bart Sipriano, to dry up completely. The court ruled in favor of the large company, but with wording that included a less than subtle warning to the legislature:

> For over ninety years, this Court has adhered to the common-law rule of capture in allocating the respective rights and liabilities of neighboring landowners for use of groundwater flowing beneath their property. The rule of capture essentially allows, with some limited exceptions, a landowner to pump as much groundwater as the landowner chooses, without liability to neighbors who claim that the pumping has depleted their wells. We are asked today whether Texas should abandon this rule for the rule of reasonable use. . . . Because we conclude the sweeping change to Texas groundwater law Sipriano [the plaintiff in the case] urges this Court to make is not appropriate *at this time* [emphasis added], we affirm the Court of Appeal's judgment.[24]

The controversy created by the obscure *East* case from the time when railroads "ruled the roost" in most of the country's economy is still alive and remains a throbbing pain to many in our state. The rule of capture still threatens landowners in areas of Texas in which no GCD exists.

Tale #2: The Case of the Dried-Up Springs

On June 21, 1954, one of the most confusing and disappointing rulings ever to be issued by a civil appeals court in Texas was rendered in *Pecos WCID No. 1 v. Clayton Williams, et al.* The Court of Civil Appeals of Texas, El Paso District, entered a judgment in favor of the defendants, Williams and others, and allowed them to continue to drill water wells on their lands and interfere with the flow of Comanche Springs in Fort Stockton. The effect of this ruling, based in part on the rule of capture, killed one of nature's most beautiful and prolific springs, the consequence of which ended the irrigated agribusiness of the right holders to the waters of Comanche Creek, which dried up entirely when the springs ceased to flow.

As is etched on its historical monument, Comanche Springs was "one of the few good watering places in this arid region." Flowing for eons, the springs were first written about by the early Spanish explorers and were the reason for the establishment of Fort Stockton. On my first visit to the location of the springs in 2007, I was overwhelmed by the sheer size of the area from which the springs flowed and struck by the over-

Comanche Springs marker. Photo by author.

all geography of flat, arid lands that make up the Fort Stockton vicinity. What a relief it must have been for the early explorers and travelers to find these huge springs along their journeys through such desolate country. Today, one can observe at least six outlets (some take a little imagination to overlook the cement and steel encasements of the nineteenth and early twentieth centuries) the water flowed through to create the now concrete-lined Comanche Creek. The first outlet I discovered was on land next to the Catholic church located on the courthouse square of Fort Stockton.

At one time this emergent outlet was honored with a special entrance of steps. I was unable to enter the locked gate to observe the depth of the outlet, but it appears to be a large cavern-type hole, and one can easily imagine the joy the resulting swimming hole created in many hearts over the years before the drying. Sadly, the chain-link gate over the outlet is covered in litter and debris. Yet one can still feel the spirit of the location.

When I visited the church next door, I was amazed to discover from my inquiries that no one in the office knew much about this main outlet. In fact, they professed to know little about the springs themselves

The main emergent hole for Comanche Springs, now despoiled. Photo by author.

other than that they had not flowed in years. I prowled all over the park of concrete and asphalt streets; the park facilities were painted in red, white, and blue.

As luck would have it, during my visit I found myself in the midst of a serious hailstorm. Seeking shelter under a barbecue pavilion, I fortunately encountered a workman who was in his thirtieth year of employment by the city. I asked him about the springs. He said occasionally they would trickle when it rained on the ranches above the springs, but in his years, he had seen this happen only a few times. Beneath the man's attitude of kind acceptance of the inevitable, I detected sadness that this unique feature of nature was gone.

The plaintiffs in this famous case were senior appropriators of the waters from Comanche Creek, which they had used for irrigation purposes on their crops for 90 years, or from just after the Civil War. Their lands were located north and east of the springs, and there was no dispute of their rights or their legitimate use of the waters of the creek, which were fed by the springs.

Around 1951, the ranchers and farmers "up-gradient" of the springs began to drill water wells.[25] The 1950s drought had begun to take its

Other dried-up Comanche Springs outlets. Photo by author.

toll in the area, and the ranchers and farmers were desperate for water for their crops and livestock; they acted to protect their lives and interests, but the unintended consequences were that a natural treasure was harmed, as were the other farmers and ranchers who depended upon Comanche Creek's water.

According to Joe R. Greenhill and Thomas Gibbs Gee, the plaintiffs alleged

- that their predecessors had owned the location and flow of the springs;
- that they had used the water beneficially for ninety years;
- that they had a right to be protected in the subsurface source of the water;
- alternatively, if it was determined they did not own the water which made up the source of supply, that they were nevertheless entitled to a fair share of the correlative rights in the source of supply or the common reservoir; and
- that the springs were not fed by percolating water but by a "well-defined" underground stream.[26]

Aerial view of Comanche Springs Park (center of photo).
Courtesy Google, USDA Farm Service Agency, Digital Globe.

The plaintiffs claimed that the mere fact that the water emerged from the springs indicated that it traveled to the surface at Comanche Springs through a "well-defined" underground stream. If they prevailed in convincing the court that this was correct, then the water taken by the ranchers and farmers was owned by the state and was not "percolating" groundwater.

There was no allegation by the plaintiffs in this case that the defendants were wasting the water. According to Greenhill and Gee, the defendants responded that

- they were landowners who used water on their own lands for irrigation and other beneficial purposes;
- they used the *East* case as precedence that they absolutely owned the water under their lands and that there are no recognizable correlative rights in percolating groundwater;

Aerial view of irrigation wells that dried up Comanche Springs.
Courtesy Google, USDA Farm Service Agency.

- that the water was percolating water;
- that groundwater is assumed to be percolating water; and
- that the plaintiffs' allegations that the water flowed in a "well-defined" underground stream were "insufficient" because they failed to provide proof of the underground stream's source, location, bed, banks, and course.[27]

The defendants also opined an argument, which is still being used, most recently in the *Del Rio* case (see tale #4). According to Greenhill and Gee, the defendants claimed "that the East case was a rule of property in Texas, that thousands of acres had been transferred with the understanding that the buyer was getting everything in and under his land, including minerals, oil and gas, and water, that thousands of acres of water rights had been transferred, and that the court should not divest landowners of ownership rights which they had so long regarded as theirs."

There was no doubt that the defendants, under the rule of capture, had every right to drill water wells and take the "diffused and percolating" water beneath their lands. The court cited Vernon's Annotated Civil Statute 7880-3c, which recognized the ownership rights of the landowner in underground water, excepting the "underflow of rivers and defined subterranean streams." A landowner owned the percolating water and could use it at his or her will in a nonwasteful manner.

The plaintiffs asked the court to declare their right to title to the springs and to declare that their rights were correlative and riparian. The court held against the plaintiffs that

- a landowner owned the percolating water under his land and he could make non-wasteful use thereof;
- there was no authority to grant the water district plaintiff's correlative right declared;
- there was no authority in the courts or in the statutes that authorized the plaintiffs to extend their appropriation, if any it had, to underground waters; and
- the bare fact that the water district plaintiff's claim that the source of the springs was a well-defined underground channel did not make it so.

The court's opinion, written by Justice Fraser, also stated that "it is clear on the authority of the Texas cases cited above that its appropriation, if any, could extend to the waters of Comanche Springs at and after their emergence from the ground, and the same is true of riparian rights. We do not find any authority in the courts of statutes authorizing plaintiff to extend its appropriation, if any it has, to underground waters."

As to the allegation that the waters were in an underground stream, Fraser wrote, "The lower court held that the allegations of plaintiff with regard to this matter were insufficient and were in effect merely a conclusion of the pleader, because plaintiff did not state sufficient facts to identify the claimed well-defined channel, either as to surface indications, probable route, source or destination, but merely states that the said waters flow in a well-defined channel."

Would the outcome have been different if the science of hydrology had been able to identify the water that flowed from the spring was from an underground stream?[28] Logically, if the water pumped "up-gradient" to the defendants' lands resulted in drying up the springs, did not the water travel in a "stream"? The only way to read the court's conclusion is that the water in the spring was "percolating" and by its nature did not flow in a "well-defined" underground channel. It is interesting to note that Judge Fraser mentioned the underground stream matter again at the end of his opinion. He cited two cases other than *East* that support the court's conclusion that one man's pumping of water that dries up a spring is not acceptable proof that the water flowed in a well-defined underground channel. Fraser made a final comment on the matter: "So it seems well decided that the mere fact that the wells of one man dried up springs or the wells of another, neither proves nor indicates a well-defined channel of underground water. We merely hold that the trial court was correct in his holding that the allegations in the petition here involved are not sufficient. Nor do we pass, therefore, on the matter of the disposition of the waters of a well-defined underground channel or subterranean river."

It appears that Judge Fraser was troubled enough over the ruling about the flow of underground water in a well-defined stream that he felt it important to further discuss the matter. It appears that if the plaintiffs had been able to provide a hydrologic expert who could provide reliable evidence that the springs did flow from an underground stream in a well-defined channel, the outcome of the case would likely have favored the plaintiffs. If the plaintiffs prevailed in proving the underground stream allegation, using one of Judge Fraser's seemingly favorite words, would the judgment be "merely" monetary damages for the plaintiffs or would the court have given the plaintiffs a permanent injunction, which would have stopped the defendants' pumping of water from their wells? Imagine the effect on the land values of the defendants—they would not be able to irrigate their pastures and crops. What would the world of Texas water rights statewide look like today if Judge Fraser's court had granted that permanent injunction? For certain, Comanche Springs would be alive and running.

Tale #3: The Catfish Farm

The rule of capture seemed to sleep in the public's consciousness until its consequences came roaring back into the news in 1991 when real estate developers Ron Pucek and Louis Blumberg dug a well for water in southern Bexar County. The well was 1,600 feet deep, and they hit water—in a big way. The artesian water well,[29] a well that blew out water from natural pressures of the Edwards Aquifer, exploded at an initial volume of 43 million gallons per day, or 48,000 acre-feet per year.

The well came in so strongly that a neighbor said he thought a freight train had rumbled by his home. The water shot some three stories into the air. The word of this discovery hit the streets of San Antonio first and, shortly thereafter, the entire United States as news services picked up the story. The amount of water from this one, free-flowing, internal-pressure water well could potentially provide *by itself* the annual water needs of 250,000 San Antonians. Another way to look at this one well's production is to compare it to the total annual withdrawal from the aquifer authorized from 1996 to 2007—450,000 acre-feet per year. The "catfish" well alone, had it continued to produce, would have exceeded 10 percent of the total allowable withdrawals for the entire aquifer.

Pucek and Blumberg knew that even though the rule of capture allowed them to take this water, the rule by this time had three limitations from case law. The *Corpus Christi v. Pleasanton* case of 1955 had established that the water could not be wasted. Therefore, the pair of developers decided the best way to put this water to use was to raise catfish as they waited for the inevitable payday this unexpected bonanza had delivered to them.[30] They opened the Living Waters Artesian Springs catfish farm. As Robert Glennon said in *Water Follies,* "They hoped to raise 750,000 catfish on the amount of water San Antonio uses to raise 250,000 human beings."[31] The characteristics of the rule of capture raised many an eyebrow, and barrels of newspaper ink were used to cry "foul" to an amazed public.

Across the state, people were incensed. How could this happen in our drought-ridden state? How could this happen in a city like San Antonio, the only city in the United States 100 percent dependent upon the same aquifer for all their drinking water? What is the rule of capture? Isn't it an oil and gas law? It all seemed grossly unfair.

On December 5, 2000, Pucek and Blumberg, catfish farmers, received $9 million from the San Antonio Water System for part of the rights to the groundwater, probably a little better return on their investment than the development plans had originally shown. Eventually SAWS acquired all the rights, and the original well has been shut in.[32] SAWS eventually purchased Living Waters Artesian Springs, Ltd., as well as most of its groundwater rights, for $30 million.[33]

Tale #4: Val Verde County Folly

The case of *City of Del Rio v. Clayton Samuel Colt Hamilton Trust* is one of the most significant water rights cases in Texas history. The city at the

The crystal-clear waters of San Felipe Springs. Photo by author.

very center of the case, Del Rio, is a city dear to my heart. Having spent 32 years in the area due to interests held in a tract of land in Mexico, I know many of the people well. The city is a wonderful place to live. It sits close to the conjunction of the Devil's River and the Pecos River with the Rio Grande, just downstream of one of the most underutilized lakes in the United States, Lake Amistad, and enjoys a pleasant climate year-round. Some of Texas' earliest prehistory stems from ancient peoples living in this fertile and beautiful area. Del Rio exists not only because of its proximity to the Rio Grande and other rivers but also because it is home to one of Texas' most beautiful and prolific springs, San Felipe Springs, which provides the city with most of its freshwater.

This case has some amazing facts, most of which were stipulated to by the parties to the lawsuit. It is highly significant to me whenever parties to a lawsuit "stipulate to" facts in the case. *Black's Law Dictionary* defines the term "stipulate" as "[a]rrange or settle definitely, as an agreement or covenant . . . [v]oluntary agreement between opposing counsel concerning disposition of some relevant point so as to obviate the need for proof or to narrow range of litigable issues."

Here are the stipulated facts in the case taken from the opinion written by Justice Karen Angelini:

- The Clayton Sam Colt Hamilton Trust owns a 3,200 acre tract of land called the "Moore Ranch" in Val Verde County. (This is located generally at the intersection of SH 90 and SH 277/377 on the way to Amistad Dam just north of Del Rio.)
- The ranch is in the extraterritorial jurisdiction (ETJ) of Del Rio.
- The ranch is not subject to regulation by any groundwater conservation district.
- The ranch has no surface water, but has groundwater which is part of the Edwards-Trinity (Plateau) Aquifer.
- In 1997, the Trust sold 15 acres to the City of Del Rio for $56,000.
- The tract is on the SH 277/377 on the west and is surrounded by the Moore Ranch on the north, east, and south.
- The warranty deed, dated January 8, 1977 provides the following: *Surface Estate Only* described as fifteen (15) acres more fully described as Exhibit "A" attached hereto and incorporated herein for all purposes.
- SAVE AND EXCEPT . . . Grantor RESERVES unto Grantor, its successors, heirs, assigns forever *all water rights associated with said tract,* however, Grantor may not use any portion of the surface of said tract for exploring, drilling, or producing any such water.

In 2000, the City, per Angelini, realized it needed to augment its municipal drinking water supply. The City drilled the subject water well on the 15 acres bought from the Trust in 2002, and it produced 500 gallons per minute (the equivalent of 440 acre-feet per year). When the well was completed, the total cost was approximately $850,000.

The local citizens I interviewed in the summer of 2009 pointed out that the City drilled the well ostensibly to test if the newly acquired 15 acres were "up-gradient" of San Felipe Springs and if there was a way to help decrease the turbidity (haziness in water caused by suspended solids generally invisible to the naked eye) in the spring water. Continuing on in her opinion, Judge Angelini reported that late in 2002 or early 2003, J. R. Hamilton of the Trust noticed the drilling and had his attorney protest the activity to the City's attorney. The Trust asked $500,000 in damages, and the City rejected the request. The Trust filed the initial lawsuit asking for monetary damages, seeking a judgment that the Trust owned the water underneath the City tract and that the City's claim to ownership to those water rights be rejected. The City counterclaimed that the deed did not leave the Trust with "right, title, or interest in any groundwater pumped to the surface by the City" and that the water that was pumped was owned by the City. The City also pled for condemnation of the water rights reserved by the Trust.

This is the ruling of the trial court:

1. The water rights reservation was valid and enforceable.
2. The City's argument that groundwater, until captured, cannot be the subject of ownership was an incorrect statement of the law.
3. Ownership of groundwater rights beneath the 15-acre tract belonged to the Trust.

The City appealed. The City argued that the Trust's water rights reservation could not prevent the City from drilling into the subsurface water. The City's interpretation of the rule of capture was that the groundwater cannot be "owned" until it was reduced to possession, and since the Trust had never drilled on the 15-acre tract, the City claimed the Trust never captured the water. The opinion of the appeals court was that the City of Del Rio does not own the water beneath the 15-acre tract and that the Trust had not conveyed any "water rights" to the City. "Pursuant to the deed, the City never obtained ownership of the groundwater."

The ruling of the appeals court was in favor of the Trust. The City then appealed to the Texas Supreme Court. On September 25, 2009, the Texas Supreme Court denied the Petition for Review. The City then requested a rehearing, and it was disposed of on December 11, 2009, subsequently sending the case into history.

There were a number of amicus curiae briefs filed in favor of the Trust with the Texas Supreme Court. The Latin phrase *amicus curiae* literally means "friend of the court," or someone who volunteers to offer a point of law or other opinion on some aspect of the case to assist the court in its determinations.

Stewart Title Company, the oldest chartered title insurance company in the state and one of the most reliable, insures interests in water rights. Stewart Title Company filed a brief supporting the Trust's position, saying, "The increased demand for policies of title insurance insuring interests in water rights suggests an increased public awareness of the significance of these rights." The company agreed that "[t]he Court of Appeals opinion correctly summarizes Texas law regarding a land owner's absolute ownership of the groundwater beneath the surface estate owned, provided the rights to the groundwater are unsevered by conveyance or reservation, and in which case the groundwater is subject to barter and sale as any other species of property."

Stewart's interest was obvious; the company has insured all types of property rights for more than 100 years, including water rights. Had the *Del Rio* case been decided for the City of Del Rio that groundwater is not owned by the surface estate until captured and taken into possession, it is this author's opinion that the entire real estate market would be placed into utter turmoil. The claims laid upon Stewart Title's insurance policies would be overwhelming, and the consequences to the valuation of all property in Texas would have been devastating.

SAWS filed an amicus brief for the Trust, as did the Canadian River Municipal Water Authority (CRMWA). Both of these major water authorities have millions of dollars invested in groundwater rights in place. SAWS stated, "SAWS is a municipal utility which provides water and wastewater services to approximately 1.3 million citizens of the City of San Antonio and surrounding areas. The judgment sought by the City of Del Rio in this appeal would detrimentally affect the ability of SAWS to secure necessary new water supplies for its customers." SAWS further stated that "SAWS has worked effectively with landowners to ensure that groundwater is acquired for urban needs in market transactions that are fair and beneficial to all involved. These transactions are occurring within the framework of groundwater district rules that recognize groundwater ownership and correlative rights, and encourage market transfer of groundwater that has never been reduced to possession." CRMWA said in its amicus brief, "With almost $200 million invested in groundwater rights and development and delivery of that water, CRMWA has a very substantial interest in upholding existing Texas law, which allows severance and independent ownership of groundwater in place, against the challenge mounted by the City of Del Rio."

One other amicus curiae brief submitted by the Texas Farm Bureau had significant opinions to offer. The Texas Farm Bureau "has over 422,159 members and is associated with independent county Farm Bureau corporations in 207 counties across the state." The bureau stated an overall concern, which is reflective of a large number of Texas rural agribusiness operators: "Texas Farm Bureau and its members—who are property owners and irrigators—believe the protection of property rights generally, and groundwater ownership as private property in particular, is of critical importance to the State of Texas." The bureau continued, "[We] are keenly interested in the legal principles established in this case, because the City of Del Rio's position in this case, and its actions in pumping underground water from a tract for which underground water rights were expressly reserved by the grantor, threaten established Texas law on private property rights in groundwater on which Texas Farm Bureau members rely." The bureau made its strongest statement on page 5 of its amicus brief: "Long-established Texas law recognizes that underground water is part of the surface estate: There is a property interest in underground water that belongs to the surface owner. Whatever right that was, the Trust reserved it and Del Rio did not receive it."

There have certainly been thousands of real estate transactions in the past and will be in the future in which the buyer of the property relied upon the terms of the purchase contract, the deed, and the title company that insured the title to all the property rights. Still other thousands of transactions have closed in which the groundwater rights were purchased, leased, severed, or transferred in some other manner. All these transactions were predicated upon the fact that the seller owned the groundwater in place based upon warranties and representations from the seller. The purchaser had the right to rely upon those representations. The ownership of the groundwater beneath the property being purchased was material and significant to the purchaser when making the decision to purchase the property.

The *Del Rio* case was the most significant case seen in modern times in relation to property rights and valuation. The long-reaching impact of a decision that declared *Del Rio* correct would have caused panic in the entire marketplace for rural land and significantly devalued most of the rural land west of IH-35 that has groundwater beneath it.

The other even more basic consequence of Del Rio's position would be that even express reservations of rights as a whole would become unreliable. While Del Rio's arguments were intellectually stimulating and represented an innovative if not flawed thought on ad valorem taxation of water in the ground not yet captured, Del Rio was simply not right in drilling a water well to take water it had agreed to in writing that it had no right to take. Del Rio represented to the Trust that the City understood it was not being conveyed the groundwater rights. Del Rio signed the contract and closing documents without being under duress and by its own choice.

This case is indicative of the intent cities have shown to find water for their citizens in any way they can. Their intent will intensify as the growth of the state in the next decades, coupled with the upcoming

The infamous Del Rio water well. Photo by author.

guaranteed droughts, causes water resources to become more scarce and precious. A major message of this book is that cities are desperate now and will be more desperate in the future for water resources; they are rightly and diligently trying to fulfill their duties to their citizens. Landowners should be aware that their individual interests in groundwater rights should no longer be taken for granted.

Photographs of the Del Rio water well in the summer of 2009 show not only a major water well on the site, which was doubtlessly expensive to drill, but also a gigantic pump, a large electrical transformer to power the system, and what appeared to me to be in excess of a mile of water main built toward the city south along the right-of-way of SH 277/377. It looked to me as if Del Rio were more than simply testing the groundwater to help with turbidity; based on its obvious investment in the ground, the City intended to make this water well an integral part of its water infrastructure. Considering almost a decade of lawsuits at all three levels of the court system, it is certain that Del Rio spent many more thousands of dollars to promote its losing position.

In the spring of 2009, Del Rio was considering a water protection ordinance that was considered by some to be vital to the city's future.

The large pump for the Del Rio water well. Photo by author.

The basis of the proposed ordinance may have been found in the provisions of state law that allow a city to protect its water supply. Changes in the property code in 2003 allow cities to use the right of eminent domain to take groundwater rights, indicating the legislature's interest in this protection in times of drought. One civil and environmental engineer opined that the ordinance was essential to protect the city's future. The engineer stated in a letter to a City of Del Rio official, "Without clean, reliable and abundant water, with which the city has been blessed, the future is certain to be worse than the present." This statement sums up the attitude of all cities in Texas toward their future water supplies. The cities' concern is fair, morally correct, and supported by history; water is life for people and cities.

The engineer's letter astutely mentions the following risks for the city, which can be applied to municipalities and individual landowners, especially those with active agribusiness interests in the arid portions of the state:

First and foremost there is a real possibility that land could be purchased or leased for extraction of water that would be transported out

Another view of the Del Rio water well. Photo by author.

of the region without any restrictions on the pumping of the aquifers. The City of San Antonio is actively seeking water sources for its future and it is not uncommon for large cities to go hundreds of miles to find and develop water supplies, including reservoirs, dams and well fields. If this occurred, and the Rule of Capture still applied as it does today, it is entirely possible that the San Felipe Springs' flows could be reduced by at least two-thirds of their current quantity.

Secondly, any landowner or leaseholder could explore and capture all the water it can find on any of the property under its control and could pump as much water as it desires, thus drying up downstream landowners' existing wells. There is no legal remedy under the Rule of Capture when a landowner captures water and that action results in taking water from other landowners. Thus everyone is then in a race to capture all the water it can and other landowners are at their mercy.[34]

This engineer was especially correct in Del Rio's case because the Del Rio area is not in a GCD, which would have the authority to regulate all the groundwater in the area. The TWDB or the local citizens should seri-

Fire plug on the site of the water well in question in *Del Rio v. Clayton Sam Colt Hamilton Trust.* Photo by author.

ously consider forming a GCD in the Del Rio area to help avoid the very real risks just described. In fact, any city that is in area outside a GCD may be well served to seriously consider promoting the formation of a district, or it may be in the situation indicated in the photograph from the Del Rio water well site: "out of service."

A FUTURE TALE STILL WAITING TO BE FULLY TOLD: THE "TAKING" CASE

The Texas Supreme Court issued a long-awaited opinion in the case *Edwards Aquifer Authority v. Day* on February 24, 2012.[35] Private landowners, groundwater conservation districts, cities, and many other stakeholders, including key trade associations, followed this case for years as it passed through the court system. The case scared many entities involved in the regulation of groundwater since the potential compensation award could prove unaffordable when applied to the thousands of permits and denied permits across the state. Many viewed the ruling as the ultimate determining factor in the affordability, possibly even the existence, of our current groundwater management systems.

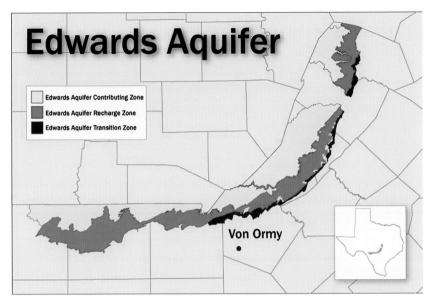

Von Ormy is the location of the Day-McDaniel conflict. Courtesy City of Van Ormy, Texas.

The unanimous decision of the Texas Supreme Court in this case consisted of two legally significant rulings. The first ruling was that landowners in Texas own the groundwater "in place" beneath their property, which clarified once and for all the ownership of groundwater in place by the surface landowner. (How one can absolutely prove the amount of groundwater in place is problematic since water is "fugitive" and moves around all the time.) The second ruling was that landowners may have a valid claim for just compensation from a government entity if the regulations and/or regulatory ruling went too far in limiting groundwater withdrawals, which opened the door to further litigation about "how much groundwater regulation is too much." If the evidence proves the government entity went too far in its regulatory efforts, those efforts could be a "taking" of the landowners' private property. Justice Nathan Hecht wrote in the opinion:

We decide in this case whether land ownership includes an interest in groundwater in place and cannot be taken for public use without adequate compensation guaranteed by Article 1, section 17 (a) of the Texas Constitution.[36] We hold that it does. We affirm the judgment of the court of appeals[37] and remand the case to the district court for further proceedings. . . . We begin by considering whether, under the

EAAA [Edwards Aquifer Authority Act], the Authority erred in limiting Day's IRP [initial regular permit] to 14 acre-feet of water and conclude that it did not. Next, we turn to whether Day has a constitutionally protected interest in the groundwater underneath his property and conclude that he does. We then consider whether the Authority's denial of an IRP in the amount Day requested constitutes a taking and conclude that the issue must be remanded to the trial court for further proceedings.[38]

The court concluded, based upon the evidence presented, that it could not determine, as a matter of law, if the EAA did or did not take Day's property. According to Hecht, "A full development of the record may demonstrate that regulation is too restrictive of Day's groundwater rights and without justification in the overall regulatory scheme."[39] The court sent the case (which was ultimately settled out of court) back to the trial court in Atascosa County (Jourdanton) for further consideration.

As clear as the Supreme Court was about groundwater ownership in place, its ruling leaves the question of how much groundwater regulation is too much before the regulation becomes a taking open for further review. According to Tom Mason and Robin Melvin, "As a practical matter, *Day* means it may take a number of landowner lawsuits that assert takings claims against groundwater districts—each based on unique facts and circumstances—before enough case law is developed to provide clearer guidance on how much groundwater regulation is too much."[40] The case arose from the plaintiffs' disagreement on the amount of groundwater they could pump from the Edwards Aquifer. The Plaintiffs asked the EAA for a permit to pump 700 acre-feet per year from a water well on their 381.4-acre ranch. Day timely applied for the permit before the deadline of December 30, 1996. In November 2000, the EAA denied the application for 700 acre-feet. Day appealed, and the matter was sent to the State Office of Administrative Hearings. The administrative law judge concluded that Day should be granted a permit for 14 acre-feet per year. The key aspect of this case for all landowners in the EAA's jurisdiction is what evidence is acceptable to prove "historic use" of groundwater.

The facts supporting the plaintiffs' request were complicated. The water well in question had not been in service since 1983 when landowners removed the pump; it still flowed under artesian pressure into a channel that led to a tank or reservoir on their land. Day offered eyewitness testimony from the period at the administrative hearing, but under cross-examination, one witness admitted a lack of knowledge of key facts concerning the amount of water pumped historically. The volume of water drawn from the well was not measured by a water meter; the amount of water historically produced could not be accurately determined. Under the existing exemption for domestic and livestock use, the plaintiffs could pump 25,000 gallons per day, equating to 28 acre-feet per year without a permit. But Day's purpose for this water was for irrigating his pasture.

The lack of documentary evidence to support historic use was fatal to Day's argument; the witnesses he called were of no help. Hecht wrote, "Day, having offered no other evidence of beneficial use during the historic period, the Authority's decision to issue an IRP for 14 acre-feet must be affirmed." The court summed up the remaining issue in the case at the end of Section III of their ruling. Addressing the EAA's warning that if its groundwater regulation can result in a compensable taking, the consequences will be nothing short of disastrous, Justice Hecht wrote, "Groundwater rights are property rights subject to constitutional protection, whatever difficulties may lie in determining adequate compensation for a taking."[41]

The EAA states: "The Legislature intends that just compensation be paid if implementation of this article causes a taking of private property or the impairment of a contract in contravention of the Texas or federal constitution."[42] Hecht wrote, "The requirement of compensation may make the regulatory scheme more expensive, but it does not affect the regulations themselves or their goals for groundwater production." Later he continued, "We cannot know, of course, the extent to which the Authority's fears will yet materialize, but the burden of the Takings Clause on government is no reason to excuse its applicability."[43]

What is the range of compensation conceivable in this case, not including legal fees and other fees of the court? The lower point in the range, of course, starts with $0 compensation due Day. What could the upper point be? Unfortunately, these critical questions will remain unanswered, as the *Day* case settled out of court on June 25, 2013, and EAA agreed to pay $950,000 to Day. The confidential settlement agreement failed to address any of the issues in the 17-year-old case.[44] All the significant questions regarding taking and compensation remain open, putting the spotlight now on a similar case—the "cat case" referred to earlier,

Bragg v. Edwards Aquifer Authority. The *Bragg* case is still working its way through the courts and is likely to end up again in the Texas Supreme Court sometime in the near future.

Notwithstanding the *Day* settlement, the latest ruling in *Bragg* may shed light on the amount of compensation that could have been awarded in the *Day* case and could be awarded in like cases in the future. Judge Tom Lee's award could be used as an example of the upper limit of compensation in cases like *Day*.[45]

Let's apply Judge Lee's finding in the *Bragg* case to *Day and McDaniel:* $3,300 per acre × approximately 381 acres = $1,257,000 (irrigated farm versus dryland farm) + $5,500 per acre-foot × 686 acre-feet = $3,773,000 (value of an acre-foot of water) = a potential total compensation of $5,030,000, or $13,203 per acre. At over $13,000 per acre, this would make the Day tract the highest-valued tract in the Von Ormy area in recorded history. The parties in the *Day* case arrived at a compromise in their settlement agreement, and it may be years (if ever) before they reveal the reasoning behind their decision to settle. Possibly, however, the lower and upper limits of like compensation awards in the future will be illuminated by the settlement amount in *Day,* on the lower end, and the previous hypothetical application of Judge Lee's ruling on the higher.

All landowners should now watch the progress of the *Bragg* case very closely. Surely many future cases involving groundwater permitting disputes will end up in court battles over "takings" and just compensation. The Texas Supreme Court's ruling in *Day* definitely opened the door of "compensatory relief" for landowners and, from the groundwater regulator's perspective, a Pandora's box; the large compensation payments that could be awarded landowners is quite worrisome. As Mark Dotzour, a Texas A&M University economist, has said many times, "Texas does not have the option of printing money like the federal government does."[46]

Of most significance to all landowners, lessees, and real estate agents is that the only way to prove historic use is to place a meter on the water well and keep accurate records and reports of its production. As mentioned earlier, many rural property owners fear water meters on their wells because they think if the meter exists, they will someday have to pay a fee per gallon to some governmental entity. Irrigators now typically pay fees in many jurisdictions based upon use. Another reason rural property owners give for their stance against meters is that the meter invades their rights associated with their property right to groundwater.

Historic use in itself can be contrary to conservation; the more water one uses, the more historic use to support a desired level of use. This, coupled with the general feeling that *my* use is always beneficial, can lead to the deliberate planting of water-hungry grasses and crops to keep historic use high with the thought that what the water property owners "own" is the "new oil." Some landowners, in the back of their minds, consider water to be so extremely valuable that they want to maintain their rights to as much of it as possible.

The other consideration all landowners should keep in mind is the "test" period (the prescribed period to determine historic usage),[47] chosen by any groundwater regulatory agency in future regulatory plans. Landowners in groundwater regulatory jurisdictions should pay close attention to their regulations and be sure to give input on the test periods when these periods are being determined.

PUBLIC POLICY THROUGH
THE CRYSTAL BALL

As Texas grows dramatically and copes with its normal periodic droughts, the issues surrounding its water and "confusing" water rights will need to be understood by everyone in order to have fruitful debates that lead to good public policy decisions. Even at times when water is plentiful due to rain and milder temperatures, the anticipated growth rate of our major metropolitan areas is expected to overwhelm our limited water resources. Individuals continue to skirmish over water rights, but the newest and most long-reaching conflicts are between thirsty, growing cities and water-starved rural agricultural interests.

According to David J. Weber, "There is a saying in the West that water does not run downhill. It runs toward money."[1] Cities can tax and issue bonds, thereby gathering money in large amounts to promote their legitimate interests in the courts. Farmers and ranchers are less able to build their coffers to the level needed to promote their legitimate interests in the courts. Going back to an earlier scenario, if a city draws too much groundwater away from a rural area, the rural area's land values drop, re-

San Antonio Splashtown on IH-35. Photo by author.

sulting in a tax base decline. Without a compensating tax rate increase, public services that depend upon the value of the property tax base in the area, such as public schools, cannot help declining in quality. Texans scream loudly about tax increases, but all want the highest quality of education for their children. If rural water goes away, we then must ask ourselves, what lifestyle do we value more, rural or urban? How in the world do the citizens and elected leaders of Texas choose between these two lifestyles? By majority vote? Water is so crucial to the sustenance of human and all animate life, and also to the economic life of an area, that the decisions made about water rights in essence are decisions about lifestyle values.

THE SPLASHTOWN CHOICE

Splashtown is a wonderful place to cool off and have fun in the summer. The owners are fine folks with a good business. For our purposes, they are simply being used as an example of the conundrum faced by water planners over values. Splashtown's season runs six months from the time the weather temperature reaches 80 degrees. The normal entry pass before sales tax costs from $19.99 to $26.99 per visit unless you buy a season pass for $49.99. Assume that 50,000 visitors per month for six months spend $20 each for a total of $6 million. The sales tax of 8.25 percent paid on this revenue equals $495,000. San Antonio Splashtown occupies only 20 acres and is located on IH-35 just before reaching the downtown area. Splashtown is a consumer of water and conserves it commendably.

However, the same amount of water used in a 20-acre cornfield in Hondo in a good year generates 100 bushels per acre. Based upon the highest price received in the last two years, $7 per bushel, this same amount of land generated $14,000 in gross revenue, which is exempt from sales taxes. The amount of water used by Splashtown, if sent to the same Hondo farm and used for irrigation, would certainly not in the best of conditions and best of market years bring the farmer anywhere near $6 million or generate almost half a million dollars in public revenue. Since sales taxes are the major source of revenue for cities in Texas, San Antonio enjoys great financial benefit from the water used by Splashtown.

What water use, therefore, is more valuable to society as a whole? Splashtown cannot use gray water because people swim in it. Farmers cannot use gray water if it is used for crops that will be consumed by humans. The same water with different uses results in gigantically differing revenue streams to the public. Do we seek the maximum utility for water use? This is an example of the very difficult questions that illuminate the tough-to-resolve issues concerning water use in Texas.

HOPE FOR OUR FUTURE: CONSERVATION AND DESALINATION

Conservation of our available water resources and development of new sources of water are obvious solutions to water shortages but will not be easy to accomplish. Maybe the most difficult hurdle will be in gaining the public will to modify daily habits of water use. History has proven to us that, due to human nature, conservation rules have to be supported by courageous enforcement policies.

The development of new water sources will require the safe management of two new types of water, desalinated water and reclaimed water. We will have to desalinate salty water, not only from our enormous brackish groundwater resources but also from plain seawater. Desalination (desal) of enough water to relieve our future water headaches on a large enough scale will cost billions of dollars. We tend to focus much more on acquisition of freshwater, or inflow, and only secondarily on the quality of the return water flow after we use it. This focus must change. Will the people of Texas be willing and able to pay the expense to make desalination and reclamation of used water viable solutions?

≈≈≈≈≈ **CONSERVATION**

In years past, nearly every drop of rain was gathered from rooftops and ground runoff on any farm or ranch in Texas. Visit any farm owned by survivors of the Great Depression in the 1930s or of the drought of the 1950s in Texas and you have a good chance of finding cisterns collecting as much rainwater as possible from the roofs of the farm buildings. I remember my grandfather, Oscar Sakewitz, a farmer in the Taylor area, stepping on the porch of his home each time it began to rain. He pulled a lever to divert the first rainfall off to the ground so as to "wash" the grit and sand from the tin roof. After a very few minutes, he reset the lever to divert all the water from the roof into his orange, aboveground cistern, which held approximately 1,200 gallons of water. He also diverted some of the rainfall to a hand-dug underground cistern or well. Grandpa understood the value of each and every drop of rain to the dryland farmer and did all he could to conserve it.

Rainwater Collection Systems

While rainwater collection systems have been around for years, they fell out of large-scale use in Texas until recently. There has been a rebirth of this practice because of private efforts and public campaigns to address water conservation, including the examples of highly visible projects such as the LCRA's Wilkerson Center for Colorado River Education, which has a number of huge cisterns to collect rainfall from the roof, or the Howson Branch Library in Austin, which installed a smaller rain collection system.

It is amazing how much rain can be collected from each inch of rain. In Texas, this runoff is diffused surface water, which is owned by the landowner. A 2,000-square-foot single-story home with a 500-square-foot two-car garage potentially can collect, in a city like Austin during a normal rainfall year of 33 inches, more than 60,000 gallons of water annually! In the years in which Austin enjoyed its average rainfall of 33

Small cistern next to the Howson Branch Library, Austin. Photo by author.

inches, if a person collected all the rainfall, that equals 5,000 gallons a month. While not drinkable without filtration, much of this water with minimal filtration could be used for washing clothes, bathing, flushing toilets, and watering landscapes. Not only does the typical rain collection system pay for itself but it also makes available for use the free bounty of nature. Rainwater collection systems save water costs for the property owner and add tangible market value to our property, resulting in a win-for-all situation.

Aquifer Storage as a Type of Mega Collection System

A similar but much more complicated way to store water from the "good years" is what San Antonio, in conjunction with the EAA, has begun to do: store excess water in "aquifer storage and recovery" (ASR) systems. Excess water is stored in existing aquifers for later use. According to Lyle Larson, a Texas House of Representatives member from San Antonio, statewide Texas can potentially store up to 5.3 billion acre-feet of water in ASR systems, a huge amount of water to better balance the good years of water availability with needy years.[2]

Simple Lifestyle Changes to Conserve Water

Here are a few things to consider about our daily use of water that are often overlooked:

- the length of your shower;
- the time of day you run your sprinkler system (or eliminating the need for a sprinkler system by replacing nonnative grasses with native drought-tolerant plants);
- the way you brush your teeth—letting the water run the entire time;
- the way you prepare dirty dishes for the dishwasher—running water over them and allowing the water to run as you load the dishwasher; and
- the water lost when waiting for the shower to heat up.

Meaningless in volume maybe on an individual basis, but just these very few examples when multiplied by millions of people every day add up to a simple, effective way to conserve water. A leaky toilet alone can waste 200 gallons of water per day, 6,000 gallons per month, adding up to 72,000 gallons per year. According to the American Water Works Association, lawn watering with in-ground irrigation systems uses 35 percent more water than homes without such systems, and homes that use automatic timers for their in-ground irrigation systems use 47 percent more than those with manual controls.[3] The Texas Water Development Board opines that "outdoor water use can account for 50 to 80 percent of home water use."[4] As I drive around the cities in Texas, it is a shame to see lost water running down the street from inefficient lawn watering of commercial and residential properties. Doubtlessly the water running down the street reenters the hydrologic system, but as it runs over the pavement, the water becomes polluted. The water used for residential and commercial irrigation systems in most cities is treated drinking water. What a waste.

Instead of throwing ice out from your glass, toss the ice into the flower bed or a potted plant. Everyone can think about ways to conserve water and stop the wasteful practices we carry out without thinking every day.

A few statistics about the amount of water you use directly or indirectly in daily life may surprise you:

- Each bath uses 70 gallons of water; a shower uses just 10–25 gallons.
- A dishwasher cycle uses 9–13 gallons, and dishwashing detergent is usually made with trisodium phosphates. (When I have poured dishwashing powder on my driveway to remove oil stains, the stains were removed, but also the top layer of concrete one-fourth inch or more down.)
- A dripping faucet uses as much as 20 gallons a day.
- A flush of the toilet uses 1–5 gallons each time; low-flow toilets use less.
- Lawn watering can use thousands of gallons during the warmer months dependent upon soil conditions, topography, grass type, and other landscape materials.

This is the footprint of indirect uses:

- One bottled drink's water footprint is 1.5 gallons.
- One day of electricity at home used 4–5 gallons to produce.
- One 18-gallon tank of gasoline used 18–45 gallons.
- One beer used 30 gallons.
- One cheese sandwich used 34 gallons.
- One cup of coffee used 37 gallons.
- One egg used 120 gallons.
- One pair of jeans used 400 gallons.[5]

These examples may be little-known facts about direct and indirect uses of water, some of which make very good targets for conservation ideas without noticeable consequence to the comfort of our lifestyles but with massive impact on our freshwater resources over time.

～～～ DESALINATION

Texas has vast resources of brackish groundwater (in the map, all the yellow areas are brackish), or water that contains mineral salts derived from the sediments associated with an inland ocean that covered the state for millions of years. While desalination technology has been available for decades in the offshore oil industry,[6] the cost for land-based desalination in the United States has been economically prohibitive for general use under current consumer water rate structures. Another prob-

The Kay Bailey Hutchison desalination plant in El Paso. Photo by author.

lem associated with desalination is the removal of the potentially toxic by-product of saltwater and salt solids. The cost of dealing with the toxic by-product is a major challenge for those in favor of desalination technology. Offshore this is not a problem—the oceans are so full of salt the tiny amount produced by offshore oil platforms is easily diluted. But the by-product is a serious problem for onshore operations due to its toxicity. The by-product, even from a possible desalination plant on the coast of Texas, would still have to be shipped out to the deeper Gulf, since raising the salinity of our bays and estuaries is environmentally hazardous. An alternative solution may be the reinjection of the by-product into deep, underground, brackish water pools, and the long-term consequences of reinjection wells scattered all over Texas are being studied today.

Perhaps one of the beneficial consequences of the severe drought of 2011, which could help advance desalination, is the gradual realization

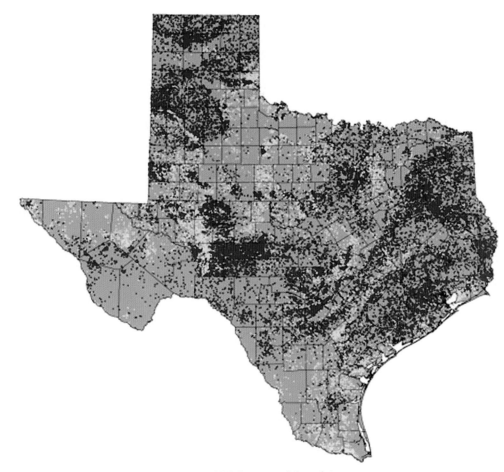

by our elected politicians that current municipal and rural water rates must increase. Many see desalination as a real source of relief for a future water-starved Texas. Weir Labatt, board member of the Texas Water Development Board, proposed a desalination plant for San Antonio in 2010. He is not the only state official talking seriously about desal to supplement our water supplies.[7]

In early 2012, Representative Lyle Larson offered a similar proposal. In order to "ensure water sustainability," his "emergency plan" called for funding up to an expected $1.1 billion, to come in part from the "rainy day" fund. His plan recommended construction of four desal plants at unspecified locations around the state at an estimated cost of $600 million. The State Water Plan of 2012 included a comment about future

Pipeline to
a mountain
reinjection well in
the far distance.
Photo by author.

desal processing; to gain a 3.4 percent share of total Texas water produced, the TWDB's estimated cost was $5.6 billion.[8]

No matter how you look at it, desalination of brackish groundwater
or even seawater is no doubt very expensive. Even if the projects started
today, gaining the right-of-way for a water line from a desal plant in Corpus Christi to San Antonio would take at least a decade, if not longer.[9]

Nonetheless, a desal plant is functioning in El Paso today, an amazing
operation, as I observed on a tour in the spring of 2011. The Kay Bailey
Hutchison Desalination Plant processes brackish water from the Hueco-
Bolson Aquifer and reinjects the salty by-product into another saltwater
pool 4,000 feet deep, 22 miles away via one major pipeline. The plant
was built in an incredibly short time after funding—two years. How did
the city beat the normal decade-long right-of-way acquisition time? The
reinjection line went solely across land that is a part of Fort Bliss; hence,

Individual
reverse osmosis
membrane filter.
Photo by author.

only one party, a friendly one at that (the US government), had to agree to the easement for the line.[10]

The Hutchison plant is said to be able to process 27.5 million gallons of water per day. The general public assumes this is the plant's output now, but I discovered during my visit that the plant's output now is around 3 million gallons daily, with a potential for 12–15 million gallons maximum daily output in the future. In order to get 12–15 million gallons daily, the plant will process 27.5 million gallons; the difference is reprocessed through the reverse osmosis membrane filter to flush out the mineral salt residue. Nonetheless, 12–15 million gallons per day will provide from 10 to 13 percent of El Paso's current overall water demand.[11]

The production cost of each gallon, compared to the amount paid by the consumer, is the same number, $1.71 per thousand gallons. Whether the production cost included all costs, such as bond and loan repay-

Solid salts per gallon. Photo by author.

ments, was not known. I will not conduct a cost-benefit analysis here; the point is obvious to me—the rate to the consumer is probably too low.[12]

The system is simple. The plant drilled a group of both brackish and freshwater wells up to 600 feet in depth. This water is mixed and then sent through reverse osmosis membranes. The amount of solid salts *each* gallon produces I estimated at about one-fourth cup.[13] I was told during my visit that the stratum in which the by-product "sludge" is reinjected is full of brine but less salty than the ancient groundwater into which it is injected; it actually dilutes the highly saline water into which it is sent.

The plant is so well organized and the control systems so well planned that I was told it takes only one person to operate the system at full capacity!

The El Paso plant proves we can make our vast brackish resources into freshwater—whenever we can afford to do so. Mark Holtzapple of

Views inside the Hutchison desalination plant. Photos by author.

Texas A&M University developed new technology that may enable desalination on a smaller scale, making it available to developers of small subdivisions of homes to provide processed brackish water much more affordably and efficiently. His system can possibly reduce the cost of desalination to under $1 million to serve 500 homes. The by-product would be sent to a saltwater reinjection well, hopefully close to any proposed subdivision, and for a fee, disposed of as oil and gas operations have done for years in Texas.[14]

Desalination opportunities are being explored by other groups throughout the state. The Guadalupe-Blanco River Authority (GBRA) and several partners are currently looking for engineering consultants to conduct a feasibility study for a regional south-central Texas power and desalination project. This project presents a regional approach for municipal and power-generation water supplies that will help address the needs of the quickly expanding south-central Texas region through 2060. While the population of Texas is expected to grow by 82 percent (roughly 20 million people) between 2010 and 2060, the population in the Guadalupe and San Antonio River basins alone is expected to increase by 1.26 million (70 percent of the expected growth in the region). Total municipal water use in the area is expected to increase twofold (340,000 in 2000 and 640,000 acre-feet per year [AFY] in 2060) while the water used for power generation is expected to increase nearly four times (35,000 AFY in 2000 to an estimated 130,000 AFY in 2060).[15]

According to Todd Votteler, the study will be managed by the Texas Sustainable Energy Research Institute and the Center for Water Research at UT San Antonio. Potential participating energy and water utilities include CPS Energy, Austin Energy, LCRA, GBRA, SAWS, Austin Water Utilities, and the City of Victoria. The project is intended to provide long-term sustainable electricity and potable water supplies for municipal and industrial use in metropolitan and rural areas in south-central Texas. Depending on the comparison of a cost-benefit analysis, the project will include the option of either a single central power-generation facility or multiple facilities spread efficiently across the region. Integral processes included in the project are seawater intake, raw water transmission, treatment facilities, desalination concentrate disposal (deep-injection wells vs. deep-sea disposal or others), and treated water distribution and storage. The approximate timeline from feasibility to construction to startup is estimated to be 10 years.

〜〜〜 **RETURN FLOW AND RECLAIMED WATER**

We tend to forget that water flows back somewhere after it is used. Water is taken from rivers and springs and is pumped from aquifers, but it also has return flow after it is used. As water returns to the river or aquifer, it picks up all kinds of human, plant, and animal waste and/or debris. Storm water carries with it into our streams the refuse of our daily lives, things such as litter, automobile fluids, leaking sanitary sewer lines,[16] fertilizers, pesticides, and a host of other chemicals—every time it rains. Walk to a major storm water inlet next to a stream, and the color of the water cannot be ignored nor can the smell.

Water planners must not only consider potable water sources but also contemplate how to be sure clean water will return to the hydrologic cycle after it is used. Detention ponds, becoming normal across the nation in construction of new real estate developments and highways, are the first step in helping to filter the toxic debris of runoff and keep it out of our watercourses and groundwater. As local, state, and federal agencies try to better protect our environment, we have to have the gumption to fund their efforts and also take personal responsibility to practice safe habits when using toxic products.

Texas law makes water pollution illegal. The Texas Water Code, Section 26.121, provides "that no person may discharge sewage, municipal waste, recreational waste, agricultural waste, or industrial waste into or adjacent to any water in the state or commit any other act or engage in any other activity which in itself or in conjunction with any other discharge or activity causes, continues to cause, or will cause pollution of any water in the state." So far, the difficulty of proving who the polluting offender is in any one instance has limited damage lawsuits to a trickle. But technology may advance to a degree that victims of polluters may find some relief in the courts. Technology advances could include more accurate underground mapping of flows of pollutants back to their ultimate source, forensic advances in determining the true perpetrator even if miles away, and even molecular "tagging" of each unique chemical compound to identify offending parties.

Reclaimed Water

Texas allows the reuse of water for beneficial purposes; "water reuse" is therefore defined as "the beneficial use of reclaimed water." The Texas Administrative Code, Chapter 30, Section 210.3, defines "reclaimed water" as "domestic or municipal wastewater which has been treated to a quality suitable for beneficial use." Reclaimed water is not "gray water," which is untreated, non-toilet household water from sinks, showers, washing machines, and baths. According to the Texas Water Development Board, "[R]eclaimed water is used for a number of different purposes including municipal and industrial use, and irrigation. Examples of municipal and industrial applications include golf course irrigation and use in cooling towers. In agriculture, water reuse could include the collection of surface runoff in ponds for supplemental irrigation or for livestock watering."[17]

Most water planning regions in Texas have made allowances for the use of reclaimed water in their regional water plans. The TAC classifies reclaimed water in Texas as two types. Type I is reclaimed water used in situations where contact with humans is likely. Examples of Type I uses are landscape irrigation at homes or public golf courses, toilet or urinal flushing, and irrigation of pastures for milking animals. Some of our fire protection now and in the future may have its water supplied from reclaimed water sources. Type II reclaimed water is used in situations where contact with humans is unlikely. Examples of Type II uses are dust control, use in chilling or cooling towers, irrigation of food crops when the water will not come into contact with the edible portion of the crop, and maintenance of "impoundments" and other natural storage areas where human contact is unlikely.[18]

The amount of reclaimed water recommended to be used by 2010 was almost 100,600 acre-feet per year statewide, increasing to approximately 915,600 acre-feet in 2060.[19] San Antonio uses reclaimed water to supplement the San Antonio River along the Riverwalk; many golf courses around the state have been using reclaimed water for years. Reclaimed water will attract much more attention in planning in the future and rightly so. The inevitable debate about reclaimed water will focus, as usual, on who owns it. Water that would normally reenter the streams or rivers from cities would be owned by the state when returned to the watercourse. Will the state claim reclaimed water under some right? Assuming that cities then never return the reclaimed water so as not to relinquish ownership, what effect will the lessened return flow have on environmental flows and the supply in rivers downstream from the cities?

These are questions for our public policymakers, who must charge in all directions at once by seeking voluntary conservation of water by our citizenry or, if necessary, mandating conservation of our water resources from all citizens even at their homes, pursuing and funding any and all reasonable new technologies, and supporting research to enhance our existing water supplies, recognizing that the manner in which humans impact the hydrologic cycle is a choice we make each and every day.

EPILOGUE

In the past, Texans have taken water for granted, and still almost everywhere water availability is as easy as reaching for and turning on the spigot. Our recent ancestors dug water wells by hand, hauled water into the house, or if they were really lucky and reasonably wealthy, pumped it by hand into buckets inside the home. They had no choice but to center their lives each and every day for at least a few minutes on the personal search for and delivery of water. In most areas of Texas we have lost the sense of urgency our grandparents or great-grandparents lived with daily over water. To this day, most land purchasers give water availability only a cursory investigation, assuming that their right to water is a "given" and that it will be easy to acquire from somewhere or someone. As our state continues to grow, we must all reach a better understanding of the ways in which we share and conserve the common pool of our most important resource, water.

Understanding water rights in Texas is challenging, especially when trying to determine what water rights a tract of land owns, whether it is your land or land you are looking to buy. Water rights to any single property or for any person exist in a "bundle" of rights. The bundle could include rights to use surface water, rights to own groundwater and diffused surface water, rights to sell or lease the water, rights to access water for domestic and livestock use—any one person's water rights in total include the bundled rights to all the types of water in Texas.

Here is a checklist to help discover the bundle of rights that make up a water right:

- Contact an attorney from the very beginning to assist you in determination of your water right.
- Ask your title company to sell you an Owner's and Encumbrances Report to assist you and your attorney to discover what documents are of record pertaining to the water rights of any tract of land. Be sure to get this report even if you already own the land because filings of record may have happened that you are not aware of, perhaps executed by past family members.

- Contact each and every agency on the list (see appendix 2) to find out their current policies and rules that pertain to the property. A good first step is to contact your Texas A&M AgriLife Extension county agent. Most county agents are up-to-date on water issues in the area and can assist you in contacting all the regulatory agencies that have jurisdiction over the property.
- Be sure to communicate in writing with the Texas Commission on Environmental Quality, any groundwater conservation district, or any other agency, like the Edwards Aquifer Authority, especially before you drill any water wells or divert any surface water from a stream or river. Avoid the fines. Even though these agencies' websites give information about exemptions, ask for a statement in writing before doing anything involving water.
- Take the time to attend all public hearings possible that directly involve water policies on a property. Your voice is welcome, and the board members appreciate citizen input.
- Always pay any water access fee in full and on time. Use your water from the location and in the amount your permit authorizes you to do.
- Be sure to disclose all known defects concerning water to any potential purchaser of any property you are selling to avoid the lawsuits involving either seller's disclosure obligations or lawsuits under the Texas Deceptive Trade Practices Act.
- Meter your irrigation wells, and consider metering your domestic and livestock wells. Use a meter whose specifications meet those approved by all the agencies that have jurisdiction over your land. Keep accurate records of the historic use. Be sure the use is always beneficial. Take a lot of dated photographs to document everything you do with water all the time. Be prepared for challenges to your historic and beneficial use when the inevitable water scarcity comes.

Remember the words of George W. Brackenridge in the letter he wrote to his brother in 1879 giving advice about which tracts of land to sell some-day: "Never dispose of those sections [of land] unless the one with water goes with them *as water renders the land valuable.*"

APPENDIX 1
SIGNIFICANT COURT CASES CONCERNING TEXAS WATER RIGHTS

The following sample of significant cases concerning water rights in Texas is not intended to represent all the court rulings that impacted our current water rights policies or to provide the reader with a legal opinion at all. However, the cases are not only interesting themselves but also indicative, when taken as a whole, of the efforts the courts have made to find the fairness and justice built into our system of government. Texas' adoption of English common law in 1840, which in essence allows laws to be modified by judicial action and interpretation, keeps our law young and alive to meet the challenges of each generation. The history of some of the key cases puts the issue of water rights into context.

TEXAS COMPANY V. BURKETT

The Texas Company became the international oil company Texaco. This landmark case was decided in 1927. These were the key rulings:

- Absence of evidence to the contrary, underground water is *presumed to be percolating* groundwater, therefore owned by the surface owner.
- A landowner need not use groundwater on the premises of his or her property and has the right to sell the groundwater captured under his or her land for off-site use by a third party.
- Spring water that was not surface water running in a streambed or water from an underground stream with defined channels was the exclusive property of the surface owner.

While ancient Spanish law did not use the word *percolating,* ownership of underground water by the surface owner and sale of water rights can be traced back in Texas history to the earliest days of Villa San Fernando (San Antonio) and are precedents to the first two conclusions of *Burkett.* Spanish law also considered springs and their underground water to be owned by the surface estate holder, another precedent for *Burkett.* The Spanish support is not mentioned in the ruling but could have been used to further strengthen the ruling since the State of Texas did, in 1927, honor Spanish land and water grants, as it had done since 1840 and still does today.

CORPUS CHRISTI V. PLEASANTON

This case was decided by the Texas Supreme Court in 1955. Since the *East* case in 1904, waste of groundwater had been recognized as an exception to the rule of capture. The *Corpus Christi v. Pleasanton* case focused on waste of groundwater. In 1927, the ruling in *Texas Company v. Burkett* confirmed that a landowner need not use groundwater on the premises of his or her property but under common law could sell the groundwater captured under his or her land for off-site use by a third party. There was no dispute that Corpus Christi, located in Nueces County, could purchase water from the Lower Nueces River Supply Company, which produced water from the Carrizo groundwater sand at various locations in Atascosa County. Corpus Christi made an agreement with the river company to acquire a portion of this groundwater, which was then dumped into the Nueces River and transported 118 miles to the city. The City of Pleasanton, located in Atascosa County, thought its water supply was threatened by this agreement and filed the lawsuit to stop the transport because the loss of water to seepage and evaporation in transit to Corpus Christi constituted waste. Pleasanton presented evidence that up to 75 percent of the groundwater was lost to evaporation and seepage before it reached Corpus Christi. The trial court ruled "by reason of the amount of water lost in the process, [the transport] constituted waste in violation of the statutes and the conservation laws of the State of Texas." The Court of Civil Appeals confirmed the trial court ruling.

The Texas Supreme Court ruled, however, that it was not waste to transport water down a natural streambed even if water was lost to evaporation and seepage: "About the only limitations applied by these jurisdictions retaining the English rule [the rule of capture] are that the owner may not maliciously take water for the sole purpose of injuring his neighbor, or wantonly and willfully waste it," said the court. Additionally, the court confirmed, "It thus appears that under the common-law rule adopted in this state an owner of land can use all of the percolating water he could capture from wells on his land for whatever beneficial purpose he needed it, on or off the land, and could likewise sell it to others for use off of the land and outside of the basin where produced, just as he could sell any other species of property."

It is interesting to note that the entire court seemed disturbed by the waste of water, especially considering that in 1955, a drought was still devastating Texas, but the majority of justices found no precedent to stop it in this case. However, the opinion did toss a challenge to the legislature:

> Undoubtedly, the Legislature could prohibit the use of any means of transportation of percolating or artesian water which permitted the escape of excessive amounts, but it has not seen fit to do so. . . . The Legislature is now in session. It will have this opinion before it before adjournment. It will recognize the problem. If it wishes to declare that the transportation of water and conduits which permit the escape of a large percentage is wasteful and unlawful it will have ample time to do it.[1]

Justices Griffin, Wilson, and Culver dissented. Justice Wilson declared his disagreement with the *East* case's rule of capture, which he refers to as the law of capture:

> This is an outpost skirmish over the waters of the Carrizo sand. Here we hold that a distant city, after purchasing a few acres of land upon which it drills four big artesian wells, can flow ten million gallons of water a day into a stream from which (under evidence and the finding of the trial court) it recovers only about 25% of the artesian water. In doing this it can disregard any injury to the effect upon the wells of the property owners drawing water from a common reservoir to irrigate local farms and to supply local communities. To this seems obviously unjust and a bad situation. . . .
>
> In the field of water law, there is not consolation to be found in the law of capture. Of what value would it be to the plaintiffs to offset defendants' wells and produce an enormous amount of water for which they have no use? This would further deplete the reservoir, reduce the pressure, and lower the standing level with consequent increase in pumping expense. Why further injure their own wells? To refer them to the law of capture in this situation is simply to say that one who has been injured may go and inflict a like injury on his neighbor. If the law of capture has any true application to underground water, it is an extremely limited one. No one can live in a vacuum. Therefore, all property rights are, to a certain extent, correlative.

The court ruling confirmed that a landowner could not pump water in a wasteful or malicious manner, and could be stopped from doing so, but did not find the loss of this water in transport to Corpus Christi to be wasteful. This is a landmark case because it reconfirmed the rule of capture as support for groundwater being a property right of the surface landowner. The case also reconfirmed that the property owner had the right to sell the groundwater and that the buyer could transport it elsewhere. The case also confirmed the *East* case's basis in *Acton v. Blundell* that groundwater could not be taken maliciously or wastefully.

STATE OF TEXAS V. VALMONT PLANTATIONS

This is a landmark case concerning irrigation rights to the surface water of the Rio Grande, which was decided in 1961. The court decided that riparian land of the Lower Rio Grande did not have an appurtenant right (one that came with or was attached to the land) to use the waters of the river for irrigation purposes since the underlying Spanish land grants were for land not classified by the king of Spain, through his viceroys and their officers, as irrigable land.[2]

Justice Jack Pope proved through his research (some say he built on the work of Will Wilson) that the lands in question were granted as pastureland. The lands of New Spain were classified by the king's delegates as pasture, arable, or irrigable lands. Pope concluded correctly that the king believed the lands in question were not able to be irrigated with water from the Rio Grande. The king granted these settlers larger tracts of land as compensation for the lands not being irrigable. The case was significant for its judicial and historical scholarship and helped lead the legislature to enact the Water Rights Adjudication Act of 1967. The case was also important because the court concluded that

- rights under titles from Spain, Mexico, and Tamaulipas were governed by the law of the sovereigns when the grants were made;
- the sovereigns did not have a system of riparian rights based upon or similar to the common law right to irrigate;
- the grants involved in the suit were not made with the implied intent or agreement that the right to irrigate was appurtenant to the lands; and
- no Texas court had considered the issue in the past.

As mentioned earlier, Texas had operated under a dual system of riparian rights as defined under English common law, which the Republic of Texas had adopted in 1840. The confusion arose because at the same

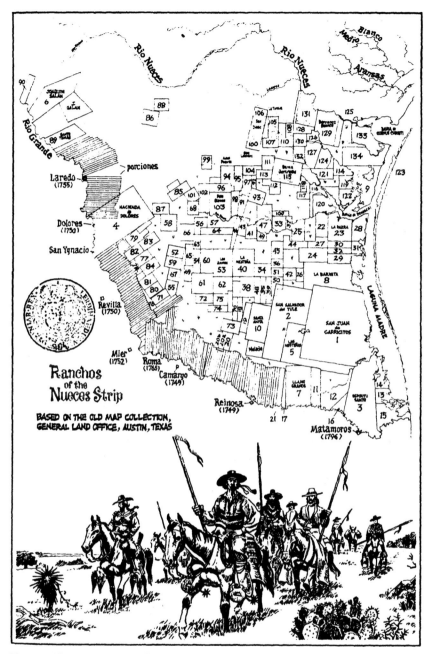

Map used in *Valmont* case, 1961. Jack Jackson's map of the long lots, many of which Justice Pope proved had no irrigation rights from Spain. Courtesy Texas A&M University Press.

time the Republic of Texas adopted the common law, it also decided to honor Spanish and Republic of Mexico land grants. Due to the work of Justice Pope in this case, establishing historical precedence to make clear that the Spanish did not have a riparian system pertaining to irrigation, as did the English, a path was set to stop the plethora of surface water lawsuits that had clogged the dockets across the state for decades. The Water Rights Adjudication Act of 1967, in my opinion, found its provenance in *Valmont Plantations.*

SMITH-SOUTHWEST INDUSTRIES V. FRIENDSWOOD DEVELOPMENT

In 1973 Smith-Southwest Industries along with others sued Friendswood Development Company, a division of Exxon. Smith-Southwest Industries alleged that Friendswood's withdrawals of groundwater caused subsidence, or lowering of elevation, of Smith-Southwest land. Friendswood, in a defensive response, filed suit on other landowners withdrawing water in the area and thus challenged the theory that all the blame lay with Friendswood. The trial court ruled in favor of Friendswood and the other defendants in summary judgment. The Court of Civil Appeals reversed, but the Texas Supreme Court affirmed, the trial court's judgment. The rule of capture protected Friendswood from liability; however, the Supreme Court ruled that from that point forward, any landowner drilling a well that caused subsidence to his or her neighbor would be liable for damages. The ruling in this case set out clearly the three limitations on the rule of capture concerning liability for withdrawing groundwater:

1. A landowner's pumping of groundwater cannot maliciously be done to harm a neighbor.
2. A landowner's pumping of groundwater cannot be done in a wasteful manner.
3. A landowner's pumping of groundwater cannot be done in a negligent manner that is the proximate cause of neighboring lands' subsidence.

A landowner may also be restricted when the groundwater is from the underflow of a river or the groundwater is regulated by a groundwater conservation district.

SIPRIANO V. GREAT SPRING WATERS OF AMERICA (OZARKA)

This case was decided on May 6, 1999. In the eastern Texas county of Henderson, Bart Sipriano and some other family members owned land whose water wells were severely depleted when Ozarka, in 1996, began to pump 90,000 gallons a day seven days a week. Sipriano lost his claim in summary judgment because of the rule of capture, which was affirmed by the Court of Appeals and the Texas Supreme Court. Sipriano had at first claimed an "exception" under the rule of capture but declined to argue it in his brief, choosing only to argue that the rule of capture should be abandoned. The Supreme Court in its ruling against Sipriano opined, "Water regulation is essentially a legislative function." It is interesting to note that the amicus briefs in favor of retention of the rule of capture came from the City of Houston, the Edwards Aquifer Authority, the Texas Alliance of Groundwater Districts, and a host of others. The court praised the legislature for its efforts to better regulate groundwater, especially commenting on the value of Senate Bill 1 in giving more authority to groundwater conservation districts. The court noted that "we are reluctant to make so drastic a change as abandoning the rule of capture and moving into the arena of water-use regulation by judicial fiat."

The significance of the *Sipriano* case is that the rule of capture was again confirmed by the highest court in Texas. Justice Nathan Hecht concurred: "The extensive regulation of oil and gas production proves that effective regulation of migrant substances far below the surface is not only possible but necessary and effective." He continued, "Petitioners [Sipriano et al.] make a strong case for replacing the rule of capture with the beneficial purpose doctrine set out in section 858 of the Restatement (Second) of Torts: While neither section 858 nor any other common law rule of water regulation is preferable to almost any effective legislative solution, absent any such solution, section 858 is preferable to rule of capture." Hecht then outlined Section 858:

Liability of Use of Ground Water
   (1) A proprietor of land or his grantee that withdraws ground
       water from the land and uses it for beneficial purposes is not
       subject to liability for interference with the use of water by
       another, unless:
       (a) the withdrawal of ground water unreasonably causes harm
           to a proprietor of neighboring land through lowering the
           water table or reducing artesian pressure,
       (b) the withdrawal of ground water exceeds the proprietor's
           reasonable share of the annual supply or total store of
           ground water, or

(c) the withdrawal of ground water has a direct and substantial effect upon a watercourse or lake and unreasonably causes harm to a person entitled to the use of its water.

Hecht concluded with hope and a subtle warning: "Nevertheless, I am persuaded for the time being that the extensive statutory changes in 1997, together with the increasing demands on the State's water supply, may result in a fair, effective, and comprehensive regulation of water that will make the rule of capture obsolete. I agree with the Court that it would be inappropriate to disrupt the processes created and encouraged by the 1997 legislation before they had the chance to work. I concur in the view that, for now—*but I think only for now*—East should not be overruled [emphasis added]." Hecht's subtle warning echoed Justice Will Wilson's warning in his dissent to *Corpus Christi v. Pleasanton* in 1955 that this court would not forever use deference to the legislature to justify maintaining the rule of capture in the face of changing circumstances. The appeals court in the Comanche Springs case made a similar comment: "It may be that the answer to this unhappy situation is legislative."

APPENDIX 2

GOVERNMENT AND OTHER RESOURCES

1. Edwards Aquifer Authority (EAA): www.edwardsaquifer.org. This is the website of the most influential groundwater district in the state. It is also an extensive site with access to everything the EAA is authorized to regulate.
2. Environmental Protection Agency (EPA): www.epa.gov. This federal website includes extensive information about issues pertaining to water across the United States.
3. Lower Colorado River Authority (LCRA): www.lcra.org. The website of the LCRA is full of good information about weather and river conditions.
4. River authorities: Use the Texas Parks and Wildlife Department site for links to all the river authorities in Texas: http://www.tpwd.state.tx.us/landwater/water/habitats/rivers/authorities.phtml.
5. San Antonio Water System (SAWS): www.saws.org. The SAWS website has extensive information about San Antonio's water supply system and also keeps up a fine internal site on the status of the Edwards Aquifer upon which San Antonio depends for its freshwater. SAWS is a water policy leader in the state and heavily influences water issues. Prudent researchers should place themselves on the mailing list to receive in advance the agendas of SAWS meetings.
6. Texas Alliance of Groundwater Districts: www.texasgroundwater.org. This is the key trade association for the groundwater conservation districts in Texas. Its link page directs the researcher to every groundwater conservation district in Texas that maintains a website.
7. Texas A&M AgriLife Extension Service: http://agrilifeextension.tamu.edu/. This site is a fine resource for water research from an agribusiness viewpoint.
8. Texas Commission on Environmental Quality (TCEQ): www.tceq.state.tx.us. This is the second most important site for water

researchers. It is divided into three main parts: air, land, and water. It is also easy to follow and has hundreds of downloadable pages of documents and reports. The TCEQ is the initial regulator of all surface water in Texas.

9. Texas Constitution and Statutes: www.statutes.legis.state.tx.us. This is the key site that links to the Texas Constitution and all statutes. Be wary of searching the statutes from an open search engine such as Google or Yahoo. The initial links are to private companies, which offer some of the statutes for free and some for a fee, and they may not be up-to-date.

10. Texas Legislature Online: www.capitol.state.tx.us. This extensive site is somewhat easy to navigate and provides live legislative actions when the legislature is in session, including copies of all of the thousands of bills. The site allows the researcher to follow the progress of all bills under consideration during the session along with testimony and journals of all the legislative committee hearings.

11. Texas Parks and Wildlife Department (TPWD): www.tpwd.state .tx.us. The TPWD site has extensive information about water as it relates to fish and wildlife management in Texas.

12. Real Estate Center at Texas A&M University: www.recenter.tamu .edu. The Real Estate Center is a public service supported by the fees of Texas' 100,000 real estate licensees. Its website is a rich source of information about water in Texas, including articles written by its staff attorney and various PhDs on staff, including economists. The website also has links to the most recent PowerPoint presentations made by the professional staff on statewide water issues.

13. Supreme Court of Texas: www.supreme.courts.state.tx.us. This site provides access for researchers to follow pending cases as they develop and also provides links to many of the briefs of ongoing matters, some of which are filed electronically. You can also choose to receive e-mail updates when documents are filed in the cases you designate from the Courts of Appeals in Texas and the Texas Supreme Court as they issue rulings.

14. Texas Water Development Board (TWDB): www.twdb.state.tx.us. This extensive site is the starting point for all water information in Texas. It is easy to follow and has literally hundreds of downloadable publications, reports, and other articles of interest

about water. The links page provides links to all regulatory agency websites along with websites of many other stakeholders. The public can download the Texas Water Plan published in 2012. The website also links to the Texas groundwater conservation districts.

15. US Fish and Wildlife Service (USFWS): www.fws.gov. This federal website has extensive information about issues pertaining to water across the United States.

Many other websites contain good information about water issues in Texas, including those of the Environmental Defense Fund, Lone Star Sierra Club, Texas Association of Realtors, Texas Farm Bureau, and many of the cities and counties in Texas. Each trade association in Texas has a website, and many of these with a stake in water issues publish policy papers online.

Access to the Lexis/Nexis website is critical to gain access to the thousands of law review articles about water issues along with the case reports on each and every court case reported in the United States. For the individual, the cost to subscribe can be considered expensive. Many universities and colleges subscribe to the service as part of the student and faculty database for research. Some public libraries may also provide access.

APPENDIX 3

TEXAS SUPREME COURT CASES AND OTHER SIGNIFICANT TEXAS CASES

The Adjudication of Water Rights in the Medina River Watershed of the San Antonio River Basin v. Alamo National Bank Independent Executor, 645 S.W.2d 596; 1982 Tex. App. LEXIS 5610 (1982)

City of Del Rio, Petitioner, v. Clayton Sam Colt Hamilton Trust, by and through Its Trustee, J. R. Hamilton, Respondent, 08-755

Chronological Documents in the Texas Supreme Court Case File:
Petition for Review—Filed: 10/30/2008
Response to Petition / Appendix—Filed: 02/05/2009
Amicus Brief—San Antonio Water System—Received: 02/19/2009
Amicus Brief—Mesa Water—Received: 02/27/2009
Amended Reply to Response to Petition—Filed: 03/25/2009
Amicus Brief—Texas Farm Bureau—Received: 03/25/2009
Petitioner's Brief on the Merits—Filed: 05/27/2009
Respondent's Brief on the Merits / Appendix—Filed: 06/30/2009
Amicus Brief—CRMWA—Received: 06/30/2009
Amicus Brief—City of Amarillo—Received: 06/30/2009
Reply Brief—Filed: 07/20/2009
Amicus Brief—Stewart Title Guaranty Company—Received: 08/05/2009
Petitioner's Response to Post-Briefing Article and Amicus Brief—Filed: 08/11/2009
Amicus Brief—San Antonio Water System—Received: 08/12/2009
Petitioner's Response to Amicus Brief—Filed: 08/20/2009

Edwards Aquifer Authority and The State of Texas Petitioners, v. Burrell Day and Joel McDaniel, Respondents, 08-0964 (For the February 24, 2012, ruling in full, see http://www.supreme.courts.state.tx.us/historical/2012/feb/080964.pdf.)

Chronological Documents in the Texas Supreme Court Case File:
Day—Petition for Review—01/30/2009

State—Petition for Review—02/02/2009
EAA—Petition for Review—02/02/2009
Amicus Brief—Medina County Irrigators Alliance—03/03/2009
EAA—Response to Petition—03/04/2009
Amicus Brief—Angela Garcia—03/06/2009
Amicus Brief—City of Victoria—03/30/2009
Amended Amicus Brief—Medina County Irrigators Alliance—
    04/08/2009
Amicus Brief—Texas Farm Bureau—Received: 04/29/200
Amicus Brief—HGSD—Received: 05/01/2009
Day—Response to State's Petition—Filed: 05/05/2009
Day—Response to EAA's Petition—Filed: 05/05/2009
Amicus Brief—Texas and Southwestern Cattle Raisers Association—
    Received: 05/05/2009
State—Response to Petition—Filed: 05/06/2009
State—Reply in Support of Petition—Filed: 05/20/2009
EAA—Reply to Response to Petition—Filed: 05/20/2009
Amicus Brief—The Alliance of EAA Permit Holders—Filed:
    06/08/2009
Supplement to Amicus Brief—The Alliance of EAA Permit Holders—
    Received: 06/09/2009
Supplement to Amicus Brief—The Alliance of EAA Permit Holders—
    Received: 06/18/2009
EAA—Petitioner's Brief on the Merits—Filed: 09/18/2009
State—Petitioner's Brief on the Merits—Filed: 09/18/2009
Day—Petitioners' Brief on the Merits—Filed: 09/18/2009
Amicus Brief—Canadian River Municipal Water Authority—
    Received: 10/27/2009
Day—Respondent's Brief to State's Brief—Filed: 10/30/2009
Day—Respondent's Brief to EAA's Brief—Filed: 10/30/2009
EAA—Respondent's Brief on the Merits—Filed: 11/02/200
Joint Amicus Brief—Texas Farm Bureau & Texas Cattle Feeders
    Association—Received: 11/02/2009
State—Respondent's Brief on the Merits—Filed: 11/02/2009
Amicus Letter—Texas Comptroller of Public Accounts—Received:
    12/15/2009
EAA—Reply Brief—Filed: 12/17/2009
State—Reply Brief—Filed: 12/17/2009
Day—Reply Brief to State's Response Brief—Filed: 12/17/2009

Day—Reply Brief to EAA's Response Brief—Filed: 12/17/2009
Amicus Brief—Texas Wildlife Association—Received: 01/12/2010
Amicus Brief—Angela Garcia—Received: 01/26/2010
Amicus Brief—Harris-Galveston Subsidence District—Received: 02/01/2010
Amicus Brief—Mesa Water—Received: 02/10/2010
Amicus Brief—Texas Landowners Council—Received: 02/12/2010
Amicus Brief—Pacific Legal Foundation—Received: 02/12/2010
Amicus Brief—Bragg—Received: 02/16/2010
Amicus Letter Brief—City of Amarillo—Received: 02/16/2010
Amicus Letter Brief—City of El Paso—Received: 02/16/2010
EAA—Petition for Writ of Mandamus—Filed: 03/05/2010
Day—Response to Post-Submission Letter Brief—Filed: 03/18/2010
Amicus Post-Submission Letter—Bragg—Received: 05/10/2010
Amicus Letter Brief—Bragg—Received: 05/25/2010
Post-Submission Amicus Brief—Texas Alliance of Groundwater Districts—Received: 05/28/2010
Amicus Letter—Duncan—Received: 06/03/2010
State—Post-Submission Brief—Filed: 06/10/2010
Day—Response to Amicus Brief—Filed: 06/10/2010
Day—Response to Post-Submission Brief—Filed: 06/28/2010
Amicus Letter—Texas Farm Bureau—Received: 07/09/2010
Edwards Aquifer Authority—Response to Amicus Letter—Filed: 08/30/2010
Amicus Curiae Brief—The Texas Farm Bureau, Texas Wildlife Association, and Texas and Southwestern Cattle Raisers Association—Filed: 07/11/2011
Amicus Curiae Brief of the City of San Antonio by and through the San Antonio Water System in Support of Petitioner San Antonio Water System—Filed: 11/3/2011
Day/McDaniel Response to the Amicus Curiae Brief of the City of San Antonio by and through the San Antonio Water System in Support of the Edwards Aquifer Authority—Filed: 11/14/2011
Edwards Aquifer Authority and the State of Texas Petitioners v. Burrell Day and Joel McDaniel, Respondents Amended Day/McDaniel Response to the Amicus Curiae Brief of the City of San Antonio by and through the San Antonio Water System in Support of the Edwards Aquifer Authority—Filed: 12/20/2011

Edwards Aquifer Authority v. Chemical Lime, Ltd., 06-0911

Petition for Review—Filed: 01/29/2006
Amicus Brief—State of Texas—Received: 12/27/2006
Petitioners' Brief on the Merits—Filed: 07/06/2007
Amicus Brief on the Merits—State of Texas—Received: 08/08/2007
Respondent's Brief on the Merits—Filed: 08/24/2007
Petitioners' Reply Brief—Filed: 10/05/2007

Barshop et al. v. Medina County Underground Water Conservation District et al., 95-0881

Bart Sipriano v. Great Spring Waters of America, 98-0247, Supreme Court of Texas (1998–1999)

Charles C. Motl et al. v. R. W. Boyd et al., 116 Tex. 82; 286 S.W. 458; 1926 Tex. LEXIS 96, Supreme Court of Texas (1926)

City of Aspermont v. Rolling Plains Groundwater Conservation District, 2008 Tex. App. LEXIS 3274, Court of Appeals of Texas, Eleventh District, Eastland (2008)

City of Del Rio v. Clayton Sam Colt Hamilton Trust, Supreme Court of Texas Court Case LEXIS 723 (2009)

Edwards Aquifer Authority v. Burrell Day and Joel McDaniel. Court of Appeals of Texas, Fourth District, San Antonio. LEXIS 9777 (2008)

Friendswood Development Company, et al. v. Smith-Southwest Industries, 576 S.W.2d 21; 1978 Tex. LEXIS 404; 22 Tex. Sup. J. 107; 5 A.L.R.4th 591; 62 Oil & Gas Rep. 218; 9 ELR 20452, Supreme Court of Texas (1978)

Glenn and Jo Lynn Bragg, Petitioners v. Edwards Aquifer Authority and Gregory Ellis, General Manager of the Edwards Aquifer Authority, Respondents, 01-0436

Guitar Holding Company, L.P., Hudspeth County Underground Water Conservation District No. 1 v. CL Machinery Company and Cimarron Agricultural, LTD. Court of Appeals of Texas, Eighth District, El Paso. LEXIS 7869 (2006)

Houston & Texas Central Railroad Company v. W. A. East, 98 Tex. Rep. 146 (June 13, 1904)

Hugh Coates, et al. v. Charles Hall, 2007 U.S. Dist. LEXIS 26294, United States District Court for the Western District of Texas, San Antonio Division (2007)

In Re the Contests of the City of Laredo, et al., To the Adjudication of

Water Rights in the Middle Rio Grande Basin and Contributing Texas Tributaries, 675 S.W.2d 257; 1984 Tex. App. LEXIS 5687, Court of Appeals of Texas, Third District, Austin (1984)

Lee, Thomas F. "Re: Glenn and JoLynn Bragg v. Edwards Aquifer Authority; Cause No. 06-11-18170-CV in the 38th District Court of Medina County, Texas" (May 2010)

Lupe Alonzo, Jim Alonzo, Joe Alonzo and Valentino Alonzo v. United States of America, 249 F.2d 189, United States Court of Appeals Tenth Circuit (1957)

Oscar C. Gordon v. San Antonio Water System, 2007 Tex. App. LEXIS 1932, Court of Appeals of Texas, Fourth District, San Antonio (2007)

Pecos County Water Control and Improvement District No. 1 v. Clayton W. Williams et al. Court of Civil Appeals of Texas, El Paso, LEXIS 2113 (1954)

San Antonio River Authority, Petitioner v. G. Garrett Lewis, et al., Respondents, No. 1-8304, The Supreme Court of Texas, 363 S.W.2d 444. Supreme Court of Texas, Austin (1962)

San Antonio River Authority v. G. Garrett Lewis, 363 S.W.2d 444; 1962 Tex. LEXIS 699; 6 Tex. Sup. J. 137, Supreme Court of Texas (1962)

South Plains Lamesa Railroad, LTD. and Kitten Family Living Trust v. High Plains Underground Water Conservation District No. 1, 52 S.W.3d 770; 2001 Tex. App. LEXIS 2497, Court of Appeals of Texas, Seventh District, Amarillo (2001)

State et al. v. Heard et al., 146 Tex. 139, 204 S.W.2d 344, Court of Civil Appeals of Texas, Austin (1946)

State of New Mexico ex rel. Eluid L. Martinez, State Engineer v. City of Las Vegas, 118 N.M. 257, 880 P.2d 868, Court of Appeals of New Mexico (1994)

State of Texas et al., Appellants, v. Valmont Plantations et al., Appellees, No. 13583, Civil Court of Appeals of Texas, San Antonio, 346 S.W.2d 853; 1961 Tex. App. San Antonio: Civil Court of Appeals, 1961

State of Texas v. Valmont Plantations, 346 S.W.2d 853; 1961 Tex App. LEXIS 2336 (1961)

The Texas Company v. Joe Burkett. Supreme Court of Texas. LEXIS 138 (1927)

United States of America in Behalf of the Pueblo of San Ildefonso v. Harley Brewer and Mrs. Harley Brewer, 184 F.Supp. 377, United States District Court D, New Mexico (1960)

United States of America v. Jose I. Abeyta, 632 F.Supp. 1301, United
States District Court D, New Mexico (1986)

United States v. Candelaria et al. 271 U.S. 432, 46 S.Ct. 561, United States
Circuit Court of Appeals for the Eighth Circuit (1925–1926)

NOTES

INTRODUCTION

1. Silverstein, "Life by the Drop," 101.

2. Water on the surface exists conjunctively with groundwater, water that is underground; surface water feeds groundwater, and groundwater feeds surface water as it flows. Black, *Black's Law Dictionary*, 302.

3. "Zero-sum" is a term used in game theory to describe both real games and situations of all kinds, usually between two players or participants, where the gain of one player is exactly offset by the loss of another player. Thus, the gains and losses sum to zero.

4. Martinez v. Maverick County Water Control and Improvement District No. 1, 219 F.2d 666, 670 (5th Cir. 1955).

5. Judon Fambrough of the Texas Real Estate Center uses the "bundle of sticks" phrase in his writings and teachings—very appropriately. "Real property" is defined as land and all the things that are attached to it.

6. Ad valorem taxes are based upon an assessment of the fair market value of a piece of land and its improvements. Each of Texas' 254 counties has a central appraisal department that annually assesses the real property and personal property values in its respective county. The county appraisers attempt to value the property at fair market value, which is defined as what a willing buyer will pay a willing seller for property with neither party under duress. From this assessment, the taxing authorities apply the tax rate for divisions of government, each of which determines how much tax revenue will be raised. Appraisal districts have not yet begun to value water rights per se, especially since it is difficult, if not impossible, to accurately determine the amount of groundwater under someone's property.

CHAPTER 1

1. The term "geological container" to describe water types in Texas can generally be traced to the fine work of Ron Kaiser of Texas A&M University.

2. "Watercourse" in Texas law is not found in the statutes but in the case Hoefs v. Short, 273 S.W. 785 (Tex. 1925): "When it is said that a stream in order to be a natural water course to which water rights attach must have bed, banks, a current of water, and a permanent source of water supply, we have only described in detail such physiographic and meteorological characteristics as make the use of the stream for irrigation practicable. When it is once shown that the waters of a stream are so confined and persistent in their course, and flow with such frequency and

volume that it is both practicable and valuable to irrigate therefrom, it is a stream to which such water rights attach.

With reference to the phrase 'definite and permanent source of supply of water,' frequently used by the courts as describing a necessary requisite of an irrigable stream, all that is meant is that there must be sufficient water carried by the stream at such intervals as may make it practicable to irrigate from or use the stream. . . . The authorities frequently say that a natural watercourse must have a permanent source of water supply. This however merely means that the stream must be such that similar conditions will produce a flow of water, and that these conditions recur with some degree of regularity, so that they establish and maintain a running stream for considerable periods of time. Farnham on Waters, Vol. 2, § 457; Ruling Case Law, Vol. 27, pp. 1065, 1066; Kinney on Irrigation, Vol. 1, § 306."

3. A full copy of the final signed bill is in appendix 1.

4. Joined together, combined so that changes in one directly result in changes to the other.

5. Interview with Kirk Holland, June 12, 2010.

6. See chapter 4 for a detailed discussion of this ownership debate.

7. An adjudicated right is settled by judicial procedure. Usufruct is the legal right of using or enjoying the fruits or profits of something belonging to another; the right to use or enjoy something; from the Latin *ususfructus* or *usus et fructus,* meaning "use and enjoyment."

8. White and Wilson, "Flow and Underflow of Motl v. Boyd," 17.

9. For example, in Colorado prior to 2010, it was illegal to capture runoff water or snowmelt from your roof.

10. Porter, presentation to United States Geological Society, Austin office, May 2010.

11. Appropriative rights allow the use of water by grant or license from a governmental authority.

12. The PDSI is based upon the analysis of tree rings in various locations in the United States, but it is more than a tree ring study. It takes into consideration other factors such as soil conditions and the characteristics of the individual trees.

13. Kelton, *The Time It Never Rained,* xiii. Elmer Kelton lived in San Angelo during the height of the 1950s drought.

14. Porter, *Maker of Modern Texas,* 176.

15. "Kindling point" is the minimum temperature at which a substance will undergo spontaneous combustion. It was so dry in Bastrop that the native trees were like "napalm" waiting to explode with the slightest provocation.

16. Interview with Tom Hatfield, October 17, 2010. This comment also appeared in Hatfield's 1964 master's thesis, which focused on the history of the then-recent 1950s drought.

CHAPTER 2

1. Porter, "Water Rights for Texas Agents," 1.

2. Fugitive water is water that has escaped from one property onto an adjacent property or from one groundwater pool to another. Groundwater is almost always fugitive to a degree due to the conjunctive relationship of water.

3. Blackstone, *Commentaries on the Laws of England,* 18.

4. Riparian water rights are based upon the land's appurtenance to the water, defined as "relating to or living or located on the bank of a natural watercourse (as a river) or sometimes of a lake or a tidewater" (www.encyclo.co.uk/define/riparian).

5. Spanish land and water grants do not have special legal significance after the Water Rights Adjudication period, but they were used to help during individual adjudication hearings. A current landowner of a Spanish land grant has no special legal ownership of groundwater. However, it is important to recognize early Texas' acknowledgment of the rights of its Spanish roots and peoples along with the historical legacy Spanish water policies gave to Texas. For further information, see Baade, "The Historical Background to Texas Water Law."

6. However, the 82nd Texas Legislature made progress toward better guidance in water policy with SBs 332, 660, 727, and 737.

7. G. Smith, "The Valley Water Suit," 580.

8. White and Wilson, "The Flow and Underflow of Motl v. Boyd," 379.

9. Texas Comptroller of Public Accounts, *Forces of Change,* 413–415.

10. Baade, "Historical Background of Texas Water Law," 11, 21.

11. Interview with Russell S. Johnson, Texas attorney and water rights expert, June 10, 2008.

CHAPTER 3

1. Fambrough, "Texas Surface Water," 1.

2. Hoefs v. Short; Galant and Johnson, "Exempt Uses," 11.

3. Texas Water Code, Section 11.021; Galant and Johnson, "Exempt Uses."

4. *Adjudication of Water Rights of the Lower Guadalupe River Segment;* Galant and Johnson, "Exempt Uses."

5. See the TCEQ website: http://www.tceq.texas.gov/permitting/water_rights/wr_faqs.html.

6. Texas Water Code, Section 11.121; Galant and Johnson, "Exempt Uses."

7. Interview with Kirk Holland, June 3, 2010.

8. I interviewed the Concho River watermaster specialist Molly Mohler on August 10, 2010, and asked how many 200 acre-feet stock ponds I could have on my land filled with water from the Concho River. The answer was as many as I could dig. However, it seems to me that if a landowner did have numerous tanks, they must be used only as stock tanks, and irrigating from those tanks would be illegal without a permit. Again, ask for a ruling before diverting any water from a watercourse, especially a river controlled by a watermaster or river authority.

9. Texas Administrative Code, Title 30 Environmental Quality, Part 1, Texas Commission on Environmental Quality, Chapter 297, Water Rights, Substantive, Subchapter C, Use Exempt from Permitting, http://info.sos.state.tx.us/pls/pub/readtac$ext.ViewTAC?tac_view=4&ti=30&pt=1&ch=297.

10. "Texas surface water is far more visible and accessible to landowners than groundwater—but landowners should be careful. Much surface water belongs to Texas, and using it without a permit can cost as much as $5,000 per day." Fambrough, "Texas Surface Water," 1.

11. See http://www.tceq.texas.gov/publications/gi/gi-228.html/at_download/file.

12. Fambrough, *Private Property,* 1.

CHAPTER 4

1. Texas Women's University v. Methodist Hospital, in Galant and Johnson, "Exempt Uses," 10.

2. Turner v. Big Lake Oil Co., in Galant and Johnson, "Exempt Uses," 10.

3. Galant and Johnson, "Exempt Uses." "A landowner could build a stock tank to capture rainwater flowing down a hill without a permit, but if the flow of water forms a channel or converges in some manner to create a defined bed as it moves down the hill before it reaches the stock tank, the person may be capturing state-owned surface water from a watercourse, which the landowner cannot do without a permit or exemption from permitting" (12).

4. The Edwards Aquifer Authority and the State of Texas, Petitioners, v. Burrell Day and Joel McDaniel, Respondents, in the Supreme Court of Texas No. 08–904, 1.

5. Ibid., 7.

6. Ibid., 11, 8, 36. Further details about this landmark case can be found in Chapter 10.

CHAPTER 5

1. Bennett and Herzog, "US-Mexico Borderland Water Conflicts," 973. Also see Dunlap, "Border Wars."

2. See "1917 Constitution of Mexico," www.latinamericanstudies.org/mexico/1917-Constitution.htm.

3. Interview with Bill Tilney, former mayor of El Paso, December 19, 2009.

4. Gwynne, "The Last Drop."

CHAPTER 6

1. Letter to the People of Texas, September 23, 2011, Texas Water Development Board, "2012 Water for Texas State Water Plan," opening page.

2. Assumes new conservation techniques will generally be used and new water sources such as those derived from desalination will be in place.

3. 2012 State Water Plan, 5, 178.

4. Notice that Region A has greater water supplies than its neighbor Region O because of its rivers.

5. Rios, "Robert Lee Prepares for Bronte Waterline."

CHAPTER 7

1. See the "Colorado County Groundwater Conservation District Management Plan," www.ccgcd.net/media/83ce3087fe13babffff803affffd524.pdf, 74.

2. The best sources for links to most of the groundwater conservation districts are Texas Water Development Board, https://www.twdb.state.tx.us, and Texas Alliance of Groundwater Districts, www.texasgroundwater.org.

3. TCEQ, "Frequently Asked Questions," http://www.tceq.texas.gov/permitting /water_rights/wr_faqs.html.

4. Texas Water Code, Section 36.117, Acts 2011, 82nd Leg., R.S., Ch. 32, Sec. 1, eff. May 9, 2011.

5. This is the calculation: 25,000 gallons per day × 365 days = 9,125,000 gallons of water; 9,125,000 gallons of water ÷ 27,154 gallons in 1 inch of rain on 1 acre = 336.05 inches of rain per year. Rainforests can be classified as such when as little as 78.74 inches of rain fall in a year. The Amazon basin averages 108 inches of rain a year. The highest level of rainfall I have found in a rainforest is an occasional 1.18 inches per day, or 430 inches a year. Any way one thinks about 25,000 gallons per day, it is a tremendous amount of groundwater to exempt from permit in Texas. Rainfall averages in Texas in Beaumont to the east somewhere around 44 inches a year; in Austin somewhere around 33 inches a year; and in El Paso at the western boundary somewhere less than 12 inches a year.

6. Currently there are seven in the state. See a map at http://www.tceq.texas .gov/assets/public/permitting/watersupply/groundwater/maps/pgma_areas.pdf.

7. This point was additionally confirmed in my on-site interview with the Concho River watermaster Molly Mohler in San Angelo on August 10, 2010. It was my understanding that landowners could pump water into as many ponds as necessary on their property for domestic and livestock use without a permit in the San Angelo jurisdiction.

8. Porter, *Spanish Water/Anglo Water.*

9. See Texas Department of Licensing and Regulation administrative rules, http://www.license.state.tx.us/wwd/wwdrules.htm.

10. Carmen McCann, ed., *The Cross Section Newsletter* 56, no. 5 (May 5, 2010).

11. See Brown, "TCEQ Drought Rule Could Result in Takings."

12. See Brown, "Brazos River Lawsuit Raises Questions."

13. Texas Farm Bureau, Frank Volleman, and Frank Destefano, Plaintiffs v. Texas Commission on Environmental Quality, Defendant, filed in the Travis County District Court December 14, 2012, 5, 6.

14. Kate Galbraith, "If Conservation Fails, Industry May Try Groundwater," *New York Times,* February 26, 2012.

15. Galant and Johnson, "Exempt Uses," 2.

16. Interview with Ray McCloskey, independent landman, January 7, 2012.

17. Agricultural exemptions lower ad valorem taxes. If lost, there is usually a five-year rollback tax due, adjusting the ad valorem taxes to reflect the loss of the exemption.

18. Many of my contacts in the pipeline industry, most of whom are attorneys who acquire right-of-way, offer this as gospel. My research indicates it may not be an exaggeration. There is a 200,000-barrel-a-day new oil pipeline approved and planned to be in use in Wilson County alone by 2013—200,000 barrels a day!

19. Jennifer Hiller, "Exact Mix of Fracking Fluids Remain a Mystery," *San Antonio Express-News,* February 2, 2013.

CHAPTER 8

1. Texas Water Code, Section 36.0015.

2. Interview with Kirk Holland, January 4, 2012.

3. Dave Harmon, "Drought Spurs More to Drill Private Wells," *Austin American-Statesman,* June 3, 2012, front page.

4. On June 15, 2011, I spoke to a West Texas GCD manager who told me his entire annual budget was only $13,000. The budget for his district, the Brewster County Groundwater Conservation District, increased to $20,000 in 2012. Another GCD in Central Texas has a $76,000 annual budget. Many GCDs simply cannot afford to keep their offices open to the public five days a week. This needs to be remedied soon. See Porter, "Financing Groundwater Conservation Districts in Texas," 57, 72.

5. The domestic and livestock exemption is set by the individual GCDs and varies across the state. The specification provided by the statute is a minimum standard for exemption.

6. See http://www.texasgroundwater.org/pdfs/2011egeupdate.pdf. Also find information at http://www.twdb.state.tx.us/GwRD/pages/gwrdindex.html, but note as of January 26, 2012, even the TWDB website has not changed MAG from "managed available groundwater" to the new term "modeled available ground-water," as discussed in the next section.

7. Since the groundwater model parameters are so critical to prudent planning of groundwater and the consequences of unrealistic models is significant, it is my opinion that the change in name is appropriate. Planning based on modeling is only as good as the model parameters. The Texas Alliance of Groundwater Districts published these comments about legislative changes made by the 82nd Legislature in 2011: "SB 660 also requires Regional Water Plans (RWPs) to be consistent with applicable desired future conditions (DFCs) and adds additional informational re-quirements for the state water plan. Notably, the bill requires TWDB and the Texas Commission on Environmental Quality (TCEQ), in consultation with the Water Conservation Advisory Council (WCAC), to develop a uniform water use calcula-tion system. These changes are consistent with the changes made by SB 181. Con-

sistent with SB 737, SB 660 changes the term 'managed available groundwater' to 'modeled available groundwater' in order to better reflect the meaning of the term. SB 660 also makes comprehensive changes to the process for establishing and adopting DFCs in the various GMAs and filing petitions for inquiry at TCEQ. Though two separate proposals for amending the DFC appeals process were introduced during the Legislative Session, neither version passed. As a result, the DFC appeals process at TWDB remains substantively unchanged."

8. See http://www.twdb.texas.gov/groundwater/management_areas/index.asp.

9. Request for an Attorney General's Opinion Regarding the Legal Authority of a County Commissioners Court to Enact a Groundwater Management Ordinance Pursuant to Texas Water Code, Section 35.019 or Texas Local Government Code, Section 232.0032; and the Validity of the Same in Certain Circumstances, RQ-1003-GA, October 11, 2011.

10. Attorney General Opinion GA-0935, May 21, 2012.

11. Votteler, "The Little Fish That Roared," 845.

12. See Edwards Aquifer Authority, "Who We Are," http://edwardsaquifer.org/eaa/who-we-are.

13. A Karst zone is an area designated by municipal governments as protected. The University of Texas at Austin's Environmental Science Institute defines Karst as "a landscape formed from the dissolution of soluble rocks, including limestone, dolomite, and gypsum."

14. Comments of Karl Dreher, water rights update luncheon, San Marcos Board of Realtors, San Marcos, November 9, 2011.

15. Interview with Kirk Holland, August 1, 2013.

16. The case is discussed in more detail later in this book. I mention it here only to stress the seemingly critical importance of water meters in proving historic use in the courts.

17. Campbell, "Texas Watermasters," used with express permission of the author.

18. Porter, *Spanish Water/Anglo Water,* 14.

19. Campbell, "Texas Watermasters," 147.

20. Ibid., 151–152.

21. Ibid., 166.

22. Ibid., 174.

23. See www.tceq.texas.gov/permitting/water_rights/wmaster/rgwr/riogrande.html.

24. A diversion right or the right to divert water from a stream in an amount during a specific time.

25. See www.tceq.texas.gov/permitting/water_rights/wmaster/stwr/southtexas.html.

26. See www.tceq.texas.gov/permitting/water_rights/wmaster/wmaster.html.

27. See http://www.lcra.org/about/overview/index.html.

28. Farzad Mashhood, "LCRA to Publish Proposed Water Plan Revision Next Week," *Austin American-Statesman,* January 17, 2012.

29. See http://www.lcra.org/water/supply/irrigation.html.

30. Quoted in Logan Hawkes, "Uncertain Future Has Texas Rice Growers Praying for Rain," *Southwest Farm Press,* November 3, 2011.

31. Justin Ellison, "Water Deal Could Ruin Texas Rice Farmers," *Farm Plus Financial,* October 3, 2011, http://www.farmplusfinancial.com/blog/general-farm -loans/water-deal-could-ruin-texas-rice-farmers/.

CHAPTER 9

1. 2012 State Water Plan, 4, www.twdb.state.tx.us/waterplanning/swp/2012.

2. The TWDB defines "total statewide water supplies" as supplies that are physically and legally available, water that can be produced with current permits, current contracts, and existing infrastructure during drought.

3. State Water Plan, 2–3.

4. Ibid., 6.

5. Letter from George W. Brackenridge to "Brother Tom," November 19, 1879, Robert Thomas Brackenridge Papers, La Prelle-Brackenridge Papers.

6. The Austin tracts are found along Lake Austin Boulevard and include Austin's Municipal Golf Course. Brackenridge donated all the land to the University of Texas. The San Antonio tract is Brackenridge Park, which Brackenridge donated to the City of San Antonio.

7. Porter, *Spanish Water, Anglo Water,* 99.

8. Silverstein, "Life by the Drop."

9. See Porter, *Spanish Water/Anglo Water.*

10. See Justice Deborah G. Hankinson's description of the farms in No. 01–0436, in the Supreme Court of Texas, Glenn and JoLynn Bragg, Petitioners v. Edwards Aquifer Authority and Gregory Ellis, General Manager of the Edwards Aquifer Authority, Respondents, on Petition for Review for the Court of Appeals for the Fourth District of Texas, Argued on October 2, 2001: "The Braggs own two commercial pecan orchards in Medina County. The first orchard is located on approximately sixty acres of land, along with the Braggs' residence and pecan processing facility. That orchard is known as the 'Home Place Orchard.' The second orchard, known as the 'D'Hanis Orchard,' is located on approximately forty-two acres. The Braggs drilled a well into the Edwards Aquifer on the Home Place Orchard in 1979. They began drilling a well on the D'Hanis Orchard in December 1994, and completed it in February 1995." Also see Judge Thomas Lee's findings in letter of May 7, 2010, in Glenn and JoLynn Bragg v. Edwards Aquifer Authority; Cause No. 06–11–118170-CV in the 38th District Court of Medina County, Texas.

11. Ellis, "Regulatory Takings and Texas Groundwater." *Black's Law Dictionary* defines the term "taking" in this way: "There is a 'taking' of property when government action directly interferes with or substantially disturbs the owner's use

and enjoyment of the property." To constitute a "taking, within constitutional limitation, it is not essential that there be physical seizure or appropriation, and any actual or material interference with private property rights constitutes a taking." Grothers v. U.S., C.A.Or., 594 F.2d 740, 741.

12. Cause No. 08–0904 in the Texas Supreme Court.

13. Judge Thomas Lee, finding letter, 2.

14. Ibid., 2, 3.

15. It is highly subjective because different crops may require differing amounts of water, irrigation techniques and equipment use differing amounts of water, and so on. What level of water constitutes an "irrigated farm" may be ultimately only in the mind of each individual buyer.

16. *Black's Law Dictionary* defines *vested rights* in this way: "In constitutional law, rights which have so completely and definitely accrued to or settled in a person that they are not subject to be defeated or canceled by the act of any other private person, and which is right and equitable that the government should recognize and protect, as being lawful in themselves, and settled according to the then current rules of law, and of which the individual could not be deprived arbitrarily without injustice, or of which he could not justly be deprived otherwise than by the established methods of procedure and for the public welfare," 1564; see also 1564n8.

17. I estimate that in the past decade at least 50 percent of the lawsuits in which I have been called as an expert witness involved some kind of disclosure of defects issue.

18. Texas Property Code, Section 5.008, (b) (4) and (5).

19. According to *Black's Law Dictionary,* "If one by exercise of reasonable care would have known a fact, he is deemed to have had constructive knowledge of such fact."

20. According to 22 TAC 531.1, "A real estate broker or salesperson, while acting as an agent for another, is a fiduciary. Special obligations are imposed when such fiduciary relationships are created." A relationship of trust and confidence is built between client and agent; therefore, the agent serves in a fiduciary capacity.

21. According to the Texas Real Estate Commission, *Ethics MCE Instructor's Manual:* "Scrupulously is defined as acting in strict regard for what is considered right or proper; punctiliously [paying great attention to detail or correct behavior] exact; painstaking. Meticulously is defined as marked by extreme or excessive care in the consideration of details; careful. Therefore, one can conclude by these definitions that the licensee must perform his or her duties in a way that exhibits a knowledge of what is right and appropriate under the circumstances and with care about details" (1).

22. 22 TAC 531.2, 3.1, 3.2, 3.3.

23. There are two types of licensees in Texas, real estate broker and real estate salesperson. The broker status is the senior status; the salesperson must have a sponsoring broker, and the broker is responsible for the authorized acts of the

sponsored salesperson. A salesperson may eventually become a broker under the procedures of the Real Estate License Act.

24. According to Mike Henry, attorney at law, negligence is "the failure to use ordinary care, that is, failing to do that which a person of ordinary prudence would have done under the same or similar circumstances or doing that which a person of ordinary prudence would not have done under the same or similar circumstances."

25. Percolating water underground is considered groundwater and is owned by the surface owner and managed by local groundwater conservation districts.

26. Porter, speech to the USGS Austin office, 2010.

27. Porter, *Spanish Water/Anglo Water,* 64–68.

28. TWBD, *Texan's Guide,* 11–12.

29. Johnson, *Texas Water Law,* 22.

30. Ibid.

CHAPTER 10

1. Houston & Texas Central Railroad Company v. W. A. East, 98 Tex. Rep. 146 (June 13, 1904).

2. Search of the newspaper files held at the Center for American History at the University of Texas at Austin found no mention of the case in the local newspapers in Denison.

3. Johnson, "Texas Water Law," 6.

4. *Black's Law Dictionary,* 344.

5. *Handbook of Texas Online,* s.v. "Denison, TX," http://www.tshaonline.org /handbook/online/articles/hed04.

6. *Handbook of Texas Online,* s.v. "Houston and Texas Central Railway," http:// www.tshaonline.org/handbook/online/articles/eqh09.

7. Mullican and Schwartz, *100 Years of Rule of Capture,* 63.

8. Plaintiff's First Amended Original Petition, W. A. East v. Houston & Texas Central Railroad Company.

9. Mullican and Schwartz, *100 Years of Rule of Capture,* 73.

10. Daniel M. Liebowitz, Representative Mark Strama's policy assistant, telephone communication with librarian at the Denison Public Library, January 12, 2008.

11. Plaintiff's First Amended Original Petition.

12. East v. Houston & Texas Central Railroad Company, 77 S.W. 647 (Civ. App. Dallas 1903).

13. Ibid., 646.

14. Ibid.

15. Findings of Fact and Conclusions of Law, W. A. East v. Houston & Texas Central Railroad Company (December 28, 1902).

16. Opelia, "The Rule of Capture in Texas," 104.

17. East v. Houston & Texas Central Railroad Company, 77 S.W. 646 (Civ. App. Dallas 1903).

18. Meyer, *Water in the Hispanic Southwest,* 178, 179. *Siete Partidas* (Seven-Part Code) refers to *Partida* 3, *Titulo* 28, *Ley* 1 (part 3, title 28, law 1).

19. Ibid., 180.

20. Houston & Texas Central Railroad Company v. W. A. East, 98 Tex. Rep. 146 (June 13, 1904).

21. Mullican and Schwartz, *100 Years of Rule of Capture,* 2.

22. Johnson, *Texas Water Law,* 12.

23. Sipriano v. Great Spring Waters of America, Inc., 22 111.1 S.W.3d 75 (Tex. 1999). Great Spring Waters of America is better known as Ozarka. Ozarka drilled a water well next to the Sipriano farm and dried up Sipriano's well. Ozarka was found to owe no liability or damages to Sipriano. Texas Supreme Court Justice Nathan Hecht warned the legislature that it should address the "rule of capture" or eventually the court would.

24. See appendix 1 for further review of this case.

25. In an interview with Kirk Holland, geoscientist, on June 7, 2011, he stated that "up-gradient" is the correct term rather than the common term "up dip."

26. Greenhill and Gee, "Ownership of Ground Water in Texas," 621–622.

27. Ibid., 622.

28. After a speech to the USGS in Austin, I asked one of its hydrologic engineers this very question. He said the Trinity Sands "percolate" to Comanche Springs, and therefore there is no "underground" stream or channel. I think it is still a very interesting question to investigate in this case.

29. An artesian well is a well drilled through impermeable strata to reach water capable of rising to the surface by internal hydrostatic pressure.

30. Porter, *Spanish Water, Anglo Water,* 129–130.

31. Glennon, *Water Follies,* 92.

32. Ibid.

33. Cervantes, "The Bad Neighbor.

34. ABE Engineering LLC to Pokrant, City Planner, City of Del Rio, May 11, 2009.

35. Edwards Aquifer Authority v. Day, S.W.3d (2012).

36. The article reads: "No person's property shall be taken, damaged, or destroyed for or applied to public use without adequate compensation being made."

37. Edwards Aquifer Authority v. Day, 274 S.W. 3d 742 (Tex. App.-San Antonio 2008).

38. Ibid., "Ruling," 1, 8.

39. Ibid., "Ruling," 45.

40. Mason and Melvin, "New Developments in Texas Water Law," 10.

41. "Ruling," 11, 28.

42. Edwards Aquifer Authority Act, Section 1.07.

43. "Ruling," 45, 46–47.

44. The confidential settlement agreement was acquired under the Texas Public Information Act.

45. For Judge Lee's full ruling, see appendix 1.

46. Comments at Realty Round Up 2007, Austin.

47. A "test" period" example: Agency X decides to grant new irrigation permits on historic use. The period used to determine historic use is January 1, 2000, to December 31, 2011. During this test period, proven by ledgers recording meter readings and/or sworn testimony, rancher Bill used an average of 12 acre-feet of water annually; hence, he qualifies for a regular permit for irrigation of same. The test period is set in the local rules. A test period selected during times of good rainfall versus times of drought could result in substantially different historic-use volumes.

CHAPTER 11

1. Weber, "Mexico's Far Northern Frontier," 282.

2. Lyle Larson, Texas Water Law Superconference, Austin, September 10, 2012.

3. McCormick and Walker, "Sprayed Away," 4.

4. Texas Water Development Board, *Conserving Water Outdoors.*

5. Porter, presentation at St. Edward's University Water Workshop, 2009.

6. Meco manufactures the typical system per Harold Hunt, Real Estate Center, Texas A&M University. Interview, September 10, 2011.

7. Water Forum, San Antonio, October 2010.

8. Farzad Mashhood, "Legislator Draws Up Water Plan," *Austin American-Statesman,* January 2012.

9. I served as an expert witness for the Texas Attorney General's Office, Right of Way Division, on several of the condemnation lawsuits on the expansion of the Katy Freeway in Houston. There were literally hundreds of lawsuits over compensation; I like to say the 30-mile expansion resulted in 30 miles of lawsuits on the way to town and 30 miles coming out of town — 60 miles of conflict. Gaining right-of-way, even with eminent domain, is time consuming and expensive. Porter, speeches to the International Right of Way Association, Austin and San Marcos, 2010.

10. Porter, on-site interview with Raymond Shay, assistant plant manager, March 5, 2011.

11. The El Paso Water Utility estimates its total demand at 120,000 acre-feet per year in 2011. An acre-foot equals 325,851 gallons of water. Dividing 120,000 acre-feet per year by 365 days equals a daily demand of 329 acre-feet. Production of 12–15 million gallons of water daily from the desal plant equals 37–46 acre-feet per day.

12. Assuming the normal home uses 10,000 gallons per month, the total monthly fee if all the water came from the desal plant at this rate would be $17.10. Of course, the rate structures are staggered and widely variable. Nonetheless, $20 or even $40

per month for 10,000 gallons of water seems to me to be inadequate to amortize debt, set aside reserves for replacement, and set aside contingent repair dollars.

13. The assistant plant manager told me they have tried to find a use for the solid by-product to cut back on reinjection. They sent samples to Vermont for use in de-icing. Vermont rejected the product because it would not work. Obviously, the cost of transport of the solid by-product long distance eliminates its use as a cost-effective de-icing product.

14. Interview with Mark Holtzapple, March 2007.

15. Interview with Todd H. Votteler, executive manager of science, intergovernmental relations, and policy, GBRA; e-mail correspondence with the assistance of his intern, Ben Haggerty, July 12, 2012.

16. The phrase "sanitary sewer" may be the ultimate oxymoron—it is the terminology used to refer to the sewer system that transports human waste to the treatment plant.

17. See TWDB, "Frequently Asked Questions," http://www.twdb.texas.gov/innovativewater/reuse/faq.asp.

18. Ibid.

19. State Water Plan, 194.

APPENDIX 1

1. Court Opinion of Corpus Christi v. Pleasanton.

2. In Texas water rights, an appurtenant right attaches to the land, not to the owner. For example, a right to use surface water for domestic and livestock purposes cannot be severed or transferred to anyone else. It remains attached to the land.

GLOSSARY

Some terms in this glossary are quoted from either chapter 11 or chapter 36 of the Texas Water Code or from *Black's Law Dictionary,* 6th edition.

Adjudicated right: A right settled by judicial procedure.

Agriculture: Any of the following activities:
  (A) cultivating the soil to produce crops for human food, animal feed, or planting seed for the production of fibers;
  (B) the practice of floriculture, viticulture, silviculture, and horticulture, including the cultivation of plants in containers or nonsoil media, by a nursery grower;
  (C) raising, feeding, or keeping animals for breeding purposes or for the production of food or fiber, leather, pelts, or other tangible products having a commercial value;
  (D) raising or keeping equine animals;
  (E) wildlife management; and
  (F) planting cover crops, including cover crops cultivated for transplantation, or leaving land idle for the purpose of participating in any governmental program or normal crop or livestock rotation procedure.

Agricultural use: Any use or activity involving agriculture, including irrigation.

Amicus curiae: Literally, "friend of the court"; someone who volunteers to offer a point of law or other opinion on some aspect of the case to assist the court in its determinations.

Appropriative rights: Rights that allow the use of water by grant or license from a governmental authority.

Appropriator: A person who has made beneficial use of any water in a lawful manner under the provisions of any act of the legislature before the enactment of Chapter 171, General Laws, Acts of the 33rd Legislature, 1913, as amended, and who has filed with the State Board of Water Engineers a record of his appropriation as required by the 1913 Act, as amended, or a person who makes or has made beneficial use of any water within the limitations of a permit lawfully issued by the commission or one of its predecessors.

Appurtenant: Belonging to; accessing or incident to; adjunct, appended, or annexed to.

Artesian well: A well drilled through impermeable strata to reach water capable of rising to the surface by internal hydrostatic pressure.

Beneficial use: Use of the amount of water that is economically necessary for a purpose authorized in Chapter 11 of the Texas Water Code, when reasonable intelligence and reasonable diligence are used in applying the water to that purpose and shall include conserved water. In Chapter 36, "Use for a beneficial purpose" means use for

(A) agricultural, gardening, domestic, stock raising, municipal, mining, manufacturing, industrial, commercial, recreational, or pleasure purposes;

(B) exploring for, producing, handling, or treating oil, gas, sulphur, or other minerals; or

(C) any other purpose that is useful and beneficial to the user.

Best management practices: Those voluntary efficiency measures developed by the commission [TCEQ] that save a quantifiable amount of water, either directly or indirectly, and that can be implemented within a specified time frame.

Conjunctive: Joined together; combined so that changes in one directly results in changes to the other.

Conjunctive use: The combined use of groundwater and surface water sources that optimizes the beneficial characteristics of each source.

Conservation:

(A) the development of water resources; and

(B) those practices, techniques, and technologies that will reduce the consumption of water, reduce the loss or waste of water, improve the efficiency in the use of water, or increase the recycling and reuse of water so that a water supply is made available for future or alternative uses.

Conserved water: That amount of water saved by a holder of an existing permit, certified filing, or certificate of adjudication through practices, techniques, and technologies that would otherwise be irretrievably lost to all consumptive beneficial uses arising from storage, transportation, distribution, or application.

Correlative: Having a reciprocal relationship in that the existence of one relationship normally implies the existence of the other. In the law governing water rights in many western states but not Texas, the correlative rights doctrine gives the individual owners of land overlying a strata of percolating waters limited rights to use the water reasonably when there is not enough water to meet the needs of everyone in the area.

Diffused surface water: Rainwater that runs off a roof or over the surface of land without flowing in a stream or channel.

Environmental flows: Uses of water for the environment.

Evidence of historic or existing use: Evidence that is material and relevant to a determination of the amount of groundwater beneficially used without waste by a permit applicant during the relevant time period set by district rule that regulates groundwater based on historic use. Evidence in the form of oral or written testimony shall be subject to cross-examination. The Texas Rules of Evidence govern the admissibility and introduction of evidence of historic or existing use, except that evidence not admissible under the Texas Rules of Evidence may be admitted if it is of the type commonly relied upon by reasonably prudent persons in the conduct of their affairs.

Firm yield: The maximum water volume a reservoir can provide each year under a repeat of the drought of record.

Fugitive water: Water that has escaped from one property onto an adjacent property or from one groundwater pool to another.

Groundwater: Water percolating below the surface of the earth.

Groundwater reservoir: A specific subsurface water-bearing reservoir having ascertainable boundaries containing groundwater.

Managed or modeled available groundwater: The amount of water that may be permitted by a district for beneficial use in accordance with the desired future condition of the aquifer as determined under Section 36.108 of the Texas Water Code.

Negligence: Failure to use ordinary care that a person of ordinary prudence would have used under the same or similar circumstances or doing that which a person of ordinary prudence would not have done under the same or similar circumstances.

Ordinary flow: Water following its normal course in a streambed and obvious to the observer.

Priority groundwater management area: An area designated and delineated by the commission [TCEQ] under Chapter 35 of the Texas Water Code as an area experiencing or expected to experience critical groundwater problems.

Public water supply well: For purposes of a district governed by Chapter 36, Texas Water Code, a well that produces the majority of its water for use by a public water system.

Real property:
(A) land;
(B) an improvement;
(C) a mine or quarry;
(D) a mineral in place;
(E) standing timber; or
(F) an estate or interest, other than a mortgage or deed of trust creating a lien on property or an interest securing payment or performance of an obligation, in a property enumerated in Paragraphs (A) through (E) of this subdivision.

Recharge: The amount of water that infiltrates to the water table of an aquifer.

Reclaimed water: Domestic or municipal wastewater that has been treated to a quality suitable for beneficial use.

Riparian: Adjacency of land to a river, stream, or creek.

River basin: A river or coastal basin designated as a river basin under Section 16.051 of the Texas Water Code. The term does not include waters originating in the bays or arms of the Gulf of Mexico.

Runoff water: Casual or vagrant water.

Run-of-the-river right: A diversion right or the right to divert water from a stream in an amount during a specific time.

Subsidence: The lowering in elevation of the land surface caused by withdrawal of groundwater.

Total aquifer storage: The total calculated volume of groundwater that an aquifer is capable of producing.

Waste: Any one or more of the following:
(A) withdrawal of groundwater from a groundwater reservoir at a rate and in an amount that causes or threatens to cause intrusion into the reservoir of water unsuitable for agricultural, gardening, domestic, or stock raising purposes;
(B) the flowing or producing of wells from a groundwater reservoir if the water produced is not used for a beneficial purpose;
(C) escape of groundwater from a groundwater reservoir to any other reservoir or geologic strata that does not contain groundwater;
(D) pollution or harmful alteration of groundwater in a groundwater

reservoir by saltwater or by other deleterious matter admitted from another stratum or from the surface of the ground;

(E) willfully or negligently causing, suffering, or allowing groundwater to escape into any river, creek, natural watercourse, depression, lake, reservoir, drain, sewer, street, highway, road, or road ditch, or onto any land other than that of the owner of the well unless such discharge is authorized by permit, rule, or order issued by the TCEQ under Chapter 26;

(F) groundwater pumped for irrigation that escapes as irrigation tailwater onto land other than that of the owner of the well unless permission has been granted by the occupant of the land receiving the discharge; or

(G) for water produced from an artesian well, "waste" has the meaning assigned by Section 11.205.

Water right: A right acquired under the laws of this state to impound, divert, or use state water. A more thorough definition of a "water right" is a right or group of rights designed to protect the use, enjoyment, and in some cases, ownership of water that travels in streams, rivers, lakes, and ponds, gathers on the surface of the earth, or collects underground.

BIBLIOGRAPHY

PRIMARY SOURCES

Arricivita, Juan Domingo. *Cronica serfica y apostolica del colegio de propaganda fide de la Santa Cruz de Querétaro* [*Apostolic Chronicle of Juan Domingo Arricivita: The Franciscan Mission Frontier in the Eighteenth Century in Arizona, Texas, and the Californias*]. Translated by George P. Hammond and Agapito Rey. Berkeley: Academy of American Franciscan History, 1992 and 1996. Originally published in Mexico by Don Felipe de Zuniga y Ontiveros, 1792.

Bexar Archives Translations at the Center for American History. The University of Texas at Austin.

Bexar County Appraisal District. San Antonio, Texas.

Bexar County District Clerk Archives. Court Journals, Indices, and Archived Pleadings. San Antonio, Texas.

Bexar County Real Property Records and Archived Records. County Clerk. San Antonio, Texas.

Black, Henry Campbell. *Black's Law Dictionary.* 6th ed. Saint Paul, MN: West Publishing, 1990.

Brackenridge Book Collection. The University of the Incarnate Word Library Special Collections. San Antonio, Texas.

Brackenridge (John Thomas) Papers. State of Texas Archives. Austin, Texas.

Brackenridge (John Thomas and George W.) Papers. Center for American History. University of Texas at Austin.

Chamber of Commerce of San Antonio, Texas.

City Map of San Antonio. Southwell Map Company, 1946.

City of San Antonio. Archives of City Council Minutes, City Clerk, Leticia M. Vacek. San Antonio, Texas.

Corner, William, ed. *San Antonio de Baxar.* San Antonio: Bainbridge & Corner, 1890.

Cortina Letters. In *Juan Cortina and the Texas-Mexico Frontier, 1859–1877,* ed. and trans. Jerry D. Thompson. El Paso: Texas Western Press, 1994.

Cutter, Donald C., ed. and trans. *Hugo Oconnor informe sobre los Presidios del Norte de Nueva Espana dado al Vcry Marques de Croix 1777* [Named by translator Hugo O'Connor's report to Teodoro de Croix, July 22, 1777]. Dallas: Southern Methodist University Press, 1994.

Davis, Chester B. *Report upon a Valuation of the Plant of the Water Works Company of San Antonio, Texas.* San Antonio: Privately published, June 1902.

Erwin, Frank C., Jr. Letter to the Members of the Board of Regents, July 10, 1973. Austin, Texas.

Espinosa, Fray Felix de Espinosa, O.F.M. *Cronica de los Colegios de Propaganda Fide de la Nueva Espana.* Mexico, 1746.

Guadalupe County District Clerk Archives. Court Journals, Indices, and Archived Pleadings. Seguin, Texas.

Herff, Peter Ferdinand. *The Doctors Herff: A Three Generation Memoir.* Edited by Laura L. Barber. San Antonio: Trinity University Press, 1973.

Institute for Texan Culture Vertical Files and Library. University of Texas, San Antonio.

Inventory of the Mission San Antonio de Valero: 1772. Austin: Texas Historical Commission, 1977.

Journal of a Texas Missionary: The diario historico of Fr. Cosme Lozano Narvais, Pen Name Fr. Mariano Antonio de Vasconcelos. Transcript of the Spanish original. Briscoe Center for American History. University of Texas at Austin.

Lacoste Papers. Center for American History. University of Texas at Austin.

LaPrelle-Brackenridge Papers. Austin History Center. Austin, Texas.

Leutenegger, Fr. Benedict, trans. *Instruccion para el ministro de la Mision de la Purissima Concepcion de la Provincia de Texas, 1787* [Instruction for the minister of the Mission Purissima Concepcion of the Province of Texas, 1787]. San Antonio: Our Lady of the Lake University, 1994.

Matson, Daniel S., and Bernard L. Fontana, eds. and trans. *Father Bringas Reports to the King, Methods of Indoctrination on the Frontier of New Spain, 1796–97.* Tucson: University of Arizona Press, 1977.

McLean, Bert J. *The Romance of San Antonio's Water Supply and Distribution.* San Antonio: Privately published for the Water Company shareholders, 1924.

Montoya, Juan de. *New Mexico in 1602.* Translated by George P. Hammond and Agapito Rey. Albuquerque: The Quivira Society, 1938.

Morrison, Andrew. *San Antonio: Her Prosperity and Prospects.* San Antonio: Privately published, 1897.

Nixon, Pat Ireland. *A Century of Medicine in San Antonio.* San Antonio: Privately published, 1936.

Olmsted, Frederick Law. *A Journey through Texas.* Lincoln: University of Nebraska Press, 2004.

Period post card and map. Private collection of the author. Austin.

Rodriguez, Jose Maria. *Memoirs of Early Texas.* Available at http://www.tamu.edu/ccbn/dewitt/rodmemoirs.htm.

San Antonio National Bank. *San Antonio and Your First National Bank through the Years.* San Antonio: Claude Aniol & Associates, 1953.

The San Jose Papers. Translated from original documents with unknown publisher, unbound, copied from the Institute of Texan Cultures, University of Texas at San Antonio, loose files.

Sanborn Maps, July 1885, 1892. *San Antonio, Texas.* New York: Sanborn Map & Publishing, 1885, 1892.

State of Texas. *Laws of the State of Texas.* Austin: State of Texas, 1862.

Stillman, Chauncey Devereux. *Charles Stillman.* New York: Privately published, 1956.

Terrell (A. W.) Papers. Center for American History. University of Texas at Austin.

United States Geographical Survey Maps.

The Zacatecan Missionaries in Texas, 1716-1834. Texas Historical Survey Committee, Office of the State Archeologist Reports, No. 23. Austin: Office of the State Archeologist, 1973.

NEWSPAPERS

Dallas Morning News, 2006

Fredericksburg Standard-Radio Post, 1986

Recorder-Times, 1983

San Antonio Daily Express, 1872–1896

San Antonio Evening Paper, 1850–1890

San Antonio Express, 1890–2007

San Antonio Herald, 1872–1890

The Semi-Weekly News, 1862–1880

Texas Democrat, 1849

SECONDARY SOURCES

The Alcalde. 1912–1922. Austin: University of Texas.

Almaráz, Felix D. *Crossroad of Empire: The Church and State on the Rio Grande Frontier of Coahuila and Texas, 1700-1821, Report No. 1.* San Antonio: University of Texas at San Antonio Center for Archaeological Research, 1979.

———. "San Antonio's Franciscan Missions." *The Americas* 44 (July 1987): 1–22.

Anonymous. *Texas in 1837.* Edited by Andrew Forest Muir. Austin: University of Texas Press, 1958.

Armstrong, Ellis L., ed. *History of Public Works in the United States 1776–1976.* Chicago: American Public Works Association, 1976.

Arneson, Edward P. "Early Irrigation in Texas." *Southwestern Historical Quarterly Online* 25, no. 2 (1921): 121–130. Available at http://texashistory.unt.edu /ark:/67531/metapth101082/m1/127/.

Austin, Mattie Alice. "The Municipal Government of San Fernando de Bexar, 1730–1800." *Southwestern Historical Quarterly Online* 8, no. 4 (1905): 277–352. Available at http://texashistory.unt.edu/ark:/67531/metapth101033/m1/284/.

Baade, Hans W. "The Historical Background of Texas Water Law—a Tribute to Jack Pope." *St. Mary's Law Journal* 18, no. 1 (1986): 1–98.

Bannon, John Francis. *The Spanish Borderlands Frontier, 1513–1821.* Albuquerque: University of New Mexico Press, 1970.

Baxter, John O. *Spanish Irrigation in the Taos Valley.* Santa Fe: New Mexico State Engineer Office, 1990.

Bennett, Vivienne, and Lawrence A. Herzog. "US-Mexico Borderland Water Conflicts and Institutional Change." *Natural Resources Journal* 40 (2000): 973.

Benoist, Howard, and Sr. Maria Carolina Flores, C.P. *The Spanish Missionary Heritage of the United States.* San Antonio: United States Department of the Interior/National Park Service and Los Compadres de San Antonio Missions National Historical Park, 1990.

Benson, Reed D. "Deflating the Deference Myth: National Interests vs. State Authority under Federal Laws Affecting Water Use." *Utah Law Review* 241 (2006).

Bhatia R., and M. Falkenmark. "Over Exploitation of Groundwater and Its Adverse Effects." Paper presented at International Conference on Web Engineering, Dublin, Ireland, 1992.

Blackstone, Sir W[illia]m. *Commentaries on the Laws of England.* Portland, ME: Thomas B. Wait, 1807.

Blake, Nelson M. *Water for the Cities.* Syracuse, NY: Syracuse University Press, 1956.

Bogener, Stephen. *Ditches across the Desert: Irrigation in the Lower Pecos Valley.* Lubbock: Texas Tech University Press, 2003.

Bolton, Herbert E. "The Mission as a Frontier Institution in the Spanish-American Colonies." *American Historical Review* 23, no. 1 (Oct. 1917): 42–61.

———. *Texas in the Middle Eighteenth Century.* Austin: University of Texas Press, 1970.

Booth, F. R. "Adjudication on Water." Paper presented to North Texas Bar Association, 1967.

Brown, Jeremy. "Brazos River Lawsuit Raises Questions about Methods Texas Should Use to Modernize Its Surface Water Rights System." UT Law Grid, posted January 29, 2013. Available at http://www.utexas.edu/law/academics /centers/energy/2013/01/brazos-river-lawsuit-raises-questions-about-methods -texas-should-use-to-modernize-its-surface-water-rights-system/.

———. "TCEQ Drought Rule Could Result in Takings." UT Law Grid, posted February 6, 2013. Available at http://www.utexas.edu/law/academics /centers/energy/2013/02/tceq-drought-rule-could-result-in-takings/.

Brown, Timothy L. "A Primer for Understanding Texas Water Law." Texas Legislative Reference Library, posted June 2006. Available at http://www.lrl .state.tx.us/legis/water_Primer.pdf.

Bullock, Bob, and Martin Hubert. "Senate Bill 1, the First Big and Bold Step toward Meeting Texas's Future Water Needs." *Texas Tech Law Review* 30 (1999): 53.

Burkholder, Mary V. *Down the Acequia Madre.* San Antonio: Privately published, 1976.

———. *The King William Area: A History and Guide to the Houses.* San Antonio: Privately published, 1973.

Burns, Robert Ignatius. "Irrigation Taxes in Early Mudjar Valencia: The Problem of the Alfarda." *Speculum* 44, no. 4 (Oct. 1969): 560–567.

Campbell, Augustus L. "Texas Watermasters: A Legal History and Analysis of Surface Water Rights Enforcement." *Texas Tech Administrative Law Journal* 7, bk. 1 (Spring 2006): 143–177.

Canseco, Susana Elena. "Landowner's Rights in Texas Groundwater: How and Why Texas Courts Should Determine Landowners Do Not Own Groundwater in Place." *Baylor Law Review* 60, no. 2 (Spring 2008): 492–525.

Caroom, Doug, and Paul Elliot. "Water Rights Adjudication—Texas Style." *Texas Bar Journal* 44, no. 10 (November 1981): 1183–1192.

Caroom, Douglas G., and Susan M. Maxwell. "Overview of Texas Water Rights and Water Development." Continuing education paper, University of Texas School of Law, 2008.

Castañeda, Carlos E. *Our Catholic Heritage in Texas, 1519–1936.* Vols. 1–7. Austin: Von Boeckmann-Jones, 1938.

Caughey, John. "The Pueblo Water Right of Laredo." Library of Sherry L. Peel Attorney at Law Austin, Texas, July 1979.

Caughey, John, and Jose Fuentes Mares. "Adjudication of the Water Rights in the Middle Rio Grande River and Its Contributing Tributaries." Library of Sherry L. Peel Attorney at Law Austin, Texas, 1979.

Cervantes, Esther. "The Bad Neighbor: Alcoa's Dirty Dealing in Central Texas." *Dollars & Sense,* 2004. Available at http://dollarsandsense.org/archives/2004 /0704cervantes.html.

Chabot, Frederick C. *With the Makers of San Antonio.* San Antonio: Privately published, 1937.

Chahin, Dinniah M. "Is the Once Mighty River Not So Mighty?: How the Distribution of Water Rights and Water Planning along the Texas Portion of the Rio Grande River Affects Future Texans." *Texas Tech Journal of Texas Administrative Law* 6 (Spring 2005): 115.

Chipman, Donald E. *Spanish Texas, 1519–1821.* Austin: University of Texas Press, 1992.

Clayton, Jeffrey J. "Here Is a Land Where Life *Is* Written in Water": Re-writing Western Water Law in the 21st Century." *University of Denver Water Law Review* 5 (Spring 2002): 525.

Clopper, J. C. "J. C. Clopper's Journal and Book of Memoranda for 1828: Province of Texas." *Southwestern Historical Quarterly Online* 13, no. 1 (July 1909– Apr. 1910): 44–80. Available at http://texashistory.unt.edu/ark:/67531 /metapth101051/m1/52/.

Combs, Susan. *Liquid Assets: The State of Texas' Water Resources.* Texas Comptroller of Public Accounts Publication 96-1360. January 2009. Available at http://www.window.state.tx.us/specialrpt/water.

Coppini, Pompeo. *From Dawn to Sunset.* San Antonio: Naylor, 1949.

Cox, I. J. "The Early Settlers of San Fernando." *Southwestern Historical Quarterly Online* 5, no. 2 (July 1901–Apr. 1902): 142–160. Available at http://texashistory.unt.edu/ark:/67531/metapth101021/m1/148/.

———. *Excavations of Portions of the San Pedro Acequia (41 BX 337) and a Search for the Arocha Acequia, Report No. 161*. San Antonio: University of Texas at San Antonio Center for Archaeological Research, 1986.

———. *10th Street Substation Excavation of the Acequia Madre (41 BX 8), Report No. 153*. San Antonio: University of Texas at San Antonio Center for Archaeological Research, 1985.

Cox, I. Waynne. *Archaeological Monitoring at Espada Road Acequia Crossing, Report No. 221*. San Antonio: University of Texas at San Antonio Center for Archaeological Research, 1993.

———. *The Spanish Acequias of San Antonio*. San Antonio: Maverick Publishing, 2005.

Cox, I. Waynne, and Brett A. Houk. *Archaeological Monitoring of the HEB-GSA Parking Lot: Impacts to the San Pedro Acequia, Report No. 279*. San Antonio: University of Texas at San Antonio Center for Archaeological Research, 1998.

Cronon, William. *Nature's Metropolis: Chicago and the Great West*. New York: W. W. Norton, 1991.

Cuevas, P. Mariano, S.J. *Historia de la iglesia en Mexico, tomo IV, 1700–1800*. El Paso: Editorial "Revista Catolica," 1928.

Cutter, Charles R. "Community and the Law in Northern New Spain." *The Americas* 50 (April 1994).

Davis, Jeff J., and Scott B. McElroy. "Revisiting Colorado River Water Conservation District v. United States—There Must Be a Better Way." *Arizona State Law Journal* 27 (Summer 1995): 597.

De la Teja, Jesús F. "Land and Society in 18th Century San Antonio de Bexar: A Community on New Spain's Northern Frontier." PhD diss., University of Texas at Austin, 1988.

———, ed. *Preparing the Way, Preliminary Studies of the Texas Catholic Historical Society, Number 1*. Austin: Texas Catholic Historical Society, 1997.

———. *San Antonio de Bexar: A Community on New Spain's Northern Frontier*. Albuquerque: University of New Mexico Press, 1995.

De Leon, Arnoldo. *The Tejano Community, 1836–1900*. Dallas: Southern Methodist University Press, 1982.

Dean, Lyn E., and Russell S. Johnson. "The Changing Face of Water Rights in Texas 2003." Continuing education paper, State Bar of Texas, 2003.

Department of the Interior. *Water Supply and Irrigation Papers of the United States Geological Survey No. 13*. Washington: US Government Printing Office, 1896.

Dobbins, Betty Eakle. *The Spanish Element in Texas Water Law*. Austin: University of Texas Press, 1959.

Doolittle, William E. "Agriculture in North America on the Eve of Contact:

A Reassessment." *Annals of the Association of American Geographers* 82, no. 3 (Sept. 1992): 386–401.

Drummond, Dylan O. "Groundwater Ownership in Place: Fact or Fiction?" The University of Texas Law School, December 2008.

———. "Texas Groundwater Law in the Twenty-First Century: A Compendium of Historical Approaches, Current Problems, and Future Solutions Focusing on the High Plains Aquifer and the Panhandle." *Texas Tech Journal of Texas Administrative Law* 173 (Summer 2003): 173–214.

———. "Texas Groundwater Rights and Immunities: From East to Sipriano and Beyond." Joint Session with the Texas Supreme Court Historical Society, 115th Texas State Historical Association meeting, 2011.

Dumars, Charles T. "Changing Interpretations of New Mexico's Constitutional Provisions Allocating Water Resources: Integrating Private Property Rights and Public Values." *New Mexico Law Review* 26 (Summer 1996): 367.

Dumars, Charles T., Marilyn O'Leary, and Albert E. Utton. *Pueblo Indian Water Rights: Struggle for a Precious Resource.* Tucson: University of Arizona Press, 1984.

Duncan, Robert. "Amicus Brief for the Edwards Aquifer Authority and the State of Texas v. Burrell Day and Joel McDaniel, Cause No. 08-0964." Letter sent to Blake A. Hawthorne, June 2010.

Dunlap, Philip. "Border Wars: Analyzing the Dispute over Groundwater between Texas and Mexico." *Law and Business Review of the Americas* 12 (Spring 2006): 215.

Eckstein, Gabriel. "Application of International Water Law to Transboundary Groundwater Resources, and the Slovak-Hungarian Dispute over Gabcikovo-Nagymaros." International Water Law Project, 2010.

———. "Precious, Worthless, or Immeasurable: The Value and Ethic of Water." *Texas Tech Law Review* 38 (Summer 2006): 963.

Elder, Robert, Jr. "Water Wars in Texas." *Cox News Service,* August 24, 2003. Available at http://madmax.lmtonline.com/textarchives/082403/s19.htm.

Ellis, Gregory M. "Regulatory Takings and Texas Groundwater." Unpublished. Available at http://rrcs-97-79-137-4.sw.biz.rr.com/water/pdf/Regulatory Takings&TexasGroundwaterLaw.pdf.

Ellis, Gregory M., and Jace A. Houston. "Overview of Regulatory Methods Available to Groundwater Conservation Districts." Speech, Texas Water Law Institute, November 5, 2004, Austin.

Ellison, Justin. "Water Deal Could Ruin Texas Rice Farmers." *Farm Plus Financial,* October 3, 2011. Available at http://www.farmplusfinancial.com/blog/general-farm-loans/water-deal-could-ruin-texas-rice-farmers/.

Everett, Donald E. *San Antonio: The Flavor of Its Past, 1845–1898.* San Antonio: Trinity University Press, 1959.

Fambrough, Judon. *Private Property: How Private Is It?* Publication 1053. Rev. 2005. College Station: Real Estate Center, Texas A&M University, 1994.

———. *Texas Surface Water: Ownership and Uses.* Publication 1508. College Station: Real Estate Center, Texas A&M University, 2001.

Fireman, Janet R. *The Spanish Royal Corps of Engineers in the Western Borderlands.* Glendale, CA: Arthur H. Clark, 1977.

Fisher, Lewis F. *Crown Jewel of Texas: The Story of San Antonio's River.* San Antonio: Maverick Publishing, 1997.

Flannery, Tim. *The Eternal Frontier: An Ecological History of North America and Its Peoples.* New York: Atlantic Monthly Press, 2001.

Foster, William C. *Spanish Expeditions into Texas, 1689–1768.* Austin: University of Texas Press, 1995.

Fox, Nicole. "Should Groundwater Be Owned by the State of Texas?" Edited by Charles Porter. Capstone class paper, St. Edwards University, August 2011.

Frkuska, Augustine. *Archaeological Investigations at the San Pedro Acequia, Report No. 103.* San Antonio: University of Texas at San Antonio Center for Archaeological Research, 1981.

Galant, Carl R., and Russell S. Johnson. "Exempt Uses of Groundwater and Surface Water." Oil, Gas, and Energy Resources Law Section Report. *State Bar of Texas* 33, no. 3 (March 2009).

Gesick, E. John, Jr. *Under the Live Oak Tree: A History of Seguin.* Seguin: Seguin Bank & Trust, 1988.

Glennon, Robert. *Water Follies: Groundwater Pumping and the Fate of America's Fresh Waters.* Washington, DC: Island Press, 2002.

Glick, Thomas F. *Islamic and Christian Spain in the Early Middle Ages.* Princeton: Princeton University Press, 1979.

———. *Southwestern Studies, Monograph No. 35: The Old World Background of the Irrigation System of San Antonio Texas.* El Paso: Texas Western Press, 1972.

Graham, Don. *Kings of Texas.* Hoboken, NJ: John Wiley & Sons, 2003.

Green, Donald E. *Land of the Underground Rain: Irrigation on the Texas High Plains, 1910–1970.* Austin: University of Texas Press, 1973.

Greenhill, Joe R., and Thomas Gibbs Gee. "Ownership of Ground Water in Texas: The East Case Reconsidered." *Texas Law Review* 33 (1955): 620–630.

Gwynne, S. C. "The Last Drop." *Texas Monthly,* February 2008. Available at http://www.texasmonthly.com/story/Last-drop?fullpage=1.

Habig, Marion A. *The Alamo Chain of Missions.* Chicago: Franciscan Herald Press, 1968.

———. *San Antonio's Mission San Jose.* Chicago: Franciscan Herald Press, 1968.

Hall, Katy. "Dry Fire Hydrants Helping Counter Rural Wildfires." March 1995. Available at http://www.texas-fire.com.

Handbook of Texas Online. Available at http://www.tshaonline.org/handbook/online.

Handy, Mary Olivia. *History of Fort Sam Houston.* San Antonio: Naylor Press, 1951.

Hardberger, Amy. "What Lies Beneath: Determining the Necessity of International Groundwater Policy along the United States–Mexico Border and a Roadmap to an Agreement." *Texas Tech Law Review* 35 (Summer 2004): 1211.

Harrison, Sylvia. "The Historical Development of Nevada Water Law." *University of Denver Water Law Review* 5 (Fall 2001): 148.

Hassan, Mohammad Masud. "GAM Run 10-050 MAG Version 2." Texas Water Development Board, February 2011.

Hays Trinity Conservation District. "Hays Trinity Groundwater Conservation District Rules." June 2007. Available at http://www.haysgroundwater.com /files/Rules/2007_HTGCD_Rules.pdf.

Highsmith, Richard M., Jr. "Irrigated Lands of the World." *Geographical Review* 55, no. 3 (July 1965): 382–389.

Hildebrand, Ira P. "The Rights of Riparian Owners at Common Law in Texas." *Texas Law Review* 6 (1927–1928): 19–50.

Horton, Alex W. "Where'd All the (Ground) Water Go? Three Approaches to Balancing Resource Efficiency with Rural Sustainability in Texas." *South Texas Law Review* 49 (Spring 2008): 691.

House, Boyce. *San Antonio: City of Flaming Adventure.* San Antonio: Naylor, 1949.

House Research Organization. "Behind the US-Mexico Water Treaty Dispute." *Texas House of Representative: Interim News* (April 2002).

Howell, Emily. "Is the TCEQ 'Hearing' Impaired?: The Impact of City of Marshall v. City of Uncertain on the Availability of Contested-Case Hearings for Water Use Permit Amendments." *Texas Tech Administrative Law Journal* 8, bk. 1 (Summer 2007): 299.

Hundley, Norris, Jr. *The Great Thirst: Californians and Water—a History.* Rev. ed. Berkeley: University of California Press, 2001.

Hunt, Robert C., and Eva Hunt. "Canal Irrigation and Local Social Organization." *Current Anthropology* 17, no. 3 (Sept. 1976): 389–411.

Hutchins, Wells A. "The Community Acequia: Its Origin and Development." *Southwestern Historical Quarterly Online,* 31, no. 3 (July 1927–Apr. 1928): 281–284. Available at http://texashistory.unt.edu/ark:/67531/metapth101088/m1 /279/.

———. *The Texas Law of Water Rights.* Austin: Texas Legislature and Texas Board of Water Engineers, 1961.

Ivey, Jake. *Mission Land Use in the San Antonio River Valley.* N.p., 1991. [Housed at the Center for Archaeological Research at the University of Texas at San Antonio Library]

Jackson, Jack. *Los mesteños.* College Station: Texas A&M University Press, 1986.

Jackson, Robert H. *Missions and the Frontiers of Spanish America.* Scottsdale, AZ: Pentacle Press, 2005.

Jackson, Robert H., and Eduardo Castillo. *Indians, Franciscans, and Spanish Colonization.* Albuquerque: University of New Mexico Press, 1995.

Johnson, Russell. *Texas Water Law: The Next Century.* Technical Report No. 1469. College Station: Texas A&M University Real Estate Center, 2001.

———. "Valuation—How Do We Do It? Water Market Transfer and Value Issues." CLE, Texas Water Law 11th annual conference, February 14, 2002.

Kaiser, Ronald. "Deep Trouble: Options for Managing the Hidden Threat of Aquifer Depletion in Texas." *Texas Tech Law Review* 32 (2001): 249.

———. "Water Marketing in Texas." Economic, Legal, and Institutional Considerations in Water Markets, 11th Annual Texas Real Estate Symposium, College Station, Texas, May 2001.

Kelly, William W. "Concepts in the Anthropological Study of Irrigation." *American Anthropologist* 85, n.s., no. 4 (Dec. 1983): 880–886.

Kelton, Elmer. *The Time It Never Rained.* Fort Worth: TCU Press, 1984.

Kunkel, Eric B. "The Spanish Law of Waters in the United States: From Alfonso the Wise to the Present Day." McGeorge School of Law, 2001.

Lamm, Freddie, and Rob Aiken. "Managing Deficit Sprinkler Irrigation of Sunflower." *Sunflower Magazine,* February 2011. Available at http://www.sunflowernsa.com/magazine/details.asp?ID=721&Cat=11.

Lea, Tom. *The King Ranch, I and II.* Boston: Little, Brown, 1957.

Leal, John Odgen. *After the Secularization of the Mission San Antonio de Valero, Known as the Alamo, 1792.* San Antonio: Bexar County, 1991.

Leutenegger, Benedict, trans. With introduction and notes by Marion A. Habig, O.F.M., and Barnabas Diekemper, O.F.M. "Memorial of Father Benito Fernández concerning the Canary Islanders, 1741." *Southwestern Historical Quarterly* 82, no. 3 (July 1978–Apr. 1979): 265–296. Available at http://texashistory.unt.edu/ark:/67531/metapth101206/m1/317/.

Maas, Arthur, and Raymond L. Anderson. *And the Desert Shall Rejoice—Conflict, Growth, and Justice in Arid Environments.* Cambridge, MA: MIT Press, 1978.

MacKinnon, Anne. "Historic and Future Challenges in Western Water Law: The Case of Wyoming." *Wyoming Law Review* 6 (2006): 291.

Mahoney, James. "Revisiting General Theory in Historical Sociology." *Social Forces* 83, no. 2 (2004): 459–489.

Marin, Carlos. "Bi-national Border Water Supply Issues from the Perspective of the IBWC." *United States-Mexico Law Journal* 11 (Spring 2003): 35.

Marks, Paula Mitchell. *Turn Your Eyes to Texas.* College Station: Texas A&M University Press, 1989.

Mason, Thomas G., and Robin A. Melvin. "New Developments in Texas Water Law, Planning and Management." Presented to the Austin Bar Association Real Estate Section meeting, March 6, 2012.

Matovina, Timothy M. *Guadalupe and Her Faithful.* Baltimore: Johns Hopkins University Press, 2005.

———. *Tejano Religion and Ethnicity San Antonio, 1821–1860.* Austin: University of Texas Press, 1995.

Matson, Daniel S., and Bernard L. Fontana, ed. and trans. *Father Bringas Reports to the King: Methods of Indoctrination on the Frontier of New Spain, 1796–97.* Tucson: University of Arizona Press, 1977.

Mauldin, Raymond P. *Exploring Drought in the San Antonio Area between 1700 and 1979.* San Antonio: Center for Archaeological Research, University of Texas at San Antonio, 2003.

McCarthy, Edmond R., Jr. "Mixing Oil and Gas with Texas Water Law." *Texas Tech Law Review,* Vol. 44, No. 4 (Summer 2012): 884–938.

McCleskey, Robert A. "Maybe Oil and Water Should Mix—at Least in Texas Law: An Analysis of Current Problems with Texas Ground Water Law and How Established Oil and Gas Law Could Provide Appropriate Solutions." *Texas Wesleyan Law Review* 1 (Spring 1994): 207.

McCormick, Lacey, and Jennifer Walker. "Sprayed Away: Seven Ways to Reduce Texas' Outdoor Water Use." July 2010. Available at http://www.texaswatermatters.org/pdfs/sprayed%20away_report.pdf.

Menger, Johnowene Brackenridge Crutcher. "M. Eleanor Brackenridge, 1837–1924, a Third Generation Advocate of Education." Master's thesis, Trinity University, San Antonio, 1964.

Meyer, Michael C. *Water in the Hispanic Southwest.* Tucson: University of Arizona Press, 1984.

Miller, Char, ed. *On the Border: An Environmental History of San Antonio.* San Antonio: Trinity University Press, 2005.

Montejano, David. *Anglos and Mexicans in the Making of Texas, 1836–1986.* Austin: University of Texas Press, 1987.

Morales, Francisco, O.F.M. "Mexican Society and the Franciscan Order." *The Americas* 54 (Jan. 1998).

Morfi, Fray Father Juan Agustin. *The History of Texas 1673–1779* [a manuscript written in 1782–1783]. Edited by Carlos Castañeda. Albuquerque: The Quivira Society, 1935.

Morgan, Bobbie Whitten. "George W. Brackenridge and His Control of San Antonio's Water Supply, 1869–1905." Master's thesis, Trinity University, San Antonio, 1961.

Mullican, William F., III, and Suzanne Schwartz. *100 Years of Rule of Capture: From East to Groundwater Management.* Report 361. Austin: Texas Water Development Board, 2004.

National Research Council. *A New Era for Irrigation.* Washington, DC: National Academies Press, 1996.

Neal, Basil Young. "George W. Brackenridge: Citizen and Philanthropist." Master's thesis, University of Texas at Austin, 1939.

Neuman, Janet C. "The Good, the Bad, and the Ugly: The First Ten Years of the Oregon Water Trust." *Nebraska Law Review* 83 (2004): 432.

Newcomb, W. W. *The Indians of Texas.* Austin: University of Texas Press, 1961.

Nickels, David L., I. Waynne Cox, and Connie Gibson. *Excavation of the San Pedro Acequia on the Grounds of the San Antonio Housing Authority, Report No. 243.* San Antonio: University of Texas at San Antonio Center for Archaeological Research, 1996.

Opelia, Eric. "The Rule of Capture in Texas: An Outdated Principle beyond Its Time." *University of Denver Water Law Review* 6 (Fall 2002): 104.

O'Rourke, Thomas P. *The Franciscan Missions in Texas (1690–1793).* N.p., 1927.

Ostrom, Elinor, and Roy Gardner. "Coping with Asymmetries in the Commons: Self-Governing Irrigation Systems Can Work." *Journal of Economic Perspectives* 7, no. 4 (Fall 1993): 93–112.

Parsons, James J. "The Migration of Canary Islanders to the Americas: An Unbroken Current since Columbus." *The Americas* 39 (Apr. 1983): 447–469.

Phelan, Richard. *Texas Wild.* New York: E. P. Dutton, 1976.

Pisani, Donald J. *From the Family Farm to Agribusiness: The Irrigation Crusade in California and the West, 1850–1931.* Berkeley: University of California Press, 1984.

———. *To Reclaim a Divided West: Water, Law and Public Policy, 1848–1902.* Albuquerque: University of New Mexico Press, 1992.

———. *Water, Land and Law in the West: The Limits of Public Policy, 1850–1920.* Lawrence: University Press of Kansas, 1996.

Porter, Charles, Jr. "The Beginnings of Spanish Settlement in the El Paso District Revisited." Presentation at Texas State Historical Association convention, Dallas, March 5, 2010.

———. "A Class Mediation Exercise for Understanding Global Water Disputes." Presentation at the World History Association of Texas Conference: Innovations in Teaching and Research, Austin, February 19, 2011.

———. "Climate Change and Water in Texas." Host and emcee, Kozmetsky Center for Excellence in Global Finance, St. Edward's University, September 12, 2011.

———. "The Convergence and Divergence of Agricultural Ideas between Spaniards and Jumano Indians along the Rio Grande." Presentation at World History Association of Texas conference, February 2010.

———. "Decisions and Consequences in the Common Pool." Speech at United States Geological Service lunch speaker series, webcast, Austin, May 8, 2010.

———. "Eyewitness Perspectives of a Village in Transition on the Far Frontier, San Antonio, 1810–1855." Presentation at San Antonio Conservation Society, June 4, 2011.

———. "Farm and Ranch for Texas Agents." Accredited continuing education course. Texas Real Estate Commission, Austin, Texas, 2008.

———. "Financing Groundwater Conservation Districts in Texas: Results of a Preliminary Study." *Texas Water Journal* 4, no. 1 (2013): 55–77.

———. "The First Missionaries in the New World: Saviors or Agents of Directed Cultural Change?" Lecture at St. Edward's University, University Programs, American Experience, CULF 1320, January 2010.

———. "From Acequias to the San Antonio Water Company: Sharing and Managing Water in San Antonio from Colonial Bexar to the Gilded Age." Presentation at St. Edward's University MLA Symposium, 2008.

———. "The History of San Antonio Water Rights." Speech at the Professional Tour Guides of San Antonio Spring Education series, March 23, 2011.

———. "The History of W. A. East v. Houston and Texas Central Railway Company, 1904: Establishment of the Rule of Capture in Texas Water Law or 'He Who Has the Biggest Pump Gets the Water.'" *East Texas Historical Journal* 50, no. 2 (Fall 2012): 107–119.

———. "How Texas Water Law and Water Rights Shaped Texas and the Perception of Texas Today." Speech at University of Texas LAMP (Learning Activities for Mature People) series, January 2012.

———. "The Hydraulic West: The History of Irrigation." In *The World of the American West,* ed. Morris Bakken, 308–335. New York: Routledge, 2011.

———. "The Impact of Private Water Pipelines on Right of Way Acquisition." Presentation at International Right of Way Association, San Marcos, September 9, 2011.

———. *Maker of Modern Texas, George W. Brackenridge.* Forthcoming, 2013.

———. "The Marriage of Interdependent Irrigation Technologies in New Spain: Prelude to Formation of a Spanish Community, Villa San Fernando." Presentation at World History Association conference, Austin, February 18, 2012.

———. "The Pivot Point for Texas Water Rights: San Antonio." Presentation at United States Geological Society Texas Water Science Center, San Antonio, June 24, 2011.

———. "Primer of Water Rights." Lecturer and organizer for Texas House of Representatives Miller, Lucio, Workman, and Strama, Austin, February 16, 2011.

———. "Querétaro in Focus: The Franciscan Missionary Colleges and the Texas Missions." *Catholic Southwest: A Journal of History and Culture* 19 (2008): 7–51.

———. "Right of Way: Gateway to Water Infrastructure in Texas." Presentation at International Right of Way Seminar, Arlington, April 20, 2012.

———. "Right of Way in Texas Water and Real Estate: Perspectives from an Expert Witness." Speech at International Right of Way Association's luncheon speaker series, Austin, March 8, 2011.

———. "Spanish Roots in Texas Water Law: Three Hundred Years of Connections and Consequences." Presentation at World History Association of Texas conference, 2009.

———. *Spanish Water/Anglo Water.* College Station: Texas A&M University Press, 2009.

———. St. Edward's University Kozmetsky Center for Excellence in Global Finance, Global Water Issues and Dispute Resolution in International River Basins. Co-host, November 8, 2011.

———. "Tales from the Common Pool: Unintended Consequences." Speech at Edwards Aquifer Authority lunch speaker series, San Antonio, August 2010.

———. "Tales from the Common Pool: Values, Obligations, and Consequences." Presentation at MLA Symposium, MLA alumni meeting, April 10, 2010.

———. Texas House of Representatives Member Paul Workman's "Water Rights and Texas." Lecturer at Texas House of Representatives, March 9, 2011.

———. "Texas Out of Water?" *Houston Chronicle,* Guest Editorial, October 23, 2012.

———. "Texas Water History." Speech at State of Texas Archives Library, March 7, 2012.

———. "Unintended Consequences." Keynote speech at Groundwater District Manager's Association, San Antonio, January 13, 2011.

———. "Unintended Consequences: A Trilogy of Tales from the Common Pool." Lecture at Texas Alliance of Groundwater Districts quarterly meeting, Austin, March 2010.

———. "Water for Central Texas—Solving the Problem." Participant in Water Panel, State Capitol, Austin, April 24, 2012.

———. "Water Policy—Should Washington County Have a Groundwater Conservation District." Lone Star Water Forum, Brenham, October 5, 2012.

———. "Water Rights for Texas Agents." Accredited continuing education course. Texas Real Estate Commission, Austin, Texas, 2008.

———. "Water Rights in the Everyday Lives of Texans." Texas Water Law Superconference, Austin, September 10, 2012.

———. "Water Rights in Texas: A History From Viceroys to GCDs." Texas Groundwater Summit, Austin, August 28, 2012.

———. "Water Rights in Texas from the Gilded Age to Ike." Presentation at Texas State Historical Association convention, 2007.

———. "Water Rights Update." Speech at San Marcos Board of Realtors luncheon, November 8, 2011.

Poyo, Gerald E., and Gilberto Hinojosa. *Tejano Origins in Eighteenth-Century San Antonio.* Austin: University of Texas Press, 1991.

Queen, Stuart A. "What Is a Community?" *Journal of Social Force* 1, no. 4 (May 1972): 375–382.

Rae, Stephen R., and Joseph E. Minor. "Early Engineering in the American

Southwest." *American Society of Civil Engineers Proceedings* 99, no. 2 (Apr. 1973): 142–157.

Ramsdell, Charles W. *San Antonio: A Historical and Pictorial Guide.* Austin: University of Texas Press, 1959.

Raup, H. F. "Transformation of Southern California to a Cultivated Land." *Annals of the Association of American Geographers* 49, no. 3 (Sept. 1959): 58–78.

Rawson, Michael. "The Nature of Water: Reform and the Antebellum Crusade for Municipal Water in Boston." *Environmental History* 9, no. 3 (2004): 411–435.

Reich, Peter L. "The 'Hispanic' Roots of Prior Appropriation in Arizona." *Arizona State Law Journal* 27 (Summer 1995): 649.

Reisner, Marc. *Cadillac Desert.* New York: Viking, 1986.

Ricard, Robert. *The Spiritual Conquest of Mexico.* Berkeley: University of California Press, 1966. Originally published in French: *Conquête spirituelle du Mexique.* Paris: University of Paris, 1933.

Riddell, John Leonard. *A Long Ride in Texas, 1855.* Edited by James O. Breeden. College Station: Texas A&M University Press, 1994.

Rivera, Jose A. *Acequia Culture.* Albuquerque: University of New Mexico Press, 1988.

Rodriguez, Sylvia. *Acequia: Water Sharing, Sanctity, and Place.* Santa Fe: School for Advanced Research Press, 2006.

Roemer, Ferdinand. *Roemer's Texas, 1845–1847.* Translated by Oswald Mueller. San Antonio: Standard Printing, 1935.

Sahs, Mary K. "Groundwater Regulation in Texas." Continuing education paper, State Bar of Texas, 2005.

Sánchez, José María. "A Trip to Texas in 1828." Translated by Carlos Castañeda. *Southwestern Historical Quarterly Online* 29, no. 4 (Apr. 1926): 249–288. Available at http://texashistory.unt.edu/ark:/67531/metapth117141/m1/275/.

Sansom, Andrew. *Water in Texas.* Austin: University of Texas Press, 2008.

Schorr, David B. "Appropriation as Agrarianism: Distributive Justice in the Creation of Property Rights." *Ecology Law Quarterly* 32 (2005): 3.

Schuetz, Mardith. "Professional Artisans in the Hispanic Southwest." *The Americas* 40 (July 1983).

Sibley, Marilyn McAdams. *George W. Brackenridge, Maverick Philanthropist.* Austin: University of Texas Press, 1973.

Silverstein, Jake. "Life by the Drop: A Special Report on Drought, Water and the Future of Texas." *Texas Monthly,* July 2012.

Skocpol, Theda, ed. *Vision and Method in Historical Sociology.* London: Cambridge University Press, 1984.

Smith, Garland F. "The Valley Water Suit and Its Impact on Texas Water Policy: Some Practical Advice for the Future." *Texas Tech Law Review* 8 (1977): 580.

Smith, Tiziana. "Overcoming Challenges in Wastewater Reuse: A Case Study of San Antonio, Texas." Thesis, Harvard College, March 2011.

Sneddon, Chris, Usa Leila Harris, Radoslav Dimitrov, and Uygar Ozesmi. "Contested Waters: Conflict, Scale, and Sustainability in Aquatic Socioecological Systems." *Society and Natural Resources* 15, no. 66 (2002): 663–675.

Taylor, Virginia H. *The Spanish Archives of the General Land Office of Texas.* Austin: Lone Star Press, 1955.

Taylor, William B. *Magistrates of the Sacred.* Stanford, CA: Stanford University Press, 1996.

Terán, Manual de, ed. *Texas by Terán: The Diary Kept by General Manual de Terán on His 1828 Inspection of Texas.* Translated by Jack Jackson and John Wheat. Austin: University of Texas Press, 2000.

Texas Alliance of Groundwater Districts. "Legislative Wrap-Up: Groundwater-Related Bills." 2011.

———. "Position Paper for the 82nd Legislature." July 2010.

Texas Comptroller of Public Accounts. *Forces of Change: Shaping the Future of Texas.* Vol. 2, pt. 1. Austin: TCPA, 1993.

Texas Farm Bureau. "Joint Position Statement on Groundwater Ownership." 2010. Available at http://www.texasgroundwaterlaw.com/uploads/1/2/9/6 /12969798/joint_position_statement_groundwater_twa_tfb_tscra.pdf.

Texas Natural Resource Conservation Commission. *Rights to Surface Water in Texas.* 2002. Available at http://www.tceq.texas.gov/publications/gi/gi_228 .html/atdownload/file.

Texas Water Code. *Water Rights, Chapter 11.* Texas Natural Resource Conservative Commission. 1977. Available at http://www.statutes.legis.state.tx.us/Docs /WA/htm/WA.11.htm.

Texas Water Conservation Association. *Confluence.* Austin: TWCA, 2011.

Texas Water Development Board. *Conserving Water Outdoors.* May 2011. Available at http://www.twdb.texas.gov/publications/brochures/conservation/doc /ConservingWaterOutdoor.pdf.

———. *A Texan's Guide to Water and Water Rights Marketing.* Austin: TWDB, 2003.

———. *The Texas Manual on Rainwater Harvesting.* 3rd ed. Austin: TWDB, 2005.

———. *Water for Texas 2007.* Austin: TWDB, 2007.

Tijerina, Andrés. *Tejanos & Texas under the Mexican Flag, 1821–1836.* College Station: Texas A&M University Press, 1994.

Torres, Luis. *Voices from the San Antonio Missions.* Lubbock: Texas Tech University Press, 1997.

Underwood, Laura. "Better Late Than Never: States Regain the Right to Regulate Stream Flows under the Clean Water Act: PUD No.1 of Jefferson County v. Washington Department of Ecology." *Texas Tech Law Review* 26 (1995): 187.

United States Environmental Protection Agency. "Drinking Water From Household Wells." January 2002. Available at http://www.epa.gov/privatewells /pdfs/household_wells.pdf.

Votteler, Todd H. "The Little Fish That Roared: The Endangered Species Act, State Groundwater Law, and Private Property Rights Collide over the Texas Edwards Aquifer." *Lewis & Clark Law School Environment Law* 28 (Winter 1998): 845–878.

Walker, Andrew. "Mexican Law and the Texas Courts." *Baylor Law Review* 55 (Winter 2003): 225.

Water Resources Center at Texas Tech University. *The Acequias of San Antonio, Historic American Engineering Record TX-1.* Washington, DC: National Parks Service, 1973.

Weber, David J. *Barbaros: Spaniards and Their Savages in the Age of Enlightenment.* New Haven, CT: Yale University Press, 2005.

———. *The Mexican Frontier, 1821–1846: The American Southwest under Mexico.* Albuquerque: University of New Mexico Press, 1982.

———. "Mexico's Far Northern Frontier, 1821–1854: Historiography Askew." *Western Historical Quarterly* 7, no. 3 (July 1976): 282.

———, ed. *New Spain's Far Northern Frontier.* Dallas: Southern Methodist University Press, 1979.

———. *The Spanish Frontier in North America.* New Haven, CT: Yale University Press, 1992.

Weber, David J., and Arnoldo De León, eds. *Foreigners in Their Native Land: Historical Roots of the Mexican Americans.* Albuquerque: University of New Mexico Press, 1982.

Weddle, Robert S. *San Juan Bautista—Gateway to Spanish Texas.* Austin: University of Texas Press, 1968.

Wegener, Elaine Hoffman, ed. *George C. Vaughan, Early Entrepreneur.* San Antonio: Watercress Press, 1984.

Weniger, Del. *The Explorer's Texas: The Land and Waters.* Austin: Eakin Press, 1984.

Wheeler, Kenneth W. *To Wear a City's Crown: The Beginnings of Urban Growth in Texas, 1836–1865.* Cambridge, MA: Harvard University Press, 1968.

White, A. A., and Will Wilson. "The Flow and Underflow of Motl v. Boyd: The Problem." *Southwestern Law Journal* 9, no. 1 (Winter 1955): 377–433.

Williams, Michael L. "Can Oil and Water Mix? The Impact of Water Law on Oil, Gas, and Mineral Production." *Texas Bar Journal* 68 (October 2005): 816.

Worster, Donald. *Rivers of Empire: Water, Aridity, and the Growth of the American West.* New York: Pantheon Books, 1985.

INDEX

Entries in **bold type** refer to illustrations.

Titles in the River Books Series

Paddling the Wild Neches
  Jim Donovan

The San Marcos: A River's Story
  Jim Kimmel

Freshwater Fishes of Texas: A Field Guide
  Chad Thomas, Timothy H. Bonner, and Bobby G. Whiteside

Paddling the Guadalupe
  Wayne H. McAlister

Texas Water Atlas
  Lawrence E. Estaville and Richard A. Earl

Flash Floods in Texas
  Jonathan Burnett

Neches River User Guide
  Gina Donovan

The Living Waters of Texas
  Ken W. Kramer and Charles Kruvand

Exploring the Brazos River
  Jim Kimmel and Jerry Touchstone Kimmel

River of Contrasts: The Texas Colorado
  Margie Crisp

Canoeing and Kayaking Houston Waterways
  Natalie Wiest

Running the River: Secrets of the Sabine
  Wes Ferguson and Jacob Croft Botter